Measuring School Performance and Efficiency:

Implications for Practice and Research

2005 Yearbook of the
American Education Finance Association

Editors:
Leanna Stiefel, Amy Ellen Schwartz,
Ross Rubenstein, Jeffrey Zabel

Routledge
Taylor & Francis Group
New York London

First Published 2005 by Eye On Education

Published 2013 by Routledge
711 Third Avenue, New York, NY, 10017, USA
2 Park Square, Milton Park, Abingdon, Oxon OX14 4RN

Routledge is an imprint of the Taylor & Francis Group, an informa business

Copyright © 2005, Taylor & Francis.

All rights reserved. No part of this book may be reprinted or reproduced or
utilised in any form or by any electronic, mechanical, or other means, now
known or hereafter invented, including photocopying and recording, or in any
information storage or retrieval system, without permission in writing from
the publishers.

Notices
No responsibility is assumed by the publisher for any injury and/or damage to
persons or property as a matter of products liability, negligence or otherwise,
or from any use of operation of any methods, products, instructions or ideas
contained in the material herein.

Practitioners and researchers must always rely on their own experience and
knowledge in evaluating and using any information, methods, compounds, or
experiments described herein. In using such information or methods they should
be mindful of their own safety and the safety of others, including parties for
whom they have a professional responsibility.

Product or corporate names may be trademarks or registered trademarks, and
are used only for identification and explanation without intent to infringe.

Library of Congress Cataloging-in-Publication Data

ISSN Pending

ISBN: 978-1-596-67006-8 (pbk)

Also Available from EYE ON EDUCATION

Money and Schools, Third Edition
David C. Thompson and R. Craig Wood

**Money, Politics, and Law: Intersections and Conflicts
in the Provision of Educational Opportunity**
2004 Yearbook of the American Education Finance Association
Edited by Karen DeMoss and Kenneth K. Wong

School Finance and Teacher Quality: Exploring the Connections
2003 Yearbook of the American Education Finance Association
Edited by Margaret L. Plecki and David H. Monk

Cost-Effectiveness and Educational Policy
2002 Yearbook of the American Education Finance Association
Edited by Henry M. Levin and Patrick J. McEwan

Education Finance in the New Millennium
2001 Yearbook of the American Education Finance Association
Edited by Stephen Chaikind and William J. Fowler, Jr.

Balancing Local Control and State Responsibility for K-12 Education
2000 Yearbook of the American Education Finance Association
Edited by Neil D. Theobald and Betty Malen

The ISLLC Standards in Action: A Principal's Handbook
Carol Engler

School Leader Internship:
Developing, Monitoring, and Evaluating Your Leadership Experience
Martin, Wright and Danzig

Introduction to Educational Administration:
Standards, Theories, and Practice
Douglas J. Fiore

Data Analysis for Continuous School Improvement, Second Edition
Victoria L. Bernhardt

Human Resources Administration:
A School-Based Perspective, Third Edition
Richard E. Smith

School Community Relations
Douglas J. Fiore

Acknowledgments

The editors gratefully acknowledge funding for the study, "Good Schools, Good Students? Measuring School Performance with Diverse Students," U.S. Department of Education, Grant Number R305T010115, which provided partial support for this book. All opinions expressed in the book are those of the authors alone. The editors also thank Joanne Keitt of the Wagner School at NYU and Kelly Bogart of the Maxwell School at Syracuse University for invaluable support in preparing the manuscript for publication.

Contributors and Editors

Hella Bel Hadj Amor is a PhD candidate at New York University's Wagner School of Public Service and a research scientist at the Institute for Education and Social Policy at NYU. She holds an MA in economics from NYU and a BS in economics from the University of Paris IX Dauphine. She specializes in education policy, public finance, and applied econometrics. She is now involved in a study of the contribution of the New York City public schools to student success at the City University of New York. Her dissertation work focuses on the cost of education in Ohio and the impact of the size and structure of Ohio school districts on school costs. She has worked on various projects, dealing with education finance and education policy at NYU and at the Milano School of the New School University in New York. She has worked for the Campaign for Fiscal Equity. Her internships have taken place at the regional Mission of the World Bank in Bangkok, Thailand, and the National Bank of Cambodia. She is a recipient of the President L. J. Oliva Community Service Award for outstanding service to the NYU community.

David Figlio is the Knight-Ridder Professor of Economics at the University of Florida and a research associate at the National Bureau of Economic Research. He is the inaugural editor, along with David Monk, of AEFA's new journal, Education Finance and Policy, to be published by MIT Press beginning in February 2006. His research on political economy issues and the design and evaluation of education and social policy has been published extensively in leading journals including the *American Economic Review, Journal of Public Economics*, and *Journal of Law and Economics*. His work has been funded by the National Science Foundation; National Institutes of Child Health and Human Development; the U.S. Departments of Agriculture, Education, and Health and Human Services; and many private foundations. He has served as a school-policy advisor to several states and foreign countries.

Dae Yeop Kim is Assistant Professor of Educational Policy, Foundations, and Administrative Studies at Portland State University's Graduate School of Education. He teaches courses in educational research, statistics, program evaluation, and educational finance. He will receive his PhD in public administration from New York University (NYU),where he specializes in public finance, public policy, and research methods. During his doctoral study, he has worked as a researcher for the Institute for Education and Social Policy at NYU and participated in research projects that have evaluated various school reform programs adopted by New York City Public Schools. His current research focuses on measurement of school efficiency, effects of high-stakes testing, and evaluation of school-based budgeting.

Steven Kimball is a researcher with the Teacher Compensation Project of the Consortium for Policy Research in Education (CPRE) at the University of Wisconsin-Madison. He completed his PhD and MS from the University of Wisconsin–Madison Department of Educational Administration. His work with the Teacher Compensation Project has included research on school-based performance award programs, National Board certification, teacher pensions, and standards-based teacher evaluation systems. Before joining CPRE, he was a legislative analyst in the U.S. House of Representatives, the U.S. Senate, and the Texas State Office in Washington, D.C.

Anthony Milanowski is a researcher with CPRE at the University of Wisconsin–Madison where he also received his PhD in industrial relations. He is coordinating the CPRE Teacher Compensation Project's research on standards-based teacher evaluation and teacher performance pay. He has taught compensation, staffing, and human resource management courses for the Schools of Business and Education at UW–Madison. Before joining CPRE, he worked in human resource management for 16 years, primarily with the State of Wisconsin. His current research interests include performance evaluation, pay system innovations, teacher selection, and the teacher labor market.

Allan Odden is Professor of Educational Leadership and Policy Analysis at the University of Wisconsin–Madison. He also is Codirector of CPRE, a national center studying how to improve state and local education policy. Formerly he was professor of education policy and administration at the University of Southern California (1984–1993) and Director of Policy Analysis for California Education (PACE), and from 1975–1984 he held various positions at the Education Commission of the States. He was president of the American Educational Finance Association in 1979–1980 and received AEFA's distinguished Service Award in 1998. His research emphases include school finance redesign, resource reallocation in schools, the costs of instructional improvement, and teacher compensation. He has written extensively, publishing more than 200 journal articles, book chapters, and research reports, as well as 30 books and monographs.

Anthony Rolle has conducted K–12 education finance and policy research for the University of Washington's Institute for Public Policy & Management, the Washington State Legislature and Democratic House Majority Whip, the Indiana Education Policy Center, and the National Education Association. His primary professional interests attempt to explore and improve relative measures of economic efficiency for public agencies. (Using relative measures of economic efficiency allows models to be developed and assessed that use the best performing public agencies as the foci of analyses; it does not give primacy to the average performing corporation of regression-based analyses.) Concomitantly, his research explores and applies measures of vertical equity to analyses of public finance mechanisms. (Using vertical equity measures recognizes that demographic differences among communities affect organizational processes and does not assume that all public agencies have the same expenditure priorities.) He received a BS from Santa Clara University, a master's degree from the University of Washington's Graduate School of Public Affairs, and a PhD from the School of Education at Indiana University. He won the American Educational Finance Association's Jean Flanigan Dissertation Award in 2002.

Ross Rubenstein is Associate Professor of Public Administration in the Maxwell School at Syracuse University, where he teaches courses in financial management, public budgeting, and education policy. He is also a senior research associate at the Center for Policy Research. His research focuses on funding equity and adequacy in education, resource allocation, performance and efficiency measurement, and merit-based financial aid for college. He has conducted training programs in public finance and budgeting for government officials from many countries and served as a staff member on Georgia Governor Roy Barnes's Education Reform Study Commission. He received his PhD in public administration from New York University and was previously on the faculty of Georgia State University.

Amy Ellen Schwartz is professor of Public Policy and Education at New York University. Her research interest is primarily in empirical public finance, with a focus on state and local government, specifically education policy and finance. Ongoing projects in K–12 education include the education of immigrant children; disparities in test scores across racial and ethnic groups; and the measurement of school performance and the relationship between performance and school organization. Her research in higher education concentrates on the costs of colleges and the impact of high school on college success. Her research on urban economic development considers the impact of housing investment and other local public services on property values. Much of her research has been published in scholarly journals including the *American Economic Review*, *Journal of Human Resources*, and the *National Tax Journal*. She has consulted on education and economic issues for government entities, including the New York City Board of Education, and a variety of nonprofit organizations including the Campaign for Fiscal Equity. She earned a PhD in economics at Columbia University.

Leanna Stiefel, Professor of Economics at New York University's Wagner Graduate School of Public Service, teaches courses in multiple regression, economics of education, and microeconomics. Her current research includes measurement of school efficiency, achievement of immigrant students, effects of school organization on student achievement, and test score gaps within schools. She is author of *Statistical Analysis for Public and Non-Profit Managers* (1990), coauthor of *The Measurement of Equity in School Finance* (1984), and author of regularly published journal articles. She is past president of the American Education Finance Association and a member of the National Center for Education Statistics Technical Planning Panel. She serves on the policy council of the APPAM and is a governor on the NYS Education Finance Research Consortium. She received a PhD in economics from the University of Wisconsin–Madison (1972), an AB with high honors from the University of Michigan–Ann Arbor (1967), and an Advanced Professional Certificate in Finance from New York University's Stern School of Business (1984).

Lori L. Taylor is an assistant professor at the George Bush School of Government and Public Service at Texas A&M University. She is also the principal researcher for the Texas Joint Select Committee on Public School Finance and House Select Committee on Public School Finance. In that capacity, she is the author or coauthor of a series of legislative reports examining the cost of education in Texas. Previously, she was the principal researcher on the Texas Cost-of-Education Project. Selected recent publications include "A New Geographic Cost of Education Index for Alaska: old approaches with some new twists" (with Jay Chambers and Joe Robinson), *Journal of Education Finance* (2004); "Competing Perspectives on the Cost of Education" (with Harrison Keller), *Developments in School Finance 2001–2002*; "Region Lags the Nation in

Education Gains," *Southwest Economy* (2003); "Updating the Texas Cost of Education Index" (with Celeste Alexander et al.), *Journal of Education Finance* (2002); "A Dose of Market Discipline: The New Education Initiatives," *Southwest Economy* (2002); "Improving Public School Financing in Texas" (with Jason Saving and Fiona Sigalla), *Southwest Economy* (2001); "On the Determinants of School District Efficiency: Competition and Monitoring"(with Shawna Grosskopf, Kathy J. Hayes and William L. Weber), *Journal of Urban Economics* (2001); "Anticipating the Consequences of School Reform: A New Use of DEA" (with Shawna Grosskopf, Kathy J. Hayes and William L. Weber), *Management Science* (1999); and "Aggregation and the Estimated Effects of School Resources" (with Eric A. Hanushek and Steven G. Rivkin), *Review of Economics and Statistics* (1996). She holds a BA in economics and a BS in business administration from the University of Kansas, and an MA and PhD in economics from the University of Rochester.

Jeffrey Zabel is an Associate Professor of Economics at Tufts University. His research interests are generally in applied microeconomics. His current research in K–12 education includes the impact of aggregation on measures of school performance, and peer group effects and student performance. Other areas of current research include social interactions and housing demand, empirical analyses of the impact of toxic waste sites on house values, and the impact of financial incentives on the labor market behavior of welfare recipients. His research has been published in academic journals including the *Journal of Econometrics*, the *Journal of Human Resources*, and the *Journal of Urban Economics*. He has consulted on the impact of critical habitat designation on housing markets and is a board member of the Boston Research Data Center. He earned a PhD in economics at the University of California at San Diego.

Table of Contents

Contributors and Editors . . . . **vii**

1   Measuring School Efficiency: What Have We Learned? **1**

Leanna Stiefel, Amy Ellen Schwartz, Ross Rubenstein, and Jeffrey Zabel . . 1

Introduction 1
Why Study School Efficiency Measurement? 3
Overview of the Volume 4
Overview of the Chapters. 5
   Part One · 5
     Adjusted Measures of School Performance: A Cross-State
      Perspective. 5
     The Good, the Bad and the Ugly:Measuring School
      Efficiency Using School Production Functions. 6
     Measuring School Performance Using Cost Functions. 7
     The Reliability of School Efficiency Measures Using Data
      Envelopment Analysis 8
   Part Two · 9
     Measuring School Performance: Promises and Pitfalls. 9
     Teacher Accountability Measures and Links to Learning . . . 10
     Revealed-Preference Measures of School Quality 11
     Rethinking Educational Productivity and its Measurement:
      A Discussion of Stochastic Frontier Analysis
      within a Budget-Maximizing Framework. 12
What Have We Learned? 13
References. 15

**2   Adjusted Measures of School Performance:A Cross-State
Perspective** **17**

*Leanna Stiefel, Amy Ellen Schwartz, Hella Bel Hadj Amor,
and Dae Yeop Kim* 17

Introduction. 17
Concept of APMs and Literature Review 18
APMs: New York City and Ohio Urban Schools: Generic APMS
   for New York City and Ohio Urban Schools 19
Data on Ohio Urban Schools and New York City Schools 21
Results. 24
Ohio APMs for Alternative Subject Tests 27
New York City APMs for Alternative Years. 29
New York City APMs for Alternative Grades. 33
Conclusions: Lessons Learned 34
References. 35

3	**The Good, the Bad, and the Ugly: Measuring School Efficiency Using School Production Functions** **37**
	Amy Ellen Schwartz and Jeffrey E. Zabel 37

Introduction. 37
Measuring Efficiency with School Production Functions 38
   The Model · 38
   Estimation Issues · 42
      Addressing Bias because of the Inclusion of Fixed Effects
        and the Lagged Dependent Variable. 42
      Addressing Bias Because of Measurement Error 43
      Addressing Bias because of the Endogeneity of School
        Resources 43
Data 44
   Test Scores · 47
   School Characteristics and Resources · · · · · · · · · · · · · · · · 47
   Student Characteristics · 48
Results. 48
   Understanding Test Score Measures· · · · · · · · · · · · · · · · · 49
   Estimating School Production Functions · · · · · · · · · · · · · · 52
   Sensitivity Checks · 55
   Comparing Efficiency Measures · · · · · · · · · · · · · · · · · · · 56
   The Good, the Bad and the Ugly: What Characterizes High
      (and Low) Efficiency? · 60
Implications and Lessons for Future Work 64
References. 66

4	**Measuring School Performance Using Cost Functions** **67**
	Amy Ellen Schwartz, Leanna Stiefel, and Hella Bel Hadj Amor. 67

Introduction. 67
Literature Review 68
   Research on Costs and District Size · · · · · · · · · · · · · · · · · 68
   Research on the Cost of Education—the Cost of Increasing Output 68
   School-Level Cost Studies · 70
The Theory of Measuring Efficiency: A Cost Function for Schools . . . 71
   Cost Functions · 71
   Cost Functions versus Production Functions· · · · · · · · · · · · 74
   Learning about Efficiency· 76
Data, Samples, and Measures. 76
Results. 78
Implications and Lessons for Future Work 88
References. 90

5	**The Reliability of School Efficiency Measures Using Data Envelopment Analysis.** **93**
	Ross Rubenstein 93

Introduction. 93
Conceptual Basis 94
Measuring Outputs 96

Table of Contents

xiii

Measuring Inputs. 96
Technical Issues. 97
Empirical Results. 98
New York City Results 100
Ohio Results · 110
Stability Across Years · · · · · · · · · · · · · · · · · · · 113
Conclusions 116
References 117

6 Measuring School Performance: Promises and Pitfalls 119

David Figlio 119

Introduction 119
Aggregation Issues in Accountability Systems 120
Aggregation Across Time · · · · · · · · · · · · · · · · · · 120
Aggregation Across Subjects Tested · · · · · · · · · · · · 122
Aggregation Across Student Subgroups · · · · · · · · · · · 123
The Scope of Measurement 124
Evaluating Schools Based on Value Added 126
Who Should Be in the Test Pool? 129
Fiscal Implications of School Accountability. 131
Conclusion. 134
References 134

7 Teacher Accountability Measures and Links to Learning. 137

Anthony T. Milanowski, Steven M. Kimball, and Allan Odden 137

Introduction 137
Standards-Based Teacher Evaluation Systems. 138
Sites and Systems 140
Cincinnati Public Schools · · · · · · · · · · · · · · · · · 141
Coventry, Rhode Island · · · · · · · · · · · · · · · · · · 142
Vaughn Charter School · · · · · · · · · · · · · · · · · · 143
Washoe County School District · · · · · · · · · · · · · · · 144
Are Standards-Based Evaluations Related to Student Achievement? . 145
Analytic Approach · 145
Test Scores 146
Teacher Evaluation Ratings 147
Summary of Results 148
Other Aspects of Standards Based Evaluation for Teacher
Accountability 151
Implications for Using Standards-Based Teacher Evaluation
as Accountability and Reward Measure 153
Improving Teacher Evaluation Systems for Use as Accountability
Systems 154
Directions for Future Research 155
References 156
Appendix 159
Measures of Student Achievement 159

8   Revealed-Preference Measures of School Quality 163

Lori L. Taylor 163

Introduction 163
Revealed-Preference Models of School Quality 164
  The Hedonic Housing Model · 164
  Discrete Choice Models of Household Location and Migration· · 171
Using Reveled-Preference Measures for Accountability
  and Adequacy 173
Conclusions 181
References 182

**9   Rethinking Educational Productivity and its Measurement:
A Discussion of Stochastic Frontier Analysis Within a Budget-
Maximizing Framework 185**

Anthony Rolle. 185

Introduction 185
A Budget-Maximizing Framework for Examining Educational
  Productivity. 188
  The Budget-Output Function: A Mathematical Representation
    of Sponsor Preferences · 188
  A Budget-Maximizing Single-Service Bureau· · · · · · · · · · · 189
  A Budget-Maximizing Multiservice Bureau· · · · · · · · · · · · 190
  Summary · 191
Using Stochastic Frontier Analysis to Determine Levels of Relative
  Efficiency 192
  Stochastic Frontier Analyses · 193
An Illustrative Example of Efficiency Measurement Using OLS
  and SFA 195
  Measuring Efficiency Using Ordinary Least Squares· · · · · · · 196
  Measuring Efficiency Using Stochastic Frontier Analysis · · · · 198
Implications for Education Finance 199
References 201

Index 205

1

Measuring School Efficiency: What Have We Learned?

Leanna Stiefel, Amy Ellen Schwartz, Ross Rubenstein, and Jeffrey Zabel

Introduction

The headline of an April 15, 2004, *Palm Beach Post* article about Florida's "Return on Education Index" proclaimed, "Web Site to Show Parents How Efficient Schools Are" (Miller, 2004). Similarly, Virginia has implemented a statewide performance review of its school system designed to "analyze how effectively each school division uses resources to boost student achievement" (State of Virginia, 2004). In 2003, during a battle over school funding, Governor Mike Huckabee of Arkansas declared, "We must insist upon a [school] system that has a level of efficiency that we can live with and afford" (Jefferson, 2003). At the same time, efficiency, with its connotations of profit-driven, assembly line automation, is not a universally-desired goal for education. Indeed, an editorial in the *Halifax Daily News* argued, "Slow, inefficient schools teach our children well" (Lafolley, 2004).

As these articles suggest, school performance and efficiency measurement have taken center stage in much of the debate and research in education policy since at least the mid-1990s. Despite the clear theoretical and practical importance of understanding the ways in which school performance can be measured, only limited research exists on alternative ways to measure how well schools are educating their students, delivering what parents want, and using resources efficiently. In this volume, the authors of eight chapters address the measurement of school performance, an issue that lies in between the study of technical characteristics of student assessments, on the one hand, and the effectiveness of accountability systems that use those assessments, on the other. Although psychometricians focus on the reliability, validity, and fairness of individual student assessments, and social scientists address whether state and local accountability systems that use those student assessments are effective ways to influence school performance, the authors of this volume consider the pros and cons of alternative measurements of school performance and efficiency, per se.

The intermediate ground between psychometric criteria and social science modeling is important. Pyschometricians often warn that standardized tests are used for purposes other than the intended ones—for example, to decide on pupil promotion—even though the tests may have less-than-desirable levels of reliability. Student test results may be especially problematic when aggregated to the school or district level to assess the performance of school and district personnel, in part because of the variety of ways in which the aggregation can be undertaken. For example, comparisons of average scores may yield very different results than comparisons of pass rates or students scoring above a minimum threshold. Perhaps when combined with other measures or aggregated in certain ways, however, test scores *can* produce meaningful measures of performance and provide insight on effective ways to organize schools and deploy resources. The intermediate ground is also essential to the literature on the effectiveness of accountability systems because accurate performance measurement is essential when we want to understand whether or not the change has produced desirable results.

Although accountability systems typically seek to measure school performance to distribute rewards for high performance, to sanction schools and students for inadequate performance, or to identify schools and students in need of remediation, the aims of social science research on school performance measurement are more basic. Before effective accountability systems can be developed, it is critical to understand the variety of output measures, model specifications, data, and quantitative techniques available for this purpose. This task is particularly complex in the provision of social services such as education because no bottom line measure of performance exists. Moreover, as all the chapters in this volume explicitly recognize, each school faces very different constraints and obstacles to maximizing aggregate student performance. Thus, one of the most vexing and important questions that must be answered is, "should valid school performance measures account for differences in student characteristics and school resources?" And if the question is answered in the affirmative (as it is in each chapter in this volume), the more difficult issue is how the student characteristics and school resources should be included in the performance measures.

This question also points out an important distinction between efficiency measurement and performance measurement. Although performance measurement may range from simple comparisons of average test scores to complex multivariate models, efficiency measurement presumes a connection between inputs and outputs. At its most basic, measures of technical efficiency seek to identify those schools getting "the most bang for their buck," where *bang* is typically a series of test score measures and *bucks* may include a variety of inputs, such as resources, organizational characteristics, and student attributes. Similarly, allocative efficiency examines whether the correct (cost minimizing) mix of inputs is deployed to produce outputs. The definition of efficiency that we use in this volume is broad, encompassing a variety of concepts, methods, and data, although most definitions stress technical rather than allocative efficiency. All the approaches share the common feature of attempting to disentangle the effects of various inputs on school outputs. Thus, although the techniques that the authors in this volume employ use different theoretical underpinnings, all attempt to measure schools' true contributions to student learning, accounting for the wide disparities in resources and student characteristics that these schools may face.

This focus on the relationship between inputs and outputs distinguishes the methods from those used in many state accountability systems and in the federal No Child Left Behind (NCLB) Act, which often focus exclusively on student performance, frequently disaggregated by subgroups. The latter systems typically do not explicitly account for disparities in the levels and qualities of resources, or of demographic differences in the composition of student bodies across schools.

Why Study School Efficiency Measurement?

As the title of this book suggests, the authors focus on school efficiency and performance measurement not simply as an academic exercise but as an issue with real implications for education policy. For example, state and federal education policy has largely focused on rewarding or sanctioning schools and school personnel based on measures of school performance. Similarly, many "natural experiments" in education seek to isolate the effects of policies and programs by comparing the performances of schools with and without specific policies.

The work presented here has several clear implications for policy and research. First, understanding the strengths and weaknesses of various measures can help policy makers to develop fairer methods of measuring school performance by taking into account the uneven distribution of resources, students, and other inputs across schools. Important incentives and disincentives are embedded in any method of performance measurement, and it is critical that we understand the potential behavioral effects of any methods that might be used for accountability purposes. It is well established that simple comparisons of test scores—and, often, of changes in test scores—will typically rank well-resourced schools serving students from more educated and high-income families at the top, whereas most schools serving more at-risk students will languish near the bottom. By controlling for these factors, school efficiency measurement provides an opportunity to identify schools that are uncommonly successful at educating their students, although their successes might not be as readily apparent.

Second, although simple test score comparisons tell us little about the causes of high performance, efficiency measures may help to shed light on the relationships between inputs, broadly defined, and test scores. The search for a definitive link between spending and performance has been, in some ways, the "holy grail" of school finance research for the past 30 years, but clearly no simple answers exist. The methods explored in this book seek to shed light on those relationships by exploring not only how to measure performance and efficiency, but also what factors appear to be systematically related to high performance and efficiency.

Third, resource constraints are a fact of life in education, and the constraints have been particularly severe in the early part of the 21st century. School efficiency measures explicitly take account of these constraints, asking how we can maximize performance given available resources. It is important to use measures that emphasize costs as well as outputs in education, lest the education system become wasteful of the public's tax dollars.

Overview of the Volume

The chapters in this volume share a number of common features. First, rather than focusing on the underlying validity or construction of the tests and other output measures commonly used to assess school performance, the authors work with available data to examine the ways in which these data can be used to analyze performance and efficiency. Second, the authors all go beyond simple test score measures to ask how various desirable outputs of schools, measured or unmeasured, can and should be combined with other features of schools or districts, such as characteristics of students or lavishness of resources, to produce meaningful measures of school performance. Third, the focus of most chapters is on the school rather than on the students, teachers, or administrators who are part of the school. Thus it is the aggregate school's performance that the authors are aiming to measure.

The book is divided into two parts. The first section reports results of studies examining four specific quantitative techniques to measure school efficiency and performance. These include adjusted performance measures, production functions, cost functions, and data envelopment analysis. A unique feature of these chapters is that they all grew out of a single project using similar data designed to assess and compare the usefulness of these techniques for school efficiency measurement.[1]

As described below and in the individual chapters, the four chapters make use of administrative data from New York City and the state of Ohio, two locations that have particularly well-developed, school-level information systems. Each chapter demonstrates the possibilities and pitfalls inherent in measuring performance and efficiency with existing data, and details the specific strengths and weaknesses of each technique.

The second half of the book includes four chapters examining alternative ways to conceptualize and measure school performance and efficiency: the use of efficiency measures in state accountability systems, stochastic frontier analysis, property values as school efficiency measures, and teacher assessment systems. The chapters reveal insights about the contribution of each performance measure. After a discussion of the major contribution of each chapter, this introduction concludes with a discussion of general themes. It is intended that these themes will prove useful to district, state, and federal policymakers as they work to improve both the ways in which schools are assessed and the accountability systems that use those assessments.

---

1 "Good Schools, Good Students? Measuring School Performance with Diverse Students," U.S. Department of Education, Grant Number R305T010115. All opinions expressed in this introduction are those of the authors alone.

Overview of the Chapters

Part One

Adjusted Measures of School Performance: A Cross-State Perspective

Leanna Stiefel, Amy Ellen Schwartz, Hella Bel Hadj Amor, and Dae Yeop Kim examine one of the simplest quantitative methods used to measure school efficiency: adjusted performance measures (APMs). An APM uses multiple regression analysis to adjust a measure or measures of school output based on the inputs facing the school, including resources, student characteristics, and organizational factors. By regressing the output on the inputs, the model holds constant school resources and estimates a predicted level of achievement. The measure of interest is the difference between each school's actual and predicted performance, or its adjusted performance measure.

Although the method is relatively straightforward and intuitive for those with a basic grounding in regression analysis, it is not without complications, for several of which the authors offer guidance. The authors' unique contribution, however, is to expand on their previous work by estimating both generic and tailored APMs for New York City and Ohio to explore the consistency of results across jurisdictions and model specifications (see Rubenstein, Schwartz, & Stiefel, 1998; Stiefel, Rubenstein, & Schwartz, 1999; Rubenstein, Schwartz, & Stiefel, 2003). The implications of these comparisons are important: If the appropriate parameters for making adjustments are relatively universal, and if complex models offer few advantages over simpler ones, the usefulness of such adjusted measures for policy making would greatly increase.

To investigate this issue, the authors first estimate generic APMs for New York City and for Ohio. The generic specification uses a standard set of output and input data that are available in most states or school districts. These data include the percentage of students passing state or local tests, student socioeconomic characteristics, school size, and some aggregate expenditure measures. Interestingly, the results are very similar for the New York City and Ohio schools, particularly when math scores are used as output measures. Thus, school rankings change little when APMs are constructed using the parameters estimated in the other location. In other words, rankings of New York City schools are relatively insensitive to the use of parameters estimated with either New York City data or Ohio data. The similarities imply that it may be possible to develop a standard set of adjustment parameters that could be shared across districts or states.

The authors go on to explore the stability of APM results using different test scores, grade levels, years of data, and model specifications. Although the results generally display fairly high levels of consistency, the authors find a negative correlation between APMs constructed using consecutive years of data and using test score gains rather than levels. This latter result points out a fundamental problem in accountability systems based on test score improvements: Gains are exceedingly difficult, and sometimes impossible, to maintain over multiple years.

In sum, the authors' results point out not only the importance of adjusting for inputs that are outside the control of schools to construct more accurate measures of performance, but also the practicality of employing these adjustments even when data or analytic capacity is limited. The authors highlight several other policy areas where such adjustments are used, but it remains to be seen whether such methods will take hold in education.

The Good, the Bad and the Ugly: Measuring School Efficiency Using School Production Functions

Performance-based accountability, a term that includes a variety of ideas, can be operationalized in several different ways. Amy Ellen Schwartz and Jeffrey E. Zabel provide a useful summary, pointing out that even when performance is measured using test scores, there are many ways to measure school performance—raw test scores, changes in raw test scores, and test scores adjusted for student and school characteristics and efficiency. In particular, efficiency measures how well both financial and student resources are used to produce test scores. For example, high-performing schools, based on either the levels or changes in their scores, adjusted or not, might turn out to be inefficient. The authors focus on developing a conceptual measure of school efficiency that is derived from a school-level education production function, and then proceed to work their way through econometric issues involved in estimating such a measure based on the fixed effects from a panel of 602 New York City elementary schools.

Zabel and Schwartz distinguish between three possible dependent variables, all derived from an original conception of an education production function: level scores (with a lagged score for the previous year and grade as a right-hand side variable), gain scores (the change in a score between adjacent grades between years), and difference scores (the change in scores in the same grade between years). Each of these allows estimates of school- or grade-specific fixed effects (interpreted as efficiency measures), but each has econometric virtues and problems. The most econometrically straightforward equation has levels of test scores as the dependent variable and the lagged test score as an independent variable; but the fixed effects in this model may suffer from three sources of bias—endogeneity because of the lagged test score, measurement error, or endogeneity of resources. The most econometrically correct estimation involves difference scores, with corrections for endogeneity, but it uses more years of data and is harder to estimate and explain than the other specifications.

Using both correlations and rankings to measure differences in the fixed effect estimations, the authors conclude that results concerning efficiency from the most straightforward estimation are quite close to the ones from the econometrically preferred approach. They also conclude that the efficiency measures are different across grades, but not across math and reading tests in a given grade.

Finally, Schwartz and Zabel make an effort to link their efficiency measures to observable characteristics of schools. They also find some evidence for a relationship between efficiency and large size, low proportions of poor and special education students, and grade span only through grade five, but point out that these relationships are suggestive, not causal.

Particularly helpful are the conclusions that efficiency measures can be calculated from relatively straightforward OLS fixed-effects models and the demonstration that efficiency measures differ from other performance-based measures. This careful work will simplify implementing a somewhat complicated model—but one that is a sorely needed addition to accountability metrics.

Measuring School Performance Using Cost Functions

Amy Ellen Schwartz, Leanna Stiefel, and Hella Bel Hadj Amor use cost functions to measure the performance of elementary and middle schools across all districts in Ohio over a three year period. Cost functions capture the minimum cost of producing a bundle of outputs given a particular technology and the prices of inputs. In theory, they should provide similar results to those of the production function approach because a cost function incorporates all economically relevant information about the technology of the organization (school).

The advantages of the cost function approach over the production function approach are that it uses multiple output measures (test scores) simultaneously rather than a single output; that the minimum number of years of data needed to estimate the cost function is less than for the production function approach; and that it assumes input prices, rather than the inputs themselves, are exogenous. This latter assumption is more realistic given that school resources are often allocated based on test scores. The disadvantage of the cost function approach is that it requires information on the prices of inputs, including teachers and staff, physical plant, books, and computers. Typically it is difficult to obtain prices for all these inputs, and it is also difficult to precisely estimate the associated coefficients given the high correlation between the prices of some inputs. In this chapter, the authors are able to use the minimum and maximum salaries for teachers holding bachelor's and master's degrees for Ohio school districts.

The efficient schools are the ones that contribute the least amount to costs holding input prices and outputs equal across all schools. Thus, the appropriate measure of school performance is its contribution to costs once all input prices and output levels are taken into account. In the cost function, estimated with panel data on schools, this is captured using the school fixed effect, which is the average of net costs across the three years of the panel for a given school.

The authors find a positive relationship between input prices and costs (as predicted by theory) but no relationship between school-level pass rates and costs (contrary to theoretical predictions). A comparison of the most and least efficient schools shows that, on average, the former spend 40% less than the latter. In addition, the most efficient schools spend 72% of their budget on instructional activities whereas the least efficient only spend 63% on instruction.

Because the cost function is estimated using fixed effects, all time-invariant variables will be included in the school efficiency measures, that is the fixed effects. The authors consider alternatives to the pure fixed effects to control for some of these time-invariant factors that are not directly attributable to the school's efficiency. These alternative efficiency measures are derived from regressions of the pure efficiency measures (the fixed effects) on the time-invariant variables. First, they include dichotomous variables representing school districts in rural, small town, suburban, urban, and major urban areas, because the cost of educating students differs across these types of areas. Second, the authors include the means of the explanatory variables over all years of the data in this second-stage regression. The correlation between the new purged and pure fixed effect measures is 0.61. The regression results show that suburban and urban districts are less efficient than rural districts, that the size of the school exhibits the expected U-shaped effect on costs, and that the presence of poor, black, and other minority students adversely affect costs.

The Reliability of School Efficiency Measures Using Data Envelopment Analysis

In this chapter, Ross Rubenstein assesses the prospects for measuring school efficiency using data envelopment analysis (DEA), a nonstochastic method that offers an alternative to the regression-based techniques described elsewhere in this volume. More specifically, DEA is a linear programming technique that constructs a nonparametric efficiency frontier that envelops all the decision-making units—in this case, schools—in the analysis. Therefore, by construction, all schools lie either on the frontier or below it, and an efficiency index can be calculated for each school. Scores range from 0, which indicates that the school is the farthest distance possible from the efficiency frontier, to 100, which indicates that the school is on the frontier.

Rubenstein notes three key ways in which DEA differs from regression-based techniques. First, DEA measures efficiency relative to the most efficient school in the analysis sample, whereas regression methods focus on averages. Second, DEA can easily accommodate multiple inputs and multiple outputs simultaneously, whereas regression methods are less suited to this—production functions easily accommodate multiple inputs only and cost functions accommodate multiple outputs only. Finally, the underlying logic of the DEA procedure allows units to gain efficiency through specialization as well as through high performance on multiple measures.

Rubenstein's chapter provides a description of the concepts and interpretation of DEA measures, then turns to a discussion of the practical issues to be confronted in empirical analysis and presents two examples—one based on a sample of schools in New York City and another using Ohio schools. The results suggest that the specification of output variables is crucial and that using level scores, rather than value-added scores, as output measures holds some advantages in this context. Further, the analyses identify groups of schools achieving higher pass rates despite serving more students with special needs and generally using lower levels of resources—schools that may be worth examining in greater depth.

Much attention is paid to drawing out and exploring the advantages and disadvantages of the DEA method. One advantage is that DEA provides an intuitive method for identifying the most efficient schools—put simply, these are the schools on the frontier. It is likely, though, that there will be more than one school on the frontier, and the technique provides little guidance for differentiating between them. At the same time, although it is possible to employ multiple

Measuring School Efficiency: What Have We Learned? 9

inputs and outputs, this is not without cost. The number of units placed on the frontier increases with the number of inputs and outputs specified. Further, the complexity of the DEA methodology makes it easily misunderstood or misused. Rubenstein concludes that considerable caution is warranted in using DEA to rank schools, particularly for the purpose of distributing rewards or sanctions. It may, however, prove to be a useful complement to other measures.

Part Two

Measuring School Performance: Promises and Pitfalls

David Figlio begins his chapter by observing that the passage of the 2001 No Child Left Behind Act (NCLB) created a new imperative for school districts across the nation to produce school performance measures for use in accountability systems. Although it is too early to measure the impacts of NCLB directly, Figlio argues that the evidence to date on state-level school accountability suggests that placing high stakes for schools based on student test scores improves student performance. At the same time, states face many choices when adopting school accountability initiatives and implementing the federal policy, and these choices may have substantial repercussions. Figlio outlines a number of these key decisions and details some of their implications. He then turns to a description of how these decisions could influence the intended and unintended consequences of school accountability initiatives and affect school finance.

His analysis begins with a discussion of three aggregation decisions that states face in designing accountability systems—will test scores be aggregated across time, across subjects, and/or across subgroups? Next he considers the implications of alternative choices in the scope of measurement—across grades and subjects—followed by a discussion of the relative virtues of measures based on level-test performance versus value added. Finally, he considers the issues surrounding the composition of the test pool and concludes with a discussion of the fiscal implications of school accountability initiatives.

His conclusions are important. He notes that although available evidence points to rising test scores directly resulting from the increased focus on test scores, there is also evidence suggesting that some of these apparent test score gains may be because of other factors besides increased focus and efficiency in education. Further, the experience to date highlights the importance of design issues in the development and implementation of accountability systems. School personnel can and will respond to the incentives created by accountability systems, producing changes in behavior and outcomes both intended and unintended—including, for example, reclassifying students to enhance school performance measures, as well as taking measures to improve performance among those tested.

Figlio concludes that the fiscal implications for schools and school districts—both direct and indirect—may have significant implications for school finance. Changes in the costs of education, such as input prices and increased special education placements, may have adequacy implications for states in their school finance systems. And the differential impacts of these systems across schools may create new equity issues or exacerbate existing uncorrected inequities. The design of school accountability and school finance systems are likely to be indelibly intertwined.

Teacher Accountability Measures and Links to Learning

The dispute over whether and how much additional resources would contribute to raising student achievement rages on. Eric Hanushek stands by his findings of "no marginal effects" in his seminal article (Hanushek, 1986), and bastions of other researchers find counterexamples (see Ferguson & Ladd, 1996; Hedges, Laine, & Greenwald, 1994). Within this heated debate, however, there is one no-combat zone where agreement reigns: Teachers do affect student achievement, although we are unable to identify which of their characteristics matter most. Moreover, the ones usually compensated, such as education and experience, seem not to matter. What, then, are policymakers to do with the findings of a positive teacher effect?

Anthony T. Milanowski, Stephen M. Kimball, and Allan Odden address this issue in their chapter on teacher accountability measures and links to learning. They claim that "standards-based teacher evaluation" systems are an answer to both how to identify specific teacher behaviors that matter to student achievement and how to provide teachers with guidance about ways to modify their behavior and produce more achievement. They argue that "instead of, or perhaps in addition to, holding teachers directly accountable for student achievement, it might make sense to hold them accountable for teaching behaviors or competencies that are causally related to student achievement."

But what is the evidence that standards-based evaluation systems are related to student performance? Based on data from four school districts that are using a rubric of criterion-referenced standards for evaluating teacher behaviors, these authors find that higher scores on the rubrics are positively correlated with larger gains in test scores for students in the teachers' classes. They first develop a hierarchical model of student achievement that includes student characteristics such as previous test scores and gender and ethnicity or race and free lunch status, with a random classroom (teacher) effect. The classroom effects are then related to teacher evaluations on the standards and other controls, with the coefficients on evaluations being positive and significant. The evidence comes from four districts, all using different tests, sometimes in different grades, and is summarized mostly with correlations that are moderate in strength (in the 0.15 to the 0.40 ranges). But given the difficulty of finding any teacher traits related to achievement, these are intriguing results. Perhaps these results are the kind that "scientifically based education research" should pursue with a randomized experiment to make sure that student, parent, or teacher selection effects or differences in grades or tests are not driving the results.

In terms of accountability measurement, if more evidence on a relationship between observable teacher behaviors and student achievement is found, and the cost of the rubrics is documented, then standards-based teacher evaluations may become a cost-effective measurement tool.

Revealed-Preference Measures of School Quality

Lori L. Taylor investigates the use of revealed preferences for primary education as a means for developing a measure of school quality. Because households are willing to move to areas with good schools and pay for schools that are perceived as high quality, these preferences should be capitalized into house prices. These capitalized values can be used to rank school performance because they are based on individual preferences for school quality that are revealed through the housing market.

Taylor lays out the basic hedonic model of house prices, in which houses are heterogeneous goods that are composed of numerous structural and locational attributes. The latter include local public goods such as schooling, accessibility, and environmental amenities, all of which will affect the price of a house. The underlying theory shows that it is possible to interpret the coefficients for these housing characteristics as the marginal willingness to pay for more of these characteristics. A problem arises because the estimated coefficients (or prices) for the individual housing characteristics may be biased if some neighborhood factors (some of which are unobservable to the researcher) are not included in the house price regression.

Taylor reviews two approaches to dealing with this omitted variable problem. One approach is to include a large number of neighborhood characteristics in the hedonic model to minimize the omitted variable bias. A second approach is the so-called "boundary fixed effects" method developed by Black (1999), whereby neighborhood fixed effects control for neighborhood. To identify school quality, there must be variations within these neighborhoods, and to achieve such variation, these neighborhoods are set up to incorporate school attendance zone boundaries. This means that households within the same neighborhood will send their children to different schools with inherently differing levels of quality.

Taylor supplements her literature survey with an interesting empirical exercise based on single-family house sales from 1997 in Dallas County, Texas. Using Black's boundary fixed-effects approach to determine if school quality is capitalized into house prices, she finds that average test scores have a positive and significant effect on house prices—a one standard deviation increase in the average test score results in a 3.2% increase in house prices. Further, Taylor finds that this impact is driven by peer effects and not by the value added of the individual school. Next, she estimates school-level fixed effects using a variation of the same model that controls for nonschool neighborhood quality and uses these fixed effects to rank schools. She considers schools in the top quartile to be "successful" schools. These schools tend to be disproportionately white and economically advantaged, but there is no significant difference in the average test scores, the percentage of Hispanic students, or the percentage of limited English proficient or special education students as compared to other schools.

Taylor compares these results to more standard measures of school performance—average test scores and school fixed effects (obtained from a test score model). Although there is variation in the school rankings using these three approaches, the revealed preference measures and the school fixed effects are the most similar. This is particularly true when Taylor considers a version of the revealed preference measure that controls for the demographic characteristics of students, the school size, and the local tax rate.

Overall, the revealed preference result offers another viable method for measuring school performance. In particular, it may be the only way to obtain a measure of school performance that includes aspects of school quality that are not captured in test scores. Yet, this approach does have its own drawbacks that are thoroughly discussed by Taylor. First, because this measure is based on housing market outcomes, it is affected by both demand and supply factors, and the latter may not directly reflect school quality. Second, no matter how much one attempts to control for all factors that affect house values, it is likely that the revealed preference measures are a noisy estimate of school quality. Thus, at best, they are a complement to standard measures such as those obtained using the education production function approach.

Rethinking Educational Productivity and its Measurement: A Discussion of Stochastic Frontier Analysis within a Budget-Maximizing Framework

In his chapter, Anthony Rolle veers from the more traditional private sector efficiency model, and instead relies on Niskanen's (1971) budget-maximizing framework. Niskanen's work, which grew out of the study of public sector bureaucracies, does not assume that organizations seek to minimize costs or maximize outputs. Instead it theorizes that public sector managers, lacking external incentives to maximize efficiency, seek to maximize their own power and prestige by enlarging the size of their budgets. The implication for school efficiency measurement is that the assumption of efficiency-maximizing behavior among school officials may not hold in practice.

The budget-maximizing theory leads Rolle to suggest that empirical analyses predicated on the assumption of cost-minimization or output maximization may be flawed. He turns instead to stochastic frontier analysis (SFA), a statistical method designed to measure technical efficiency by comparing organizational performance to the best observed performance in a sample. Like data envelopment analysis, it focuses not on average performance but on extreme performance—those schools lying on the efficiency frontier. Unlike DEA, which is a nonstochastic method, the stochastic frontier analysis includes an error term partitioned into a random component and a component representing technical efficiency. This potentially provides a more precise measure of efficiency. Rolle then supplies a simple empirical example using data from Tennessee school districts. He uses expenditures per pupil as an input measure and average ACT scores as an output. He finds that that, on average, districts spend approximately 20% more than predicted by the model, though the estimates range up to 140% more. Based on his results, such as the finding that twice as many districts are rated efficient as inefficient, Rolle concludes that Tennessee districts do not appear to fit the budget-maximizing framework.

His chapter concludes with a list of five fundamental questions that we should ask, providing a timely reminder that we must be careful to step back and consider the goals of educational policies before attempting a "one-size-fits-all" approach to efficiency measurement.

What Have We Learned?

The most important lesson of these chapters is that performance and efficiency are separate concepts and must be measured differently. Although performance can be measured using school outputs, such as test scores (or graduation rates, college attendance rates, and so on), efficiency requires that resources, including students, teachers, and perhaps community attributes, be taken into account as well. If efficiency is not included in school performance assessments, then society runs the risk of missing important opportunities to use scarce educational resources more productively. At a time when the public sector is struggling with how the nation's resources should be allocated among large competing interests such as foreign affairs, protection of cities, and health care, the education enterprise can ill afford to show little improvement in its output if it is allocated more public dollars. In other words, it can ill afford to leave efficiency out of its measurements of school performance. All the authors in this volume study measures that account for both the inputs and outputs of education, and thus provide the reader with seven different ways to quantify efficiency.

Not every approach analyzed by the authors of chapters is equally useful to policymakers who are looking for school performance measures that could be implemented, perhaps as part of accountability systems, in the short run. Can these measures be regarded as useful, promising, or not ready for prime time? We focus only on the utility of these measures for use by policymakers. All the authors have advanced our understanding of the conceptual and practical issues embedded in each of these approaches.

In the useful category, representing school efficiency with the coefficients from fixed effects (or dummy variables for each school) from regression equations based on panel data of outputs (such as test scores) on inputs, provides the most attractive measure. Relatively straightforward estimation techniques work well to determine fixed-effect coefficients, and the largest implementation problem would seem to be the annual accumulation of data on schools, so that panels of data can be maintained.

Promising, but not so immediately useful, are fixed effects estimated from cost functions, APMs, rankings taken from teaching evaluations, and DEA measures. School-level cost functions are promising because they resolve the problem in production functions of focus on one output. They are not, however, ready for prime time, in part because schools do not act autonomously and do not have prices of inputs to which they can respond. If school districts continue to allow more independent budgeting behavior and forms of organization (such as charter and privately-run schools), this situation may change, making cost estimations more plausible.

Likewise, APMs have attractive features and are promising. They can be estimated yearly and do not demand the data accumulation that are required to estimate fixed effect production functions; they are more understandable to users than are fixed effects; and they have the possibility of being universal, that is, having coefficients that are similar across jurisdictions. They are a cheap version of the fixed effects from production functions and are better than having no efficiency measure at all.

Measures based on teacher performance on standardized assessments would be very helpful for the professionals that deliver education services to children. Although the evidence provided in this book makes this a measure to watch, more research is needed to clarify the strength of the link between the scores on the teacher evaluations and student performance in the teachers' classes.

Finally, DEA analysis is promising because it allows multiple outputs to be measured and because it focuses on schools that are doing the best rather than better than average. But it is less than ideal as a measure because of its limitation in terms of the number of inputs and its tendency to identify a large number of efficient units, particularly if large numbers of outputs are included. DEA could be useful as a way to identify schools for further study or audit purposes. Schools that appear very good or very bad may be doing something exceptional that should be investigated. Private industry has used DEA for this purpose and perhaps it could be tried in education as well. But as a way to rate efficiency, it could both provide too many winners and, in some cases, may do so on the basis of extraordinary success on one indicator but abysmal performance on all others.

Two measures that are not ready for prime time use by policymakers are property-value-based and Niskanan-based estimates. Each presents a different challenge in terms of its utility. Although impacts of test scores on residential property values incorporate willingness to pay by families into the measure of performance and thus do not require a guess about how much a gain in scores or a reduction in costs is worth to the public, their virtue is also a problem. Market prices are based on the current income distribution and have built into them whatever market imperfections exist (such as possible discrimination in sales or mortgages). Thus, these measures presume that the current distribution of income is desirable and that imperfections are acceptable. It is perhaps better to let the political process decide what to do once measures are established.

Measures based on Niskanan's budget maximizing bureaucrats take us in a different direction from the market, toward the so-called realism of the political process. These measures might better represent how public bureaucracies behave, but again, as a normative measure of school performance, they could fall short of the public's aspirations for its schools. Budget-maximization theory's application through stochastic frontier analysis, however, provides many of the same potential advantages as data-envelopment analysis and could provide a useful technique for identifying exemplary schools.

Finally, there are extensions of the work on efficiency measurement that will be worth pursuing. In this book, the authors focus on how to measure efficiency. Once it is possible to attach a metric to efficiency, research to help determine what drives that metric is imperative. By thinking of the fixed effects from an educational production function as a measure of efficiency, one should ask what determines their coefficients. In other words, open up the "black box" of the fixed-effects estimates to determine what is left out of the model: Is it how schools are organized? Is it principals? Is it something that districts provide?

Also consider the implications of using these measures for rewarding or sanctioning schools. That is, if some jurisdiction decided to use the efficiency scores as the basis of their accountability system, would schools then seek to maximize their efficiency? And, if they did, what kinds of changes would they try to make in their resource use, in their student body, or in their production processes?

As the states and federal government continue to implement school accountability systems, attention needs to be given to the metrics used to measure school success. Efficiency should not be missing from these metrics and the authors of the chapters in this book have provided alternative ways to obtain information on this important concept.

References

Black, S. (1999). Do better schools matter: Parental evaluation of elementary education. *Quarterly Journal of Economics*, 114(2), 577–599.

Ferguson, R., & Ladd, H. (1996). How and why money matters. In Helen Ladd (Ed.), *Holding schools accountable*, Washington DC: Brookings Institution.

Hanushek, E. A. (1986). The economics of schooling: Production and efficiency in public schools. *Journal of Economic Literature*, 24, 1141–1177.

Hedges, L. V., Laine, R. D., and Greenwald, R. (1994). Does money matter? A meta-analysis of studies of the effects of differential school inputs on student outcomes. *Educational Researcher*, 23, 5–14.

Jefferson, J. (2004). Huckabee: Inefficient schools drain higher ed dollars. *Associated Press State and Local Wire*, August 13, 2003.

Lafolley, S. (2003, April 26). Slow inefficient schools teach our children well. *Halifax Daily News*, p. 13.

Miller, K. (2004, April 15). Web site to show parents how efficient schools are. *Palm Beach Post*, p. 8A.

Niskanen, W. (1971). *Bureaucracy and Representative Government*, Chicago: Aldine.

Rubenstein, R., Schwartz, A. E., & Stiefel, L. (2003). Better than raw: A guide to measuring organizational performance with adjusted performance measures. *Public Administration Review*, 63(5), 607–615

Rubenstein, R., Schwartz, A. E., & Stiefel, L. (1998). Conceptual and empirical issues in the measurement of school efficiency. *National Tax Journal, Proceedings from 91st Annual Conference:* 267–274.

State of Virginia, (2004) Accountability and efficiency reviews. Retrieved August 12, 2004, from http://www.governor.virginia.gov/Initiatives/Ed4Life/EfficiencyReview.htm

Stiefel, L., Rubenstein, R., & Schwartz, A. E. (1999). Using adjusted performance measures for evaluating resource use. *Public Budgeting and Finance*, 19(3), 67–87.

2

Adjusted Measures of School Performance: A Cross-State Perspective

Leanna Stiefel, Amy Ellen Schwartz,
Hella Bel Hadj Amor, and Dae Yeop Kim

Introduction

State legislators, governors, mayors, parents, and now, with the passage of the No Child Left Behind Act of 2001 (NCLB), the federal government find themselves in uncommon agreement that schools should be made responsible for their students' academic achievements. Doing so, however, requires school performance to be measured and schools falling above or below the acceptable performance level identified. There are many ways that such performance could be measured, some more demanding of data and technical expertise than others. Less-demanding means are attractive both because many states will be able to implement them and because the public can be taught to understand them. [1]>

This chapter discusses one of the least-demanding methods of measuring school performance—the use of residuals from school-level, multiple-regression equations in which raw performance indicators are dependent variables. We call these measures adjusted performance measures (APMs) because they adjust the output measure (usually a test score) for student and school characteristics beyond the control of an individual school. We estimate APM regressions for schools in New York City and urban districts in Ohio in an effort to gain an understanding of how the adjustment parameters—that is, the coefficients in the APM regressions—differ across settings. Are there universal adjustment parameters, or do we need to estimate adjustment parameters separately for different jurisdictions? This is important because fully implementing even the APM methodology may be beyond the capacity of some

---

1 For example, the *New York Times* published a version of school-level performance measures. See Josh Barbanel (1999a, 1999b, 1999c, 2000) who used test scores as outcome measures with statistical controls for income and sometimes English proficiency. Each school was compared to schools with a similar mix of students.

administrative units, perhaps as a result of limitations in data availability or an insufficient number of schools for the regression. In these cases, it is possible that parameters estimated from another state's data may be transferred (and used) for creating the APMs.[2] Besides the question of whether parameters can be transferred across jurisdictions, questions about the effects of a number of other changes are important, including whether different outcomes, years, or grades yield the same parameters or the same measures.

We also estimate a set of tailored APM regressions in which we take full advantage of the data in Ohio, which includes data for multiple outcomes. We then compare the results of these tailored APM regressions—both the adjustment parameters and the APMs themselves—to ascertain whether adding additional information on outcomes yields different adjustment parameters, and, perhaps more important, different APMs. Finally we estimate the New York City APMs for two different years and two different grades to explore whether the adjustment parameters or APMs differ along these dimensions.

In the second section of this chapter, we describe the concept of APMs more fully and review the literature on such methods. In the third section, we compare similar specifications of APM regressions for Ohio urban schools and New York City schools. In the fourth section, we tailor the Ohio APMs based on more complete test data available for Ohio urban schools and compare these tailored measures to the basic ones estimated for Ohio. In the fifth and sixth sections, we discuss different years and different grades, respectively, for the basic New York City APMs, and in the final section, we provide conclusions on lessons learned.

Concept of APMs and Literature Review

Adjusted performance measures are derived from school-level regression equations in which outputs, usually test scores, are the dependent variables, and the independent variables include a variety of student and school characteristics that are outside the control of a school. That is, this method computes school-performance measures after adjusting for differences in school resources, student educational needs, and the like, which characterize the school environment. Usually, but not always, a past year's score is included as an independent variable to approximate the value added of achievement over the school year. The APM is calculated as the difference between the actual school output and the output predicted from the regression equation, or the estimated residual from the regression.

More specifically, if $P_{i,t}$ represents the performance measure for school i in year t, $Z_{i,t}$ is the set of uncontrollable variables affecting i's performance in year t, and $P_{i,t-1}$ represents the performance measure for school i in year $t-1$, then we estimate:

---

2 The Environmental Protection Agency (EPA) uses a conceptually similar method to measure benefits of river cleaning by applying parameters for benefit equations estimated in one part of a state (or the country) to data from another. Such methods have been found by researchers to give reliable results, and they save the EPA considerable resources in doing cost and benefit studies. (See Desvousges et al., 1992; Parsons & Kealy, 1994.)

Productivity and Its Measurement

$$P_{i,t} = \beta_0 + \beta_1 Z_{i,t} + \beta_2 P_{i,t-1} + \varepsilon_{i,t} \text{ such that } i = 1,2.....\text{N and } t = \text{year} \qquad (1)$$

where N is the number of schools in the analysis, β_0 is the intercept of the equation, β_1 is the vector of coefficients capturing the marginal impacts of changes in the Z's on $P_{i,t}$, β_2 is the marginal contribution of changes in $P_{i,t-1}$ on $P_{i,t}$, and $\varepsilon_{i,t}$ is an error term with the usual properties. Denoting estimates of β_0, β_1, and β_2 as b_0, b_1, and b_2, respectively, the *APM* for school i in year t, $APM_{i,t}$ is found as:

$$\text{APM}_{i,t} = P_{i,t} - b_0 - b_1 Z_{i,t} - b_2 P_{i,t-1} \text{ for all } i = 1, 2, \ldots, N \text{ and } t = \text{given year} \qquad (2)$$

Thus, $APM_{i,t}$ is the estimated residual (or the prediction error) from the estimation of (1).

The use of residuals to gauge comparative performance is not new to the school accountability movement of the 1990s. As early as 1976, Edward Gramlich wrestled with a way to judge how responsible New York City was for its fiscal crisis of the mid-1970s. Gramlich estimated a regression equation relating expenditures per capita to various expenditure determinants using data on the 30 largest U.S. cities and interpreted the residual as a measure of New York's distance from its expected or predicted spending (Gramlich, 1976). And, we are not the only ones to think of the residual as a natural measure of school performance as well. Ladd and Walsh (2002) describe similar methods in use in both South Carolina and North Carolina, although the estimated equations are different in the two states, and they estimate performance measures using student-level data. Finally, in recent work, we have explored performance measures using school-level APMs and compared them to fixed effects estimated from production function models (Rubenstein, Schwartz, & Stiefel, 1998; Stiefel, Rubenstein, & Schwartz, 1999; Rubenstein, Schwartz, & Stiefel, 2003). Our objective in this chapter is to move the literature forward by comparing the APMs from urban schools in two jurisdictions to ascertain if the parameters of APMs can be generalized across jurisdictions, to investigate whether there are any significant differences between APMs based on relatively simple models and those generated using more sophisticated models, and to test for the effects on parameters and measures of changes in years and grades. Although most analysts intuitively think that the best measures of performance can be derived from student-level data and the estimation of education production or cost functions (see Schwartz & Zabel; Schwartz, Stiefel, & Bel Hadj Amor, both in this volume), school-level data are much more commonly available and their use more accessible to policymakers and the public. Therefore it is useful to continue to pursue the strengths and weaknesses of such school-level measures.

APMs: New York City and Ohio Urban Schools: Generic APMS for New York City and Ohio Urban Schools

To compare the parameter estimates based on data from two quite different jurisdictions, we construct a straightforward "generic" APM equation that requires only variables available for both the State of Ohio and New York City. Restricting ourselves to variables for which both the city and state have data turns out to be a significant constraint, as New York City has been producing fairly sophisticated annual school reports for nearly a decade and has more complete data on student characteristics, performance, and resources available. Ohio tests students on a wider range of subject areas, however, allowing an investigation of the extent to which results for reading and math tests, which are most commonly available, are sufficient to gauge school performance.[3] The generic specification uses the percentage of students passing a fourth-grade reading test as the dependent variable and each school's percentage of passing students in last year's fourth grade as an independent variable. Use of percent passing and last year's fourth-grade score, rather than third grade, are concessions made because of data limitations in Ohio, where testing only occurs in grades 4, 6, 9, 10, and 12. In principle, value added would be best captured by measuring test scores on third- and fourth-grade tests in consecutive years, for the same set of students. Second best would be to use school-level data to measure the change from a school's third to fourth grade, thereby tracking many, if not all, of the same students. Unfortunately, these data are unavailable. Using the fourth-grade test scores in both years can be viewed as a noisy approximation to value added, or, perhaps more accurately, as capturing the amount by which school performance has improved, rather than as a value-added measure.[4]

Student characteristics are captured by the percentage of students in a school eligible for the federal free-lunch program (proxy for poverty) and the percentage of students in the school who are Black, Hispanic, Asian, and other races, respectively. Race and ethnicity, although not causal factors in determining school test scores, have been found repeatedly to correlate with these scores. Because using any school performance, including APMs, may have incentive effects that influence the types of students attracted to each school, we believe it is important to include such variables as controls. We discuss this issue of incentives further in the conclusions.

School characteristics include school enrollment and a set of dummy variables capturing the different grade spans served by the school. We include these grade-span dummy variables because elementary schools in both New York City and Ohio are constituted in several different configurations of grades, and in other work we have found these differences to be significant determinants of school performance (see Schwartz & Zabel in this volume). Here we divide our sample of elementary schools with fourth grades into three categories of grade spans: those with grades 3 to 5, those serving grades 3 to 6, and those serving grades 3 to 8 (all of these schools may also serve some early childhood grades). Substantively, these organizational traits might matter to performance in a par-

---

3 Tailored regression results for New York City, where data are available on additional student characteristics, are available from the authors.

4 Fourth grade is chosen because in both jurisdictions most elementary schools include a fourth grade, whereas other grades for which tests are available in both locations, such as sixth grade, are sometimes in middle schools rather than elementary schools. (Ohio tests in grades 4, 6, 9, 10, and 12.) In addition, fourth-grade reading is a relatively uncontroversial measure of appropriate learning, whereas in higher grades, such as eighth, other areas of study become more important. In New York City, we have only third through eighth graders, and thus a high-school comparison could not be executed.

Productivity and Its Measurement   21

ticular grade because of their impact on the allocation of resources, which might differ depending on the presence of older grades. They might also matter to peer effects, either positive or negative, that occur when older students attend with younger ones. School size, as measured by enrollment, has been found to affect student outcomes inversely (Fowler & Walberg, 1991; Stiefel et al., 2000) and is also included.

Finally, we include two measures of school resources: teacher/instructional expenditures per pupil and nonteacher/noninstructional expenditures per pupil. Although there is a long and contentious literature on the effect of resources on student performance (see, for example, Hanushek, 1986, 1997; Greenwald, Hedges, & Laine, 1996), relatively little of this research has made use of school-level resource data; most research relies on district-level data. Further, relatively few studies have made use of data that breaks the spending down further than a single aggregate per pupil number. Although there is some debate about whether and how controllable these resources are by schools, in both Ohio and New York City most expenditures are district, rather than school determined. Equally important, most of those are allocated by formulas that follow teacher positions or allocate administrative expenditures based on student body size, and thus they are uncontrollable at the school level.

Data on Ohio Urban Schools and New York City Schools

In 1997–1998 the state of Ohio educated more than 1.8 million students, in 612 school districts, 119 of them categorized as urban rather than suburban, town, or rural by the Ohio Department of Education (ODE).[5]

That year, the entire state had 3,767 schools, with 3,004 of them elementary and middle schools and 2,035 of them serving fourth-grade students. Of these, 744 schools belonged to one of the 94 urban districts and had complete (and valid) data for all variables used in our analysis.[6] We use these 744 urban fourth-grade schools in this analysis.[7]

In the same year, New York City educated 1.1 million students in more than 1,100 schools, 938 of them elementary or middle schools. Of these, 622 schools had test data for fourth-grade students in 1997–1998, as well as the previous year, and data for all other independent variables. We use these 622 in our analyses.

---

5 A list of the Ohio urban school districts is available on request.

6 We use an algorithm developed by Evans, Murray, & Schwab (1997) to remove outliers with respect to expenditure data, reducing the original sample of schools with fourth grades from 1,623 to 1,595.

7 Data on 5,263 school buildings are reported in the 1998 Ohio data. In addition, 4,441 school buildings are found in the 1997 data. When these two datasets are merged, we obtain a sample of 5,336 observations. Data on the percentage of students passing the fourth-grade proficiency tests in reading and math in both years are available for 1,976 buildings. We further limit our sample to buildings containing grade spans 3 through 5, 3 through 6, or 3 through 8, which leaves 1,623 buildings, of which 744 are urban.

Ohio data come from the ODE, some available on their Web site, others provided directly by ODE.[8] New York City data come from the New York City Department of Education (DOE), again some publicly available and some obtained through a special request to the DOE.[9,10]

Figure 2.1 presents descriptive statistics for urban schools with fourth grades in Ohio (panel A) and in New York City (panel B). The dependent variable, percent passing fourth-grade reading (R4PASS), is defined by ODE each year for each school in Ohio, and for New York City, we constructed the percent passing fourth-grade reading as the percentage of the students performing at the 50th percentile on the state test. The implication is that the criteria determining passing likely differ between the two samples and, in fact, the mean percentage of students passing in New York City schools is about 20 percentile points higher than in Ohio urban schools. New York City schools educate about 25 percentage points more poor (free lunch) students than Ohio urban schools and have about the same mean percentage of black students, but significantly more Hispanic and Asian students. Ohio's urban schools essentially educate black students and white students, whereas New York City schools educate a large percentage of Asian and Hispanic students as well. The distribution of schools across the various grade spans is somewhat similar in Ohio and New York City, but New York City schools are almost twice as large on average.

In Ohio, we subdivide educational expenditure into two categories: instructional and noninstructional. The latter includes operations, administration, pupil support, and staff support. In New York City, we distinguish classroom-teacher and nonteacher expenditures from one another. Classroom-teacher expenditures include full-time teacher salaries, preparation-period payments, per diem per-session payments for substitute teachers, and fringe benefits. Although classroom or instructional expenditures per pupil are similar in New York City and Ohio (around $3,700 per pupil), noninstructional expenditures are significantly lower in Ohio urban schools (around $1,900 versus $4,500).

---

8 The three sources are the Educational Management Information System (EMIS), the Expenditure Flow Model (EFM), and the Report Cards. See http://www.ode.ohio.gov/ for publicly available data.

9 The Department of Education was known as the Board of Education at the time.

10 The four sources for New York City are: Annual School Reports (ASR), the School Based Expenditure Reports (SBER), school-level test data, and individual student-level data. See http://www.nycenet.edu/ for publicly available data on school reports and expenditures.

Figure 2.1. Descriptive Statistics for Ohio Urban and New York City Schools, 1997–1998

Variable	N	Mean	Minimum	Maximum
A. Ohio Urban Schools				
Percent Passing Grade 4 Reading 1997–1998	744	33.90	2.10	93.80
Percent Passing Grade 4 Math 1997–1998	744	28.86	1.20	100.00
Percent Passing Grade 4 Citizenship 1997–1998	744	43.47	1.30	100.00
Percent Passing Grade 4 Writing 1997–1998	744	45.53	1.50	100.00
Percent Passing Grade 4 Science 1997–1998	737	35.14	1.60	100.00
Percent Passing Grade 4 Reading 1996–1997	744	40.21	6.30	100.00
Percent Passing Grade 4 Math 1996–1997	744	27.80	1.20	88.00
Percent Passing Grade 4 Citizenship 1996–1997	744	41.47	2.10	100.00
Percent Passing Grade 4 Writing 1996–1997	744	55.26	4.20	100.00
Percent Passing Grade 4 Science 1996–1997	737	28.75	1.40	94.10
Percent Free-Lunch Students	726	49.51	2.81	100.00
Percent Free Lunch is 0 When Data are Missing	744	48.31	0.00	100.00
Dummy = 1 If Pct Free Lunch Not Missing	744	0.98	0.00	1.00
Percent Black Students	744	32.51	0.00	100.00
Percent Hispanic Students	744	1.86	0.00	57.20
Percent Asian and Other Students	744	1.36	0.00	39.50
Grade 3 Through 5 Dummy	744	0.54	0.00	1.00
Grade 3 Through 6 Dummy	744	0.43	0.00	1.00
Grade 3 Through 8 Dummy	744	0.03	0.00	1.00
Enrollment	744	421.82	104.00	1327.00
Instructional Expenditure per Pupil	744	3695.55	1995.00	5576.00
Noninstructional Expenditure per Pupil	744	1867.81	518.00	4042.00
Total Expenditure per Pupil	744	5563.36	3287.00	8982.00
B. New York City Schools				
Percent Passing Grade 4 Reading 1997–1998	622	55.03	5.60	98.10
Percent Passing Grade 4 Math 1997–1998	622	64.47	10.00	100.00
Percent Passing Grade 4 Reading 1996–1997	622	53.84	0.00	96.97
Percent Passing Grade 4 Math 1996–1997	622	63.74	0.00	100.00
Percent Free-Lunch Students	622	75.23	6.30	100.00
Percent Black Students	622	35.66	0.20	97.60
Percent Hispanic Students	622	35.55	1.30	98.10
Percent Asian and Other Students	622	10.78	0.10	94.30
Grade 3 Through 5 Dummy	622	0.54	0.00	1.00
Grade 3 Through 6 Dummy	622	0.39	0.00	1.00
Grade 3 Through 8 Dummy	622	0.07	0.00	1.00
Enrollment	622	792.58	116.00	2672.00
Instructional Expenditure per Pupil	622	3732.44	2397.70	8990.60
Noninstructional Expenditure per Pupil	622	4477.23	2572.08	12834.81

Results

Figure 2.2 presents results of the APM regressions for Ohio urban schools in the first column and New York City schools in the second column. The regressions are weighted by school enrollment to correct for heteroskedasticity.[11]

The results are strikingly similar across states—in both Ohio and New York City, the coefficients on the previous year's fourth-grade percent passing is positive and significant, on percent free-lunch students is negative and significant, and on percent black students is negative and significant. Enrollment is insignificant in the regressions for both samples. Nonteacher (noninstructional) expenditures have a negative, significant coefficient indicating that we need to control for differences in the resources allocated to individual schools. All equations have high explanatory power (R^2 of .68 in Ohio and .79 in New York City).[12]

---

[11] Because the dependent variable is an average for each school, schools with larger enrollments may have more precisely estimated averages, resulting in decreasing variance as enrollment increases. In addition, the Cook-Weisberg test for heteroskedasticity using fitted values of R4PASS rejected the hypothesis that there was no heteroskedasticity.

[12] We also estimated a specification that includes student characteristics alone and another that adds school characteristics but does not include school resources. In these models, too, the results across states are very similar and explanatory power is high (R^2 of .67 or higher). In the latter specification, grade-span dummies are negative and often significant indicating that the schools serving grades 3 through 6 or 3 through 8 perform less successfully, on average, than the schools serving the reference group, schools serving grades 3 through 5 only. Results are available on request.

Figure 2.2. Grade 4 Reading APM Regressions

Dependent Variable is Percent Passing Grade 4 Reading 1997–1998		
Independent Variables	*Ohio*	*NYC*
Intercept	20.4457 ***(4.2492)	41.3098***(4.7876)
Student Characteristics:		
Percent Passing Grade 4 Reading 1996–1997	0.4729***(0.0302)	0.6176***(0.0308)
Percent Free-Lunch Students[a]	−0.2146***(0.0251)	−0.0870***(0.0297)
Percent Black Students	−0.0596***(0.0168)	−0.0655**(0.0262)
Percent Hispanic Students	0.0270 (0.0601)	−0.0860***(0.0297)
Percent Asians and Others	0.0886(0.1190)	0.0664**(0.0336)
School Characteristics:		
Grade 3 Through 6 Dummy	−1.7474**(0.7504)	−1.5197**(0.7525)
Grade 3 Through 8 Dummy	−2.8432(2.0710)	−1.4321(1.2921)
Total Enrollment	0.0011(0.0023)	−0.0011(0.0011)
Resources:		
Teacher/Instructional Expenditures Per Pupil[b]	−0.0009(0.0008)	−0.0005(0.0009)
Nonteacher/Noninstructional Expenditures Per Pupil	−0.0015*(0.0009)	−0.0011**(0.0005)
F	141.19	231.16
R-squared	0.6797	0.7909
Number of Observaions	744	622

Notes:

[a] In Ohio, the regression includes a dummy that takes value 1 if the school reports free-lunch data and 0 if it does not. The coefficient on the dummy is positive (close to 6.5) and significant at the 5% level. Thus, on average, schools that report free-lunch data have higher pass rates than those that do not report data on this variable. Note that percent free lunch is available in 98% of the schools.

[b] NYC reports teacher and nonteacher expenditures; Ohio reports instructional and noninstructional expenditures.

1) All regressions are weighted by enrollment share.

2)   * indicates significance at the 10% level.
    ** indicates significance at the 5% level.
    *** indicates significance at the 1% level.

3) Standard errors are reported in parentheses.

The striking similarity in the regression coefficients in the APM equations estimated for the New York City and Ohio urban schools offers the tantalizing prospect that adjustment parameters might be stable or constant across settings. We tested this in two ways. First, we tested for equality of all slope coefficients, but the test rejected the hypothesis of equal coefficients at conventional levels ($F = 2.16$). Thus, at least some of the coefficients differ significantly across jurisdictions for reading.[13]

It is interesting that similar analyses estimating APM equations using the pass rates in math rather than reading yield coefficients for Ohio and New York City samples that are insignificantly different from one another. That is, a joint test of the equality of the coefficients in the two equations indicated no significant difference between them.[14] The similarity of the coefficients of the APM regressions—the adjustment parameters—is intriguing. If adjustment parameters are relatively stable across jurisdictions, then adopting a single, standard set of parameters to use for adjusting performance measures for a large set of schools may be possible. In particular, borrowing adjustment parameters from neighboring or similar jurisdictions or using a standard set might be particularly attractive for small school districts with few schools that might otherwise have to rely on raw, unadjusted performance measures.

The second method we used to investigate the stability of the reading test adjustment parameters across our two samples focused on evaluating whether and to what extent the differences between the estimated parameters were substantive, or, put differently, policy relevant. Although the coefficients may be statistically different, as a group, these differences may not be very important when viewed from the policymaking or decision-making perspective. Although differences in coefficients seem to imply that each state needs to estimate its own equation for reading, it is not clear that school rankings would differ significantly if one state were to borrow another's estimates. We investigate this by constructing APMs for the schools in each jurisdiction using the coefficients estimated from the other jurisdiction, following the spirit of the methodology in Blinder (1973) and Oaxaca (1973).[15, 16] We then compare the rankings of schools based on APMs computed with their own coefficients with rankings based on APMs computed with the other coefficients, using Pearson (r) and Spearman Correlations (S).

---

13 We also tested for the equality of all slope coefficients *except* the ones on the lag test scores, because the lag score has an extremely high t statistic and is likely to be driving the similarity in all coefficients. This test was rejected at the 2% level ($F = 2.21$).

14 Math regression results are available from the authors.

15 Blinder and Oaxaca decomposed differences in wages for males and females into components based on differences in personal characteristics and differences in returns to those characteristics.

16 For New York City, the indicator dummy for not-missing free-lunch data takes a value of one for all observations. Therefore, it is not included in the New York City APM regressions.

This comparison yielded interesting results. The rankings of Ohio urban schools are largely invariant to the choice of adjustment parameters ($r = .9750$; $S = .9704$), and the same is true for New York City schools as well ($r = .9354$; $S = .9238$). It is not clear which is more surprising. On the one hand, New York City is frequently viewed as being different from everywhere else, suggesting that its adjustment parameters would be idiosyncratic. On the other hand, there is greater diversity (and variation) in the composition of the students attending New York City schools, and thus the New York City data are more likely to yield precise parameter estimates for some variables that are likely to be capturing factors important to the adjustment procedure. For example, in New York City there are substantial percentages of Asian and Hispanic students (11% and 36% respectively), and there is considerable variation in the representation of Asians and Hispanics across schools, suggesting that the coefficients can be precisely estimated in the New York City analysis. In Ohio, however, these variables show little variation across schools. The resulting significant coefficients for these variables in New York City and insignificant coefficients in Ohio are, then, unsurprising. The implication is that these variables might not be given adequate weight in the adjustment for New York City schools when using the Ohio parameters. One interpretation of our results, then, is that the variation in Ohio schools might be sufficient to yield adequate parameter estimates, although standard errors are large. How is it, on the other hand, that the New York City parameters do so well for the Ohio schools? Here, the explanation lies in part in the low representation of Asian and Hispanic students. Because Ohio schools have so few Asian and Hispanic students (1% and 2% on average), using the New York City coefficients does not affect the value of the Ohio APMs.

Although much additional work needs to be done to understand the stability or generalizability of adjustment parameters for school test scores, these results suggest that this work should be done—it may, after all, be possible to create a set of standardized adjustment parameters to use across jurisdictions, states, or school districts, affording small school districts insight into the relative performance of their schools they might not otherwise have.

Ohio APMs for Alternative Subject Tests

Ohio tests fourth-grade students in several different subject areas (reading, math, citizenship, writing, and science), and pass rates by school on these tests provide information for a new set of APM equations. The independent variables in these equations are identical to the ones used in the reading equations because there are no appropriate school-level data to supplement these in the Ohio data. Figure 2.1 provides descriptive statistics for school pass rates on the additional tests, and we see that they bracket the pass rates in reading, ranging from a high mean of 55.26% for the lagged writing rate to a low mean of 28.75% for the lagged science rate. Figure 2.3 presents the regression coefficients for the four additional regressions. (Reading is presented in Figure 2.2). The regressions for math, citizenship, and science yield results similar to reading, differing only in the higher coefficient on the lagged passing rate. The writing equation has a low lagged coefficient similar to reading, but the coefficients on the school resources are different. Here the grade-span dummies are insignificant, but the enrollment coefficient is positive and significant.

Figure 2.3. Ohio Tailored APM Regressions

Dependent Variable is Percent Passing Grade 4 Test 1997–1998				
Independent Variables	*Math*	*Citizenship*	*Writing*	*Science*
Intercept	12.6297*** (4.4720)	25.5174*** (4.8095)	24.4299*** (6.1024)	20.3520*** (4.5484)
Student Characteristics:				
Percent Passing Grade 4 Test 1996–1997	0.6138*** (0.0282)	0.5927*** (0.0289)	0.4564*** (0.0373)	0.6037*** (0.0316)
Percent Free-Lunch Students[a]	−0.1525*** (0.0253)	−0.2027*** (0.0281)	−0.2159*** (0.0357)	−0.1892*** (0.0273)
Percent Black Students	−0.0404** (0.0182)	−0.0242 (0.0190)	0.0017 (0.0238)	−0.0617*** (0.0183)
Percent Hispanic Students	0.0401 (0.0649)	0.1469** (0.0682)	0.1280 (0.0854)	0.0644 (0.0656)
Percent Asians and Others	−0.0010 (0.1285)	−0.0453 (0.1349)	0.3021* (0.1696)	−0.1121 (0.1297)
School Characteristics:				
Grade 3 Through 6 Dummy	−2.0789** (0.8108)	−2.7938*** (0.8497)	−0.6538 (1.0639)	−2.4716*** (0.8227)
Grade 3 Through 8 Dummy	−2.4972 (2.2392)	−4.2425* (2.3456)	−1.3744 (2.9384)	−2.7066 (2.2564)
School Enrollment	0.0001 (0.0025)	−0.0014 (0.0027)	0.0069** (0.0033)	0.0008 (0.0026)
Resources:				
Instructional Expenditure per Pupil	0.0012 (0.0009)	0.0004 (0.0009)	−0.0007 (0.0011)	0.0013 (0.0009)
Noninstructional Expenditure per Pupil	−0.0008 (0.0010)	−0.0010 (0.0010)	−0.0003 (0.0013)	−0.0007 (0.0010)
F	131.28	142.07	63.31	147.18
R-square	0.6636	0.6810	0.4875	0.6907
Number of Observations	744	744	744	737

Notes:

1) All regressions are weighted by enrollment share.

2) * indicates significance at the 10% level.
   ** indicates significance at the 5% level.
   *** indicates significance at the 1% level.

3) Standard errors are reported in parentheses.

[a] As in Figure 2.2, these regressions include a dummy that takes value 1 if the school reports free-lunch data and 0 if it does not. For all four subjects, the coefficient on the dummy is positive (it ranges from 5.8 to 6.5), and significant at the 10% level or above.

Productivity and Its Measurement 29

How much of a difference would the use of these tests make for the ranking of urban schools in Ohio? Somewhat surprisingly, given the similarity in estimated coefficients between the APM regression equations, the Pearson and Spearman correlation coefficients between all tests are quite low. The highest Pearson correlation (between citizenship and science) is 0.6502 and the lowest (between writing and science) falls to 0.3974. For the Spearman, the range is similar, with the highest between math and science (0.6281) and the lowest between math and writing (0.3380). The rankings are sensitive to the test and thus, at least in Ohio, either policymakers must make a choice about which tests should be used to rank schools or devise a methodology for combining rankings (or deriving rankings) based on performance on several tests. One method would be to create the APM using a dependent variable constructed as the weighted average of pass rates on the different exams. Alternatively, the APM could be constructed by weighting the residuals based on different APM regressions to get an average APM, or minimum values could be set for each test, with schools needing to be above on all of them.[17] The latter is akin to New York State's policy on Regents high-school exams, where, when fully implemented, students will have to pass five different exams to receive a diploma.

New York City APMs for Alternative Years

To gauge how APMs change over consecutive years, we estimate the following four New York City generic reading regressions, with percent passing as the dependent variable: 1996–1997 grade 4 with grade 4 lag, 1997–1998 grade 4 with grade 4 lag, and the same two equations in level form (without the lag).[18] Figure 2.4 shows these regression results in columns 1 and 2 for the lag equations and columns 3 and 4 for the level equations. An F test of the equality of slope coefficients across years for each specification does not reject the hypothesis of equal coefficients at conventional levels ($F = 1.42$ and 0.40). Nevertheless, the similarity of slope coefficients does not guarantee similarity in APMs of schools across years because the values of the variables change each year. Panel A of Figure 2.5, which shows Pearson and Spearman correlation coefficients for pairs of APMs, sheds light on how similar the APMs are. In the top of the Figure 2.5, based on the lag equations from columns 1 and 2 of Figure 2.4, the 1996–1997 and 1997–1998 APMs are reported for the following: (i) 1996–1997 coefficients with 1996–1997 values of variables and 1997–1998 coefficients with 1997–1998 values of variables, (ii) 1997–1998 coefficients with 1996–1997 and 1997–1998 values of variables, (iii) 1996–1997 coefficients with 1996–1997 and 1997–1998 values of variables, (iv) 1996–1997 and 1997–1998 coefficients with 1997–1998 values of variables, and (v) 1996–1997 and 1997–1998 coefficients with 1996–1997 values of variables. Right below on panel A of Figure 2.5 are the same set of APMs using the level regressions from columns 3 and 4 in Figure 2.4.

---

17 The choice of weights is neither straightforward nor dictated by technical considerations. Rather, the weights would have to be chosen to reflect the goals and values of education policymakers.

18 We also estimate similar equations for grade 5 and find no qualitative differences in any results and so do not report them.

Figure 2.4. NYC Alternative Generic Regressions for Alternative Years

	Lag Specification		Level Specification	
Dependent Variable is Percent Passing Grade 4 Reading 1996–1997 or 1997–1998	(1)1996–1997 Grade 4	(2)1997–1998 Grade 4	(3)1996–1997 Grade 4	(4)1997–1998 Grade 4
Intercept	38.7618*** (4.5595)	41.3098*** (4.7876)	108.5321*** (4.2645)	109.8101*** (4.3205)
Student Characteristics:				
Lagged Percent Passing Grade 4 Reading	0.7018*** (0.0326)	0.6176*** (0.0308)		
Percent Free-Lunch Students	−0.1000*** (0.0295)	−0.0870*** (0.0297)	−0.3473*** (0.0361)	−0.3155*** (0.0353)
Percent Black Students	−0.0373 (0.0264)	−0.0655** (0.0262)	−0.2005*** (0.0337)	−0.1808*** (0.0329)
Percent Hispanic Students	−0.0430 (0.0301)	−0.0860*** (0.0297)	−0.2192*** (0.0386)	−0.2188*** (0.0372)
Percent Asians and Others	−0.0095 (0.0335)	0.0664** (0.0336)	0.0411 (0.0445)	0.0877** (0.0432)
School Characteristics:				
Grade 3 Through 6 Dummy	−1.4699** (0.7323)	−1.5197** (0.7525)	−3.4100*** (0.9673)	−3.5807*** (0.9594)
Grade 3 Through 8 Dummy	−1.2407 (1.4697)	−1.4321 (1.2921)	−3.4408* (1.9516)	−3.2517** (1.6589)
Total Enrollment	−0.0028*** (0.0010)	−0.0011 (0.0011)	−0.0034** (0.0014)	−0.0033** (0.0014)
Resources:				
Teacher Expenditures per Pupil	−0.0007 (0.0010)	−0.0005 (0.0009)	−0.0008 (0.0013)	−0.0010 (0.0012)
Nonteacher Expenditures per Pupil	−0.0007 (0.0005)	−0.0011** (0.0005)	−0.0017** (0.0007)	−0.0022*** (0.0006)
F	252.80	231.16	129.53	128.05
R-square	0.8090	0.7909	0.6610	0.6531
Number of Observations	608	622	608	622

Notes:

1) All regressions are weighted by enrollment share.

2) * indicates significance at the 10% level.
   ** indicates significance at the 5% level.
   *** indicates significance at the 1% level.

3) Standard errors are reported in parentheses.

Productivity and Its Measurement   31

Figure 2.5. Correlation Coefficients of APMs
from Generic Regressions for Alternative Years and Grades

A. Alternative Years					
	Grade 4 Lag Specification				
	(i)	(ii)	(iii)	(iv)	(v)
Pearson Correlation	−0.2313	−0.2085	−0.2996	0.9807	0.9830
Spearman Correlation	−0.2018	−0.1762	−0.2786	0.9737	0.9773
	Grade 4 Level Specification				
	(i)	(ii)	(iii)	(iv)	(v)
Pearson Correlation	0.5668	0.5683	0.5664	0.9941	0.9946
Spearman Correlation	0.5509	0.5494	0.5537	0.9921	0.9924
B. Alternative Grades					
	Lag Specification				
	(i)	(ii)	(iii)	(iv)	(v)
Pearson Correlation	0.0291	0.0416	0.0052	0.9799	0.9785
Spearman Correlation	0.0570	0.0885	0.0329	0.9716	0.9730
	Level Specification				
	(i)	(ii)	(iii)	(iv)	(v)
Pearson Correlation	0.5774	0.5731	0.5702	0.9889	0.9897
Spearman Correlation	0.5586	0.5556	0.5543	0.9856	0.9871

Notes:
1) 1996–1997 coefficients with 1996–1997 values of variables and 1997–1998 coefficients with 1997–1998 values of variables
2) 1997–1998 coefficients with 1996–1997 and 1997–1998 values of variables
3) 1996–1997 coefficients with 1996–1997 and 1997–1998 values of variables
4) 1996–1997 and 1997–1998 coefficients with 1997–1998 values of variables
5) 1996–1997 and 1997–1998 coefficients with 1996–1997 values of variables

What do these correlations demonstrate? In panel A of Figure 2.5 for the lag specification, they show first that the APMs from the two years are negatively correlated (correlation i), second that the year of the analysis makes a very big difference, resulting again in negative correlations (correlations ii and iii), and third that, conversely, a change in the year of the parameters make no difference (correlations iv and v). In the bottom of panel A of Figure 2.6 for the level specification, all five correlations are moderately high, with the highest for changes in the year of the parameters, showing that different years of data and especially different parameters have only a moderate influence on the correlations. Why do we find these results? With the lag specifications, the results regarding parameters are expected, given all the previous findings on the transferability of parameters, but the negative correlations when the year of data changes can be explained by an example. When a school makes considerable improvements one year, going for example from 65% to 80% passing a fourth-grade reading test, then either because of a conscious decision that 80% is a good percent or because more change is very hard, the school may show little additional progress on next year's fourth grade, but instead may maintain close to the 80% next year as well. Another school, on the other hand, might rise from a low to a high percent the following year. This kind of pattern will mean a low or negative correlation, at least until all schools reach a desired performance level and maintain it over years. On the other hand, the level equations do not evaluate performance on improvement, and the raw level scores are much more likely to be correlated across years, with some attenuation for the adjustments for student and school characteristics.

Figure 2.6. NYC Alternative Generic Regressions for Alternative Grades

Dependent Variable is Percent Passing Grade 4 or 5 Reading 1997–1998

	Lag Specification		Level Specification	
	(1) **1997–1998** **Grade 4**	**(2)** **1997–1998** **Grade 5**	**(3)** **1997–1998** **Grade 4**	**(4)** **1997–1998** **Grade 5**
Intercept	41.3098*** (4.7876)	35.3207*** (4.4350)	109.8101*** (4.3205)	101.5597*** (4.5109)
Student Characteristics:				
Lagged Percent Passing Reading	0.6176*** (0.0308)	0.6584*** (0.0292)		
Percent Free-Lunch Students	−0.0870*** (0.0297)	−0.1372*** (0.0288)	−0.3155*** (0.0353)	−0.3592*** (0.0367)
Percent Black Students	−0.0655** (0.0262)	−0.0539** (0.0259)	−0.1808*** (0.0329)	−0.1910*** (0.0342)
Percent Hispanic Students	−0.0860*** (0.0297)	−0.0841*** (0.0294)	−0.2188*** (0.0372)	−0.2537*** (0.0386)
Percent Asians and Others	0.0664** (0.0336)	0.0165 (0.0331)	0.0877** (0.0432)	0.0635 (0.0448)
School Characteristics:				
Grade 3 Through 6 Dummy	−1.5197** (0.7525)	−1.1314 (0.7423)	−3.5807*** (0.9594)	−3.5064*** (0.9970)
Grade 3 Through 8 Dummy	−1.4321 (1.2921)	−2.5146** (1.2812)	−3.2517** (1.6589)	−3.4457** (1.7376)
Total Enrollment	−0.0011 (0.0011)	−0.0011 (0.0011)	−0.0033** (0.0014)	−0.0015 (0.0014)

Resources:				
Teacher Expenditures per Pupil	−0.0005 (0.0009)	0.0013 (0.0009)	−0.0010 (0.0012)	0.0004 (0.0013)
Nonteacher Expenditures per Pupil	−0.0011** (0.0005)	−0.0014*** (0.0005)	−0.0022*** (0.0006)	−0.0021*** (0.0007)
F	231.16	281.61	128.05	139.21
R-square	0.7909	0.8236	0.6531	0.6747
Number of Observations	622	622	622	622

Notes:
1) All regressions are weighted by enrollment share.
2) * indicates significance at the 10% level.
   ** indicates significance at the 5% level.
   *** indicates significance at the 1% level.
3) Standard errors are reported in parentheses.

New York City APMs for Alternative Grades

We perform the same conceptual experiment for different grades as we did for different years. Because the year chosen to look at different grades does not affect results, we report only 1997–1998 equations for fourth and fifth grades. Figure 2.6 shows grades 4 and 5 regressions in lag specification (columns 1 and 2) and in level specification (columns 3 and 4). An F-test for the equality of slope coefficients across years for each specification does not reject the hypothesis of equal coefficients at conventional levels ($F = 1.40$ and 0.73), but once again, to see how related the APMs are, we construct panel B of Figure 2.5, to show 10 Pearson and Spearman correlations. The top section of panel B of Figure 2.5, displays the following correlations for the lag specification: (i) grade 4 coefficients with grade 4 values and grade 5 coefficients with grade 5 values, (ii) grade 4 coefficients with grade 4 and grade 5 values, (iii) grade 5 coefficients with grade 4 and grade 5 values, (iv) grades 4 and grade 5 coefficients with grade 4 values, and (v) grades 4 and 5 coefficients with grade 5 values. The bottom section of Figure 2.5 shows the same set of correlations for the level specifications.

Once again the lag specifications show that parameters are transferable (correlations iv and v) but not data on specific grades (correlations ii and iii). The level specifications show moderately high correlations across years even when the data vary by year.

Conclusions: Lessons Learned

Raw performance scores correlate well across grades and years, but raw scores are problematic as performance measures.[19] By not adjusting for the student mix and school characteristics outside an individual school's control, raw scores not only are unfair but may provide perverse incentives for schools to gain control over their student mix to increase test scores.[20] For example, when given some leeway about whether to accept transfer students from other districts or schools, a school might be more likely to accept only students expected to earn high scores. Using APMs, as described above, for school accountability can help mitigate such incentives, but APMs are not without their own challenges.

One challenge is that APMs created using a lag score (value-added or improvement measures which adjust for students' prior performance) yield school rankings that vary across years and test grades—different years and different grades may lead to significantly different school rankings. Some schools identified as performing at a high level in fourth-grade math, for example, may be identified as an average or even low performer in reading, say, or fifth-grade math. The implication is that evaluating school performance using APMs requires policymakers and educators to make choices about what is important for accountability. For example, should schools be held accountable for performance for all grades and subjects or is there some subset that is paramount—say, fourth-grade reading? Because the rankings differ across tests and grades, these decisions are crucial to determining the rankings. More important, these decisions extend beyond the purview of the analyst.

Of course, an alternative would be to use APMs based on level specifications rather than value-added models, in which case the performance measures are *not* adjusted for the prior performance of the students. Level specifications may be considered attractive, in part, because they show higher correlations across years and grades—meaning that rankings are relatively robust to the choice of test grade and year. Further, there is a closer correspondence between the APMs and the raw achievement levels. Many people prefer the level specification because, while improvement is desirable, if the level of performance is still low, rewards may not seem justified.

A second challenge is that calculating APMs requires adjustment parameters be estimated through multiple regressions, which may be beyond the capacity of some jurisdictions. Our research has identified a potential solution to this problem. It may be possible to combine the adjustment parameters estimated in one jurisdiction with the actual data in another jurisdiction (i.e., test scores, demographics, school charac-

---

19 Using the Ohio data, we find that raw performance scores also correlate well across test subjects. Ohio also tests students in math, citizenship, writing, and science. Generic regressions were run with these subjects (results available on request) and similar results obtain for math, citizenship, and science. Yet, Pearson and Spearman correlations between tests are quite low so that the test matters to the rankings.

20 For example, Rubenstein, Schwartz, & Stiefel (2003) find that raw test scores are not highly correlated with APMs.

teristics) to create usable APMs for the latter jurisdiction. This feature of transferability, which was found to be strikingly pervasive across jurisdictions, grades, and years, can be valuable to districts that do not have estimated APMs to use, or in evaluations of charter or privately contracted schools, where estimating a separate equation is not possible for lack of a sufficient sample. Transferability of parameters might also be of use nationally as all states could be evaluated using the same equation, with, for example NAEP scores as dependent variables. Such an equation could be estimated across all states, with additional controls for the urbanicity or rurality of the state, perhaps, and states could be evaluated based on a common metric.

Overall, APMs are an inexpensive and accessible method of measuring performance while accounting for differences in the characteristics of school populations and resources. They present a fairer way to evaluate school performance than the use of raw scores alone, and they can even be used across jurisdictions. They do not, however, circumvent the difficult, subjective decisions that policymakers must confront about which subjects are important to test, which grades are important to emphasize, and which years to evaluate.

References

Barbanel, J. (1999a, March 21). Testing, testing: How the city's third graders performed in 1998. *New York Times*, 8.

Barbanel, J. (1999b, March 28). Report cards point to struggles for middle and high schools. *New York Times*, 10.

Barbanel, J. (1999, April 11). How the county's third graders are reading. *New York Times.*, 12.

Barbanel, J. (2000, March 19). The report card for middle and high schools. *New York Times*, 12.

Blinder, A. S. (1973). Wage discrimination: Reduced form and structural estimates. *Journal of Human Resources*, 8, 436–55.

Desvousges, W. H., Naughton, M. C., & Parsons, G. R. (1992). Benefit transfer: Conceptual problems estimating water quality benefits using existing studies. *Water Resources Research*, 28, 675–82.

Evans, W. N., Murray, S. E., & Schwab R. M, (1997). Schoolhouses, courthouses, and statehouses after Serrano. *Journal of Policy Analysis and Management*, 16(1), 10–31.

Fowler, W. J. and Walberg, H. J. (1991). School size, characteristics and outcomes. *Educational Evaluation and Policy Analysis*, 13, 189–202.

Gramlich, E. M. (1976). The New York City fiscal crisis: What happened and what is to be done? *The American Economic Review*, 66(2), 415–29.

Greenwald, R., Hedges, L. V., & Laine, R. D. (1996). The effect of school resources on student achievement. *Review of Educational Research*, 66(3), 361–396.

Hanushek, E. A. (1986). The economics of schooling: Production and efficiency in public schools. *Journal of Economic Literature*, 24(3), 1141–77.

Hanushek, E. A. (1997). Assessing the effects of school resources on student performance: An update. *Educational Evaluation and Policy Analysis*, 19(2), 141–64.

Ladd, H. F., & Walsh R. P. (2002). Implementing value-added measures of school performance: Getting the incentives right. *Economics of Education Review*, 21(1), 1–18.

Oaxaca, R. (1973). Male-female wage differentials in urban labor markets. *International Economic Review*, 14, 693–709.

Parsons, G. R., & Kealy, J. K. (1994). Benefit transfer in a random utility model of recreation. *Water Resources Research*, 30, 2477–84.

Rubenstein, R., Stiefel, L., & Schwartz, A. E. (2003) Better than raw: A guide to measuring organizational performance with adjusted performance measures. *Public Administration Review*, 63(5), 607–15.

Rubenstein, R., Schwartz, A. E., & Stiefel, L. (1998). Conceptual and empirical issues in the measurement of school efficiency. *Proceedings of the 91st Annual Conference on Taxation* (pp. 267–74). Washington, D.C.: National Tax Association.

Stiefel, L., Rubenstein, R., & Schwartz, A. E. (1999). Using adjusted performance measures for evaluating resource use. *Public Budgeting and Finance*, 19(3), 67–87.

Stiefel, L., Berne, R., Iatarola, P., & Fruchter, N. (2000). High school size: Effects on budgets and performance in New York City. *Educational Evaluation and Policy Analysis*, 22(1), 27–39.

3

The Good, the Bad, and the Ugly: Measuring School Efficiency Using School Production Functions

Amy Ellen Schwartz and Jeffrey E. Zabel

Introduction

Measuring the efficiency of public schools in a way that disentangles the efficiency of the school itself (the effective use of administrators, teachers, pedagogical techniques, and so on) from the characteristics of the clients it serves (the students) is difficult but critical to creating performance measures that can be used to identify successful practices, guide school reforms, and reward or sanction school personnel. Although some would argue that raw test scores are, in and of themselves, sufficient to distinguish between good and not-so-good schools, the economic theory of the production of education suggests an alternative approach. According to this view, although test scores provide a measure of school output, assessing school efficiency requires the understanding of the education production function, which captures the process by which the inputs to schooling are translated into outputs. As in the case of manufacturing firms, production functions can be specified to allow for differences in the efficiency of schools, controlling for a wide range of differences in the conditions, clients, and resources that constrain production possibilities. This chapter estimates measures of school efficiency using school-level production functions and explores the sensitivity of these measures to alternative econometric specifications. An important goal of this chapter is to identify a method for estimating efficiency measures that can be used as part of a broad range of policy and management applications. Thus, we discuss practical, as well as theoretical, considerations in the construction and interpretation of school-efficiency measures and attempt to evaluate the value added of more sophisticated techniques (over less-sophisticated measures) in distinguishing between efficient and inefficient schools. We compare the resulting efficiency measures to raw test scores and illustrate the use of these measures for exploring the differences between efficient and inefficient schools.

As discussed by Schwartz and Stiefel (2001), estimating the efficiency of schools is, in some measure, quite similar to estimating the efficiency of firms. There are conceptual and empirical challenges to be faced in measuring outputs and inputs (including both the choice of appropriate measures as well as whether and how to adjust for quality differentials), and challenges in capturing environmental, organizational, and institutional effects. Further, it is especially difficult to disentangle the causality of the relationships between outputs and inputs, particularly the contributions of peers.[1]

Investigations of school efficiency have, in the past, been limited significantly by data scarcity and quality. For this study, we have assembled a rich panel data set on public schools in New York City, the largest urban school district in the country, that includes information on school-level expenditures, test scores, and pupil and teacher characteristics over four years. These data are uncommonly rich—there are relatively few jurisdictions in the United States that collect and maintain such data at the school level—which means that they offer the opportunity to gain insight into performance measurement under what might be viewed as a best-case scenario. Unfortunately, constructing useful and reliable performance measures even with these unusually rich data still presents challenges, including, for example, the potential for bias due to measurement error, endogeneity, and correlation between the fixed effects and the lagged test scores, which are included in value-added production functions. Therefore, we include a discussion of lessons for practice, directions for additional research and data collection priorities for the future.

Measuring Efficiency with School Production Functions

The Model

At the heart of much of the research on school performance is a production function for education. Borrowing from the models originally used to describe the production process of manufacturing firms, an education production function links the inputs used and the outputs produced by the education firm (or plant)—the school. Denote the output of school s, for students in grade g, in year t, as Q_{sgt}. A school-level production function can be written as:

$$Q_{sgt} = f_{sgt}(ST_{sgt}, P_{sgt}, SC_{sgt})$$ (1)

where ST_{sgt} represents the characteristics of students and their families (e.g., the prevalence of poverty, limited English proficiency), P_{sgt} represents the character-

---

1 See Schwartz & Stiefel (2001) for an overview of the literature and a discussion of the state of the art in estimating school efficiency, including alternative approaches.

Measuring School Efficiency Using School Production Functions 39

istics of peers, and SC_{sgt} represents the school inputs and characteristics (e.g., teachers, principals, enrollment, grade span).

Given school- and grade-level data for a set of schools over a number of years—on the quantities of inputs used, characteristics of schools, students and districts, and the quantities of output produced—and an assumption about the form of the production function (that is, the mathematical form), this relationship can be statistically estimated and the results used to identify more- and less-efficient schools. Notice that equation (1) has been written to allow for a different production function to capture the production process for each school, grade, and time period (that is, f has subscripts s, g, and t), because there may be differences in the production technology across schools, grades, and/or time. As an example, the relationship between class size (one measure of inputs) and academic performance (output) may well differ between the early and later grades. Or, as is of particular interest here, some schools may be able to produce more output with a given level of inputs, other things equal, than some other set of schools. Put differently, some schools may be more efficient than others.[2] To be concrete, an education production function (EPF) that allows for these differences can be written as:

$$TS_{sgt} = \beta_{0g} + \beta_{1g}TS_{s,g-1,t-1} + \beta_{2g}ST_{sgt} + \beta_{3g}SC_{sgt} + T_{gt} + S_{gs} + \varepsilon_{sgt} \qquad (2)$$

where the ST_{sgt} and SC_{sgt} variables are as defined earlier, and T_t and S_s are time and school effects to be estimated and ε_{sgt} is an error term. We refer to this model as the fixed-effects model (FE) in the remainder of the chapter. Both TS_{sgt} and $TS_{s,g-1,t-1}$ represent average test scores. Note that TS_{sgt} is the test score for grade g in school s and time t, whereas $TS_{s,g-1,t-1}$ is the test score for the same school (s) but measured in the lagged year *and lagged grade.* Notice also that the coefficients, β, and the time, school, and grade effects differ across grades.[3] This is consistent with the specification used by Todd and Wolpin (2003), in which the impact of previous experience is allowed to vary by age (grade). Note that the peer group variables, P_{sgt}, are not explicitly included in equation (2). Because the level of observation is the grade, the peer group variables will be subsumed in the other grade-level variables ($TS_{s,g-1,t-1}$ and ST_{sgt}).

This formulation, developed in Schwartz and Zabel (2002), reflects (1) the definition of the output of education, Q_{sgt}, as the change in education between grades $g-1$ and g, and (2) an assumption that this change is measured as a

---

2 Notice that we have included no specific reference to districts in the notation. Because schools do not change districts, the use of district notation besides the school reference would imply spurious generality.

3 Schwartz and Zabel (2002) discuss the derivation of this model and the relationship between the estimated coefficients and the smaller set of underlying structural parameters. Their results imply that the coefficients on each of the explanatory variables are scaled by a grade-specific measure of the relationship between educational attainment and test scores. Thus, slope coefficients and time and school effects are grade specific, even though the coefficients in the underlying education production function are not grade dependent.

weighted difference in test scores between grades, where the weights capture differences in the relationship between the test score and the education level of a student in each year. These imply that an EPF can be specified as an equation with the test score as the dependent variable and with the lagged-grade lagged-year test score included as a right-hand-side regressor.[4]

The school effect, S_{gs}, measures the persistent difference between the output of school s and the output of other schools, conditional on their inputs, student characteristics, and so on. Thus, it provides a measure of (relative) school efficiency, capturing the extent to which each school systematically produces gains in education more (or less) than the others of each school holding all observable inputs constant. Thus, the schools with the largest estimated school effects may be considered the most efficient because they systematically produce more education from the same set of inputs as schools with smaller estimated school effects. Likewise, schools that obtain the lowest school effects are considered to be the least efficient schools because they systematically produce less education from the same set of inputs as schools with larger estimated school effects. To be clear, in education production functions, as in production functions estimated for manufacturing firms, the fixed effect is, in some sense, a measure of our ignorance capturing both differences in productive efficiency and the contribution of any other omitted (perhaps unobservable) variables.[5]

Note also that equation (2) includes grade-specific school effects, which provide estimates of school efficiency for each grade. We will examine the relationship between efficiency across grades, and we will also estimate a different EPF—and different efficiency measures—for reading and math test scores and examine the extent to which efficiency in reading is related to efficiency in math education.

This production function also includes a time effect, T_{gt}, that captures general changes in productivity, common to all grades and schools, not accounted for by the observable inputs—changes in district retention policies, for example. All other coefficients are assumed to be time invariant. Except the school fixed

---

4 These types of models are often estimated using student-level data We do not do so here for two reasons. First, we are fundamentally interested in estimating the coefficient on a school level variable—the fixed effect. Because we specify a linear estimating equation, aggregating from the student to the school level should not change the coefficients (assuming the model is correctly specified). Zabel, Stiefel, and Schwartz (2004) carry out a theoretical and empirical analysis of the ways that the use of student-level versus school-level data affects measures of school efficiency. They find that the efficiency measures are not greatly affected by sample composition or aggregation. Second, an important consideration in our analyses is the practical feasibility of creating these measures. Using student-level data increases the data and analysis requirements substantially, perhaps, prohibitively.

5 Further, the fixed effect captures the impact of any time-invariant variables that may influence performance, such as neighborhood effects. See Bartelsman

Measuring School Efficiency Using School Production Functions 41

effects, the coefficients on all other variables are assumed to be constant across schools.

Note that two common models are special cases of equation (2). One can be derived by restricting $\beta_{1g} = 1$ and subtracting $TS_{s,g-1,t-1}$ from both sides of equation (2) yielding:

$$\Delta_g TS_{sgt} = \beta_{0g} + \beta_{2g} ST_{sgt} + \beta_{3g} SC_{sgt} + T_{gt} + S_{gs} + \varepsilon_{sgt} \tag{3}$$

where $\Delta_g TS_{sgt} = TS_{sg,t} - TS_{s,g-1,t-1}$. Now, the dependent variable is the gain in test scores. Thus, we refer to this as GAIN model. Although gain models are common in the literature, whether the restriction $\beta_{1g} = 1$ is appropriate is an empirical, rather than theoretical, matter. If β_{1g} is not, in fact, equal to one, then equation (3) may produce biased estimates of all the parameters in the model, including the school-efficiency measure. We estimate efficiency measures based on the GAIN model, for comparison purposes, and to gain insight into how well this commonly used model serves.

A second model, perhaps less popular than the GAIN model, can be derived by setting $\beta_{1g} = 0$. In this case, the lagged test score is excluded from the model, yielding a production function that does not include controls for prior academic performance:

$$TS_{sgt} = \beta_{0g} + \beta_{2g} ST_{sgt} + \beta_{3g} SC_{sgt} + T_{gt} + S_{gs} + \varepsilon_{sgt} \tag{4}$$

This might be called the "level" model because it explains the level of test-score performance. Although models such as this have been estimated in previous research, more recent work has generally relied on value-added models such as equation (2) or (3), following the intuition (confirmed by a growing body of empirical work), that prior academic performance is an important determinant of current performance. We test the assumption that $\beta_{1g} = 0$ to verify, empirically, that the FE model (equation [1]) is preferred to the level model.

Notice that although we have thus far assumed a linear form for the production function for education, there is little theoretical basis for this assumption. The linear production function assumes the marginal product of any of the inputs is constant over all ranges—that is, there is no diminishing marginal product. Further, it assumes the marginal product of each input is independent of the utilization of other inputs. These may not in fact be right, and it is relatively easy to adapt these models to accommodate alternative assumptions. Nonlinearities in production can be accommodated by including squares and cross products of input variables, for example. We explore nonlinearities by including ST_{sgt}^2 as a regressor.[6]

---

and Doms (2000) for a related discussion of efficiency measurement in manufacturing firms.

6 Another type of nonlinearity may occur if the production of education gains depends on the initial education level. Intuitively, gains may be easier to make

Estimation Issues

Although the production function model in equation (2) is relatively simple, estimation presents several challenges. The most straightforward method is to estimate equation (2) using OLS as it is written, which includes estimating the school fixed effects (the requisite measures of school efficiency) directly. Unfortunately, the fixed-effects estimator (FE) ignores three sources of bias. First, bias may derive from the inclusion of both a lagged dependent variable ($TS_{s,g-1,t-1}$) and fixed effects among the independent variables, which induces a correlation between $TS_{s,g-1,t-1}$ and the error term.[7] Second, bias may arise from measurement error in test scores—again, implying that $TS_{s,g-1,t-1}$, will be correlated with the error term, ε_{sgt}.[8] As shown in Schwartz and Zabel (2002), the correlation between $TS_{s,g-1,t-1}$ and ε_{sgt} may cause attenuation bias, such that the coefficient estimate for β_{1g} will be biased downwards, with potential bias on other coefficients of unknown direction. Third, bias may arise from the potential endogeneity of school resources.

Addressing Bias because of the Inclusion of Fixed Effects and the Lagged Dependent Variable

To eliminate the first source of bias, we transform the model to exclude the fixed effects by differencing, as follows. First, write equation (2) to capture production in $t - 1$:

$$TS_{sg,t-1} = \beta_{0g} + \beta_{1g}TS_{s,g-1,t-2} + \beta_{2g}ST_{sgt-1} + \beta_{3g}SC_{sgt-1} + T_{gt-1} + S_{gs} + \varepsilon_{sgt-1} \quad (2')$$

Because equation (2') includes the same set of school fixed effects as equation (2), subtracting (2') from (2) yields an equation without the school fixed effect:

$$\Delta_t TS_{sgt} = \beta_{1g}\Delta_t TS_{s,g-1,t-1} + \beta_{2g}\Delta_t ST_{sgt} + \beta_{3g}\Delta_t SC_{sgct} + \Delta_t T_{gt} + \Delta_t \varepsilon_{sgt} \quad (5)$$

where $\Delta_t TS_{sgt} = TS_{sgt} - TS_{sg,t-1}$ (and other variables are defined similarly). We refer to equation (5) as the difference model or DIFF. It is worth emphasizing that we difference using the EPF for $TS_{sg,t}$ (2') and not $TS_{sg-1,t-1}$ (the lagged dependent variable) to sweep out the school effect, which is grade specific. That is, although the EPF uses the test score from the previous year for the previous grade as a regressor, here we use the test score for the previous year for the same grade, which means that S_{gs}, which is grade specific, cancels out and does not appear in equation (5).

---

if initial scores are low. Or, high test scores in previous periods may reflect greater propensity to learn or better ability to teach, facilitating larger subsequent gains. As shown in Schwartz and Zabel (2002), the EPF can be adapted to allow for this; however, empirical investigation provided little evidence that the additional complexity introduced by this nonlinearity was warranted.

7 Intuitively, this correlation occurs because the model explaining $TS_{sg-1,t-1}$ will have the same fixed effects as the model explaining $TS_{sg,t}$.

8 Again, the measurement error is explicit in the $TS_{sg-1,t-1}$ production function.

Measuring School Efficiency Using School Production Functions   43

Unfortunately, estimating equation (5) using OLS may still yield biased estimates if $\Delta_t TS_{s,g-1,t-1}$ and $\Delta_t \varepsilon_{sgt}$ are correlated.[9] This can be addressed by using an instrumental variables estimator—providing that suitable instruments can be found. That is, we need a set of variables that are not correlated with the error term but are correlated with the change in test scores. Fortunately, $\Delta_t TS_{s,g-2,t-2}$ and $TS_{s,g-2,t-2}$ are both valid instruments because neither is correlated with $\Delta_t \varepsilon_{sgt}$ (Hsiao, 1986).

Addressing Bias Because of Measurement Error

Bias because of measurement error in the lagged test score means that $TS_{s,g-1,t-1}$, is correlated with the error term, ε_{sgt}. It follows that $\Delta_t TS_{s,g-2,t-2}$ and $TS_{s,g-2,t-2}$ are not valid instruments because both are correlated with the error term $\Delta_t \varepsilon_{sgt}$ in equation (5). (Recall that a valid instrument will be uncorrelated with the error term but correlated with the endogenous variable.) In this case, $\Delta_t TS_{s,g-1,t-3}$ and $TS_{s,g-1,t-3}$ are valid instruments that can be used to correct for both biases.

Notice however, that putting these together means that the fully consistent DIFF estimator requires a minimum of four years of data. This is a fairly strong requirement. As discussed in greater detail below, efficiency measures can only be constructed for schools operating continuously for four years and for which data on test scores, inputs, and so on can be assembled. Thus, we explore the differences between school-efficiency measures obtained from the DIFF and FE models to gain insight into whether the estimates differ sufficiently to justify the cost of more sophisticated and data-intensive modeling.

Note that because the school fixed effects are not directly estimated in DIFF, they must be calculated after estimation. It is relatively easy to do so. The fixed effect for a school can be computed as the mean difference between the predicted and actual value of the dependent variable for that school over time.

Finally, notice that because the gain model in equation (3) does not include a lagged dependent variable, OLS will yield unbiased estimates. Put differently, if $\beta_{1g} = 1$ is justified, then applying OLS to the gain model will result in unbiased estimates of the school-efficiency measures.

Addressing Bias because of the Endogeneity of School Resources

Finally, bias may arise because of the potential endogeneity of school resources either because resources are jointly determined with test scores, or resource allocations depend directly on test scores (implying reverse causality). Although this is particularly troubling in a study utilizing district-level or

---

9 Note that $\Delta_t TS_{s,g-1,t-1}$ includes $\varepsilon_{s,g-1,t-1}$ and $\Delta_g \varepsilon_{sgt}$ includes $\varepsilon_{s,g,t-1}$. These two error terms will be correlated if they both include a common component that is specific to the school and the time period, $t - 1$. This could arise if, for example, the exams for grades g and $g - 1$ are given on the same day and there is a fire drill that disrupts both exams.

cross-district data, it is less likely to be an important problem in the New York City context for two reasons. First, the distribution of resources across schools in New York City is largely determined by the characteristics of students and schools in the prior year, because school budgets must be created before the beginning of school in September. (Thus, the specific performance of a school in year t cannot directly affect the allocation of resources in that year.) Second, and more important, the distribution of resources within a single school district reflects the relatively complex interaction of student needs, parental enrollment decisions, and teacher preferences over work assignments, regulations, mandates, and politics; and it responds relatively sluggishly to school variables, such as test scores. (See Iatarola, 2002 for more on the distribution of resources in New York City public schools.)

In any event, the potential endogeneity of school resources can, again, be addressed using an instrumental variables approach, assuming appropriate instruments can be found. We estimate the DIFF, FE, and GAIN models using a set of lagged variables as instruments—the lagged values of enrollment, the percent of students with limited English proficiency, the percent of full-time special education students, and the percent of students eligible for free lunch. We then compare the resulting efficiency measures to those previously estimated to gauge the importance of correcting for this potential endogeneity in estimating school efficiency.

Data

In 1999–2000, New York City educated 1.1 million students in 1,161 schools, 936 of which were elementary and middle schools. This study uses a balanced panel of 602 elementary schools serving third, fourth, and fifth grades during 1995–1996 through 2000–2001. Our study sample is limited to schools with valid reading and math scores for all three grades and all five years.

We use data on school resources and characteristics from the New York City Department of Education's (DOE) School-Based Expenditure Reports (SBER) and the Annual School Reports (ASR) and pupil-level data also provided by the DOE. School-level variables on grade-specific student background characteristics include gender, race/ethnicity, recent immigrant status, free/reduced-price lunch eligibility and test-score data for the third-, fourth- and fifth-grade students, including reading and math test scores and percentile scores on the Language Assessment Battery (LAB), a test designed to assess English proficiency. Figure 3.1 provides descriptive statistics for 1999–2000.

Figure 3.1. Descriptive Statistics (i)—
Academic Year 1999–2000

Variable	N	Mean	Min	Max
Test scores				
Grade 3: Reading (z-score)	602	0.03	−0.86	1.47
Math (z-score)	602	0.04	−0.89	1.29
Grade 4: Reading (z-score)	602	0.02	−0.95	1.58
Math (z-score)	602	0.03	−0.95	1.54
Grade 5: Reading (z-score)	602	0.03	−0.85	1.53
Math (z-score)	602	0.04	−1.08	1.35
School characteristics and resources:				
Total enrollment as of 10/31	602	802.86	100.00	2200.00
Terminal Grade is 5th grade	602	0.57	0.00	1.00
Terminal Grade is 6th grade	602	0.34	0.00	1.00
Terminal Grade is 8th grade	602	0.09	0.00	1.00
Total classroom teacher expenditure per pupil in $1000 (ii)	602	3.88	2.56	6.91
Total nonteacher expenditure per pupil in $1000 (ii)	602	5.29	2.64	16.19
Teacher–pupil ratio	602	0.07	0.05	0.13
Percent teachers fully licensed/permanently assigned	595	82.66	40.00	100.00
Percent teachers with >5 years of experience	595	58.33	13.30	93.90
Percent teachers more thantwo years in this school	595	65.09	13.30	89.70
Percent teachers with masters degree or higher	593	78.18	33.30	100.00
Student characteristics:				
Percent full-time special-education students	602	4.86	0.00	18.40

Variable	N	Mean	Min	Max
Student characteristics Grade 5:				
Percent students having reading test scores	602	91.72	63.58	100.00
Percent students having math test scores	602	92.92	62.91	100.00
Percent females	602	50.70	32.50	69.14
Percent students eligible for free lunch	602	73.23	5.98	100.00
Percent students eligible for reduced-price lunch	602	6.86	0.00	28.57
Percent black students	602	36.32	0.00	100.00
Percent Hispanic students	602	33.94	0.00	100.00
Percent Asians, Native Americans and unknowns	602	11.39	0.00	95.89
LAB Percentile	602	25.57	1.00	99.00
Percent students LAB = <40 percentile (iii)	602	7.58	0.00	37.90
Percent students taking LAB test (iii)	602	9.49	0.00	41.94
Percent resource room students (iv)	602	8.71	0.00	33.33
Percent recent immigrants (v)	602	5.59	0.00	29.88

Notes:

i) Reported means are not pupil weighted.

ii) All expenditure figures are measured in 1997 dollars, deflated using the CPI.

iii) LAB refers to the Language Assessment Battery. According to the New York City Board of Education, this test is given to identify and evaluate English language proficiency for students whose home language is other than English. Students earning a score less than or equal to the 40th percentile are eligible for ESL and bilingual services.

iv) Resource room includes students receiving resource room, consultant teacher and related services.

v) Recent immigrants are students who entered the U.S. school system within the last three years.

Test Scores

In the period of this study, the DOE administered different tests to students in different grades. Students in the third and fifth grades were given the CTB/McGraw Hill Test of Basic Skills (CTB) in reading and the California Achievement Test (CAT) in mathematics, although students in the fourth grade were administered new state English Language Arts (ELA) reading and mathematics tests in 1998–1999 and 1999–2000. To make these different tests comparable over the years and to one another, we normalized test scores based on city-wide averages and standard deviations for the third, fourth, and fifth grades. [10] As shown in Figure 3.1, the range in performance across schools is substantial. On the high side are schools in which performance averages 1.5 standard deviations above average. At the other extreme are schools in which average performance is quite low—nearly a full standard deviation below average.

School Characteristics and Resources

The New York City public schools vary widely in characteristics and resources. To begin, although the average school enrolls 803 students, the largest school is almost three times that size (2,200), whereas the smallest enrolls only 100. At the same time, schools differ in their grade spans. By construction, all of our sample schools serve grades three, four, and five, however only 57% end there. Roughly one-third continue through sixth grade and 9% continue through eighth.

Interestingly, although all the schools are funded by a single school district, spending and teacher resources vary significantly. Although the average school spends nearly $3,900 per pupil on classroom teachers, such spending varies from a low of roughly $2,500 to a high of $6,900. Spending on other items is even more disparate—whereas the average is nearly $5,300 per pupil, the minimum is roughly half that and the maximum more than three times as much.[11] Teacher resources are similarly variable—the teacher–pupil ratio ranges from 5 teachers per 100 students to 13 teachers per student, with an average of roughly 7. And, teacher characteristics differ across schools—in some schools nearly all the teachers are licensed and permanently assigned, whereas in other schools, such teachers are in the minority. Although these disparities may be viewed as cause for concern regarding equity, for our purposes this variation is crucial, allowing estimation of the EPF.

---

10 Underlying CTB and CAT scores for 1995–1996 through 1998–1999 were Normal Curve Equivalent (NCE) scores, ELA reading and state math tests for 1998–1999 and 1999–2000 and CTB and CAT tests for 1999–2000 were scale scores.

11 Classroom teacher expenditures include full-time teacher salaries, preparation period payments, per diem per session payments for substitute teachers, and fringe benefits.

Student Characteristics

The diversity in the New York City public schools extends to demographic and student educational needs. Because our regression analyses focus on fourth- and fifth-grade performance, we turn next to the characteristics of these grades. Figure 3.1 shows the characteristics of fifth-grade students. Fourth-grade students are quite similar in these characteristics.[12] Although the average fifth grade is roughly half female, the female share ranges from a low of roughly one-third to more than two-thirds. On average, roughly three-quarters of the students are eligible for free lunch and another seven percent for reduced-price lunch. Again, there is considerable diversity. Some schools have few poor students, whereas others are entirely composed of poor students.

Racial diversity is considerable. Although the average fifth grade is more than a third black and a third Hispanic, Asians and Native Americans comprise more than a tenth of the class, while just under a fifth are white. Roughly 5.6% of the students in the average school are recent immigrants. To be sure, this "average" school is hardly typical. Racially homogenous schools of all kinds exist, and schools dominated by two racial groups (for instance, black and Hispanic students) are common. Some schools have no recent immigrants, but others have substantial shares.

Finally, utilization of special-education and supplemental services varies widely—in the use of resource room (or part-time special education), full-time special-education and English-language instruction. As shown, the average school has a student body in which roughly 5% attend full-time special-education programs; some schools have no such students and others have substantially more. On average, nearly 10% of fifth-grade students take the LAB test, and nearly 9% score low enough to be eligible for bilingual or English-as-a-second-language instruction.

Results

Because our focus in this chapter is on school-efficiency measures, we devote little attention to the coefficient estimates in the EPFs. Instead, we concentrate on exploring efficiency measures estimated various ways, as described above. We begin with an analysis of the raw test scores, both because these are the dependent variables in our EPF regressions, but also because they are popularly relied on as measures of school performance; and we are interested in assessing whether they differ substantively from the econometrically estimated efficiency measures.

We estimate the EPFs using four outputs: reading and math in fourth and fifth grades. Third-grade scores are used in the fourth-grade EPFs, but the absence of second-grade test scores precludes the estimation of a third-grade EPF.

---

12 Note that the table reports the characteristics of the average school and have not been student weighted.

Understanding Test Score Measures

The EPF models rely on three test-score measures as the dependent variables: (i) levels, TS_{sgt}, as in equation (2); (ii) **gains**, defined as the change in test scores between grade g–1 in period t-1 and grade g in period t ($\Delta_g TS_{sgt}$, as in equation [3]); and (iii) **differences** in test scores, defined as the change in test scores between grade g in period t–1 and grade g in period t, $\Delta_t TS_{sgt}$, as in equation (5). Recall that the **gain** in test scores captures the average change in student-level test scores between adjacent years. The **difference** in test scores captures the average change in scores in the same grade between adjacent years (and thus might be interpreted as capturing school improvement rather than the gains made by any set of students).

Figure 3.2 shows correlations between the three test-score measures for academic years 1997–2000.[13] To begin, correlations in the levels are quite high—ranging from 0.87 to 0.94. Within grades this is unsurprising, given the common set of students. The high cross-grade correlations may mean that so-called *good* schools are consistently good and *bad* schools are consistently bad. Or, these correlations could suggest that high-scoring students consistently choose schools that high-scoring students have chosen in the past, whereas low-scoring students choose schools chosen by low-scoring students in the past.

---

13 Notice that although we have data for 1996–2000, the first year of the test-score data are only used as the lagged dependent variable in the EPF regressions. Using a lagged dependent variable means we lose a year of data.

Figure 3.2. Pearson Correlation Coefficients between Raw Test Scores, N=602

	Level Grade 4 Reading	Level Grade 4 Math	Level Grade 5 Reading	Level Grade 5 Math	Gain Grade 4 Reading
Level Grade 4 Reading	1.00				
Level Grade 4 Math	0.93	1.00			
Level Grade 5 Reading	0.90	0.88	1.00		
Level Grade 5 Math	0.87	0.91	0.94	1.00	
Gain Grade 4 Math	0.36	0.24	0.18	0.18	1.00
Gain Grade 4 Math	0.15	0.24	0.08	0.08	0.51
Gain Grade 5 Reading	−0.06	−0.07	0.14	0.05	0.06
Gain Grade 5 Math	−0.06	−0.06	0.05	0.13	0.02
Diff Grade 4 Reading	0.22	0.10	−0.07	−0.06	0.45
Diff Grade 4 Math	0.11	0.19	−0.08	0.10	0.17
Diff Grade 5 Reading	0.01	0.00	0.20	−0.08	0.11
Diff Grade 5 Math	0.00	0.00	0.11	0.17	0.08

Gain Grade 4 Reading	Gain Grade 5 Reading	Gain Grade 5 Math	Diff Grade 4 Reading	Diff Grade 4 Math	Diff Grade 5 Reading	Diff Grade 5 Math
1.00						
0.01	1.00					
0.04	0.50	1.00				
0.17	0.41	0.19	1.00			
0.43	0.15	0.40	0.54	1.00		
0.10	0.43	0.18	−0.07	−0.09	1.00	
0.13	0.20	0.38	−0.07	−0.07	0.63	1.00

Notes:
i) Level test scores are measured in z-scores; gain scores are defined as the change in level test scores between grade $g–1$ in period $t–1$ and grade g in period t; and Diff scores are defined as the change in level test scores between grade g in period $t–1$ and grade g in period t.

ii) Reported correlations are based on four-year averages (1996–1997 through 1999–2000) of the three test-score measures.

The correlations between the gain measures are considerably lower. Within grade, the correlations are roughly 0.5 whereas the cross-grade correlations are close to zero. The implication is that a school posting high gains in one area or grade may well post low gains in another area or grade. Put differently, there is little evidence that schools producing big gains in fourth grade will also produce big gains in fifth grade. Note, also, that there is very little correlation between test-score levels and gains. Schools with high-scoring students may well produce low gains.

Turning to the difference measures, the correlations in Figure 3.2 suggest lower correlations among the difference measures than the correlations in levels. Correlations between reading and math differences for the same grade are 0.54 and 0.63 for the fourth and fifth grades, respectively. Cross-grade correlations are slightly *less* than 0 and, again, there is very little correlation between test-score differences and gains.

The implication of this analysis of test scores is that the choice of output measure matters to an assessment of school performance. Schools reporting high test-score levels may well have low gains, and mediocre differences. Many combinations are possible and there is little consistency to be relied on.

Estimating School Production Functions

We turn next to estimating two EPF models described above: (i) the fixed-effects (FE) model, as in equation (2), (ii) the difference model (DIFF), as in equation (5). Figure 3.3 shows the results, along with the results of estimating the gain model (GAIN), as in equation (3), for comparison purposes.

Figure 3.3. Selected Coefficient Estimates for Education Production Functions

	Grade 4			Grade 5		
	FE	DIFF	GAIN	FE	DIFF	GAIN
Lagged test score	0.3504*** (0.0137)	0.2907 (0.2016)	—	0.4358*** (0.0130)	0.6783*** (0.1210)	—
Teacher–pupil ratio	1.2690 (1.4304)	0.8767 (3.1920)	−0.4138 (1.7739)	−2.2478* (1.2942)	−4.1648 (2.9175)	0.9918 (1.5580)
Teacher–pupil ratio squared	−3.9594*** (1.0654)	−3.1629 (3.7385)	−4.2304*** (1.3217)	−0.1819 (0.9650)	1.3131 (3.3950)	0.6960 (1.1616)
Nonteacher class-room expenditure	−0090 (0.0188)	−0.0069 (0.0328)	0.0199 (0.0233)	0.0476*** (0.0170)	0.0329 (0.0296)	0.0539*** (0.0205)
Nonteacher class-room expenditure squared	−0.0056*** (0.0021)	−0.0031 (0.0035)	−0.0088*** (0.0027)	−0.0030 (0.0019)	−0.0018 (0.0030)	0.0008 (0.0023)
(Teacher–pupil ratio) × (Nonteacher class-room expenditure	1.1031*** (0.3798)	0.8181 (0.7216)	1.3910*** (0.4711)	0.3285 (0.3445)	0.1906 (0.6498)	−0.2031 (0.4145)
Number of observations)	4,816	2,408	4,816	4,816	2,408	4,816
Adjusted R^2	0.8199	0.1350	0.0367	0.8103	0.1081	0.0002
p-value for the joint significance of school inputs	0.0010	0.0927	0.0006	0.0000	0.0475	0.0000
Marginal effects: Teacher–pupil ratio	0.0050	0.0019	0.0017	−0.0045	−0.0069	−0.0047
Nonteacher ependiture per pupil	0.0055	0.0090	0.0144	0.0203	0.0142	0.0240

Notes:

i) Dependent variables for the FE, DIFF, and GAIN equations are level, difference, and gain test scores, respectively.

ii) All regressions are estimated using pooled reading and math data.

iii) Regressions also include total enrollment; dummies for years, grade spans, and schools with students who take the LAB test; the percentage of students who are enrolled in full-time special education programs; the percentages of teachers fully licensed and permanently assigned, with master's degrees, with more than five years of teaching experience, and working more than two years in their current school; and the percentages of fourth- (or fifth-) grade students who are female, free/reduced-price lunch eligible, black, Hispanic, Asian or other, recent immigrant and resource room participant and who have reading (or math) test score, take the LAB test, score in the 40th percentile or lower on the LAB; and a set of missing indicators.

(iv) Lagged test score in the DIFF equations for the fourth grade is instrumented by the third lags of third- and fifth-grade reading and math test scores. The lag in the fifth-grade DIFF equation is instrumented by the third lags of third- and fourth-grade reading and math test scores.

(v) Standard errors are reported in parentheses.

(vi) * indicates significance at the 10% level.
** indicates significant at the 5 % level.
*** indicates significance at the 1% level.

As shown in Figure 3.3, we use a set of student and school characteristics as explanatory variables when estimating the EPFs, and a single equation is estimated for each grade—that is, the reading and math observations are pooled and a single regression estimated for each grade. (The appropriateness of this pooling assumption is explored below.) Following the discussion above, the FE model is estimated in levels and the DIFF model is estimated using changes, both for the dependent and independent variables. To review, consistently estimating the parameters of the DIFF model requires instrumental variables. For the EPFs for fourth-grade reading and math, we use the third lag of third and fifth-grade reading and math scores as instruments (the third rather than the second lag is needed to alleviate the measurement error bias, see Section 2.2). For the EPFs for fifth-grade reading and math, we use the third lag of third and fourth-grade reading and math scores as instruments.

As shown in Figure 3.3, the adjusted R^2s for the fourth- and fifth-grade FE models are relatively high (0.82 and 0.81), and the coefficients on the lagged test score are statistically significant with estimates of 0.35 and 0.44. The implication is that neither the gain model (that assumes this coefficient is one) nor the level model (that assumes this coefficient is zero) is correct—statistical tests indicate that the coefficients on the lagged dependent variables from the FE model are neither one nor zero.

The results for the school input variables (teacher–pupil ratio and nonteacher expenditures per pupil) are mixed. As described above, both squares and cross-products of these variables are included to allow for nonlinear returns. For both models, the school input variables are significant as a group at the 1% level.[14] To get a sense of how these variables affect test scores, we compute the impact on standardized test scores of a decrease in the number of pupils per teacher from 15 to 14 (15 is about the mean) and from an increase in nonteacher expenditures from \$4,750 (about the mean) to \$5,250 (each increase is roughly 1/3 of a standard deviation).[15] All these impacts are small and, for all but two cases, insignificant at the 5% level.

As shown in Figure 3.3, the magnitudes of the DIFF coefficients for grade 4 are quite similar to those for the FE model, although the standard errors are generally much larger. This highlights one of the drawbacks of using the DIFF model. The stringent data requirements result in a decrease in degrees of freedom and hence less-precisely estimated parameters, larger standard errors, and weaker results. In the grade 5 model, on the other hand, the coefficient estimate of the lagged test score rises from 0.44 to 0.68, and although the standard error also increases, it remains statistically significant.

---

14 Both the increases in the teacher–pupil ratio and in nonteacher expenditures are positive for both models.

15 The discussion refers to pupils per teacher even though the regressions used the teacher–pupil ratio. This was done for ease of interpretation but the numbers are based on the estimates in the regressions reported.

Sensitivity Checks

Although the theory allows for different efficiency measures for each grade and subject area in a school, whether efficiency varies across grades and/or subject areas is an empirical question. In the regressions in table 3, we report the results for pooled regressions which combine both math and reading EPF equations. Is this appropriate? Could we have estimated only a single equation for all grades and tests? That is, are school-efficiency measures estimated for different tests in the same grade significantly different from one another or can we legitimately rely on one, jointly estimated, efficiency measure for the fourth grade? Similarly, are fourth- and fifth-grade efficiency measures sufficiently different from one another, either all together or by subject area, to warrant separate estimation? This gets to the heart of one of the questions we posed earlier. Are there good schools and bad schools, or are schools good at some things and not so good at others?

To investigate this, we estimated EPFs under two assumptions: (i) EPFs are exactly the same across grades as well as tests and only one efficiency measure is estimated, and (ii) the coefficients on all inputs but the school-efficiency measures are the same and only the efficiency measures and intercept are allowed to vary across grade or test.[16]

We begin by examining whether the coefficients and school-efficiency measures are grade-specific; we compare the coefficients estimated using the FE model for EPFs for fourth- and fifth-grade reading and for fourth- and fifth-grade math. (Results are not reported here in the interest of conserving space.) Statistical tests reject the null hypothesis that the coefficients and school-efficiency measures are equal across grades. We then examine whether it is only the school-efficiency measures that differ even while the other coefficients are similar (as in [ii] above). Again, statistical tests indicate significant differences in the efficiency measures across grades both for math and reading. Thus, the results provide evidence that grade-specific EPFs are necessary.

That said, do we need test-specific EPFs within each grade? Here, we test whether there is a common production function across tests for the same grade. Note that most of the independent variables are the same in the two models. Of course, the dependent variable and its lag differ, as does the percentage of the students taking the exam, but all others are the same. Given the high correlation in the within grade test scores, shown in Figure 3.2, it is perhaps unsurprising that the results suggest the EPFs are quite similar: Statistical tests fail to reject the null hypothesis that the coefficients or the school-efficiency measures are equal.

Comparing efficiency measures directly yields a similar picture. In particular, correlations between the efficiency measures estimated in separate EPFs for fourth- and fifth-grade reading and math under both (i) and (ii) are all greater

---

16 The test means are normed to zero for all schools. Because we only analyze schools with test scores for all five years, the means for the included schools are no longer zero and are unlikely to be equal across tests or grades.

than or equal to 0.95. The implication is that one EPF per grade is sufficient, even though different grades require their own EPFs.

A second concern is that the school resources may be endogeneous in principle—either because resources are allocated to schools based on their performance or because they are jointly determined. Thus, we investigate the potential endogeneity of school resources using five instrumental variables—lagged values of enrollment, percent of limited English proficient students, percent of full-time special education students, and percent of students eligible for free lunch.

The first-stage regressions have adjusted R^2s around 0.50 and the instruments are jointly significant at the 1% level. Results provide little evidence of endogeneity. Although there are some large changes in the point estimates of the school input coefficients, these are predominantly in variables that are not significant. Further, the correlations between school-efficiency estimates from the models where we do and do not account for the potential endogeneity of resources are high. Finally, testing for endogeneity of resources using the Hausman test provides no evidence of endogeneity, even at the 10% level of significance.[17] (Regression results are not shown in the interest of brevity, but are available from the authors.)

Our conclusion from these sensitivity checks is that the EPFs in Figure 3.3 are appropriately estimated and we turn next to exploring the estimated efficiency measures.

Comparing Efficiency Measures

Given the challenges posed by estimating more sophisticated and appropriate production functions, it seems important to consider whether this greater difficulty is worth the additional effort. We address this issue by investigating the extent to which more sophisticated measures yield different guidance about school efficiency. Although statistical tests may reveal significant differences in estimated coefficients, our interest in this chapter is in the efficiency measures.

We begin by comparing the correlations among the school-efficiency measures generated from three models: the fixed-effects model (FE), the first difference model (DIFF) that corrects for the two biases inherent in FE, and the Gain model (GAIN). We include the latter in this analysis because it is a popular model, and it does not suffer from the two biases that FE does. The results are presented in Figure 3.4a.

---

17 As noted in the first section, consistently estimating DIFF requires instrumenting for the difference in the lagged test score which is correlated with the error term. We carry out a Hausman test for the exogeneity of the difference in the lagged test score and firmly reject this test. Here we have evidence that this variable is endogenous and IV is necessary.

Figure 3.4a. Pearson Correlation Coefficients between School-Efficiency Measures, N = 602

	Grade 4 FE	Grade 5 FE	Grade 4 DIFF	Grade 5 DIFF	Grade 4 GAIN	Grade 5 Gain
Grade 4 FE	1.00					
Grade 5 FE	0.59	1.00				
Grade 4 DIFF	0.98	0.56	1.00			
Grade 5 DIFF	0.28	0.85	0.28	1.00		
Grade 4 GAIN	0.42	−0.03	0.41	0.01	1.00	
Grade 5 GAIN	−0.18	0.60	−0.19	0.82	−0.10	1.00

Among the three models, the school-efficiency (Fig. 3.4a) measures from FE and DIFF have the highest correlation; 0.98 and 0.85 for the fourth- and fifth-grade measures. This provides an initial rationale for recommending the use of the FE model because the resulting efficiency measure is highly correlated with the efficiency measure from the econometrically best model (DIFF) yet imposes less severe data requirements. Note that the correlations across grades are relatively low for all three models. In fact, the correlation between the fourth- and fifth-grade measures is negative for GAIN. These correlations suggest there can be divergence in output across grades within a school.

Figure 3.4b. Percentage of Schools with Discrepant Classifications across Methods: Top Decile, Bottom Decile, Middle Deciles, N = 602

	Grade 4	Grade 5
FE vs. DIFF	6.0	15.0
FE vs. GAIN	29.6	23.9
DIFF vs. GAIN	30.1	14.6
Note: Schools are designated to the top, bottom, or middle group based on their efficiency scores generated from the FE, DIFF, or GAIN model.		

Notice that for many purposes, we may be more interested in identifying outlier schools—that is, schools that are particularly good, perhaps to be rewarded or emulated, and schools that are particularly bad, for sanctioning, reform, or intervention. Thus, we turn next to exploring the congruence between these measures in the identification of outliers. We begin by defining the set of top and bottom schools as those schools in the top and bottom deciles, respectively. That is, we sort schools by efficiency measures into three groups; those in the top decile, those in the bottom decile, and those in the middle eight deciles. We then examine the pair-wise cross-tabulations of the rankings of the different models between FE and DIFF to see which will indicate how many of the top-ranked schools, according to FE measures, are also top-ranked schools according to DIFF, and so on. These cross tabulations suggest a fair amount of agreement between FE and DIFF. As shown in Figure 3.4b, only 6.0% of schools are ranked differently for FE than DIFF in the fourth grade. The fifth-grade results, however, disagree for 15.0% of the schools, which is somewhat more problematic. The disagreement is more substantial across other methods. The worst case is that DIFF and GAIN assessments differ for 30.1% of the schools in the fourth grade. What is unclear from these statistics, however, is whether the discrepancies are driven by small differences in the designation of schools around the boundaries. These disagreements may be because of schools moving from the first to the second decile, for example, which is somewhat less troubling than disagreements across several deciles.

Figure 3.4c. Percentage of Schools with Rankings that Differ across Methods by More than One Decile, N = 602

	Grade 4	*Grade 5*
FE vs. DIFF	2.2	34.4
FE vs. GAIN	59.6	53.3
DIFF vs. GAIN	61.3	38.7
Note: School rankings are based on school-efficiency scores generated from the FE, DIFF, or GAIN model.		

To get a better feel for the magnitude of this problem, we examine the frequency of large disparities across methods. That is, for each set of efficiency measures, we sort the schools into efficiency deciles, and conduct a set of pair-wise comparisons between measures, computing the percentage of schools for which the two decile assignments differ by more than 1 (e.g. first and third or sixth and ninth). By allowing for at least one decile between efficiency measures, we exclude cases where a marginal shift in relative performance implies a shift in deciles: for example, where a school moves from the top of the eighth decile according to one measure and just at the bottom of the ninth decile according to the rankings of another measure. The results are presented in Figure 3.4c. Here, the FE and DIFF measures are quite similar for the fourth grade—only 2.2% of the schools differ in ranking by more than one decile. The discrepancy is larger in the fifth grade—34.4%. Both FE and DIFF differ markedly, however, from the GAIN based measures. For example, for the DIFF and GAIN measures, 61.3% of the schools differ in ranking by more than one decile based on fourth-grade scores.[18] Taken together, the results imply that the FE model yields school-efficiency measures that may be viewed as quite similar to the DIFF measures, which are methodologically preferred.

---

18 The fact that there is a higher percentage of discrepancies in Figure 3.4c compared to Figure 3.4b is not surprising. Figure 3.4c reports disparities in efficiency measure rankings across all ten deciles, whereas Figure 3.4b disparities for only the top and bottom deciles.

Measuring School Efficiency Using School Production Functions

Of course for policy purposes, the critical question is: How different is the guidance offered by the econometrically estimated efficiency measures from that offered by raw test scores or, for that matter, test-score gains? Figure 3.5a shows the correlation between the three efficiency measures and the four-year average level, gain, and difference test scores by grade. The results indicate that the school-efficiency measures generated from FE are most highly correlated with level test scores. This is, perhaps, unsurprising because the dependent variable is the test-score level in the FE model, whereas the dependent variable is a test-score change in the DIFF and GAIN models. Thus, it is similarly unsurprising that school-efficiency measures generated from GAIN are highly correlated with test-score gains. Turning to the DIFF model, for fourth grade, the DIFF efficiency measure is not highly correlated with test-score *differences* or *gains.* For fifth grade, the DIFF efficiency measure is not highly correlated with test-score *differences or levels.* The implication is important. Compared to the methodologically preferred DIFF measures, raw test scores, whether measured as gains, levels, or differences may well give misleading guidance about school efficiency.

Figure 3.5a. Pearson Correlation Coefficient between School-efficiency Measure and Average of Reading and Math Test Score, N = 602

	Level		Difference		Gain	
	Grade 4	Grade 5	Grade 4	Grade 5	Grade 4	Grade 5
FE	0.72	0.57	0.11	0.10	0.43	0.38
DIFF	0.68	0.13	0.09	0.09	0.36	0.53
GAIN	−0.08	−0.14	0.15	0.21	0.75	0.74

Note: Correlations are based on school-efficiency measures generated from the FE, DIFF, or GAIN model and four-year average level, difference, or gain test score.

Further evidence can be found in Figure 3.5b, which compares the decile rankings of DIFF (as used in Figure 3.4) to decile rankings based on the raw test scores. We calculate the percentage of schools that differ in ranking by more than one decile using the mean over all four years—and for each year separately for the three average raw test scores. In every case, the raw test scores perform poorly. The FE based measures are clearly better guides to school performance than raw scores.

Figure 3.5b. Percent Discrepancy between School Efficiency from DIFF and Average of Reading and Math Test Score, N = 602

	Level		Difference		Gain	
	Grade 4	Grade 5	Grade 4	Grade 5	Grade 4	Grade 5
Mean	51.2	66.4	70.9	71.6	61.5	57.5
1997	53.3	67.6	65.3	65.9	66.3	60.3
1998	51.0	66.4	71.6	70.3	66.8	63.3
1999	51.8	68.1	73.9	75.9	63.3	63.8
2000	52.5	69.1	71.6	71.1	69.1	65.3

Note: Numbers show the percentage of schools that differ in ranking by more than one decile between the efficiency measures based on the DIFF model and the level, difference, or gain test score.

Note that aggregating test scores result in little, if any, improvement. First, taking the average of the reading and math scores makes little difference when compared to the individual tests. The correlations in Figure 3.5b calculated separately for reading and math tests (not shown) are strikingly similar to the statistics presented. Second, taking the mean across years also makes little difference. Although more information is typically better, in this case, more is not much better. This is because the mean test scores for a given year are strongly influenced by the quality of the students and this does not change much over the years. This is contrary to the advice offered by Kane and Staiger (2002) and others who advocate using more years of data, such as the means of several years of test scores, to improve accuracy.

In summary, the FE measures most closely mirror the methodologically superior DIFF measures—there are relatively few discrepancies in the rankings suggested by these two. Although estimating efficiency with the DIFF model is clearly preferable, unfortunately, it requires a lot of data—a minimum of four years and three (consecutive) grades—and somewhat more sophisticated analyses. Thus, our results suggest that if the DIFF model is impracticable, the FE model is a reasonable alternative. Equally important, raw test scores—either in level, difference, or gain form—do not emerge as good or even *adequate* substitutes for the DIFF efficiency measures. And the GAIN model, which has enjoyed recent popularity, seems to be a poor substitute as well.

The Good, the Bad and the Ugly: What Characterizes High (and Low) Efficiency?

We next turn to examine the characteristics of schools identified as either high or low efficiency. Although there is some disagreement among the measures, we next determine if there is a set of schools for which both measures agree. That is, there are 25 schools that have efficiency measures in the top 10% for both fourth and fifth grade—the so-called *best* schools—and 25 schools that

Measuring School Efficiency Using School Production Functions 61

have efficiency measures in the bottom 10% for both grades—the worst schools.[19]

Further, 76 schools are in one of the top three deciles for both grades but not in the top decile for both—a set of schools we term good—and another that are in bottom three deciles for both measures but not in the bottom decile for both—the bad schools (81 schools). Interestingly, there is a fifth group, a set of 28 schools in the top three deciles for one measure and the bottom three for another; the ugly schools. What distinguishes these schools from each other?[20]

As shown in Figure 3.6, the mean characteristics of these schools show a remarkable consistency. As might be expected, average scores are lowest in the worst schools, low in the bad schools, better in the good schools, and highest in the best schools—the ugly are somewhere in the middle. The pattern in the gain is less evident. On average, gains are very close to zero. It is only in the worst schools that the average gain (actually loss) exceeds -0.03 standard deviations. The pattern in school size is, perhaps, somewhat surprising. The best schools are the largest, exceeding 900 students, as are the ugly, and the worst schools are the smallest, averaging less than 600 students. Good and bad schools lie predictably in the middle. And the same pattern obtains for grade enrollment.

Figure 3.6. Variable Means
for Worst, Bad, Good, Best, and Ugly Schools

Variable	Worst (N = 25)	Bad (N = 81)	Good (N = 76)	Best (N = 25)	Ugly (N = 28)	(Worst) (Best)
Raw test scores						
Grade 4:						
Reading level	−0.50	−0.36	0.46	0.69	−0.18	−1.19***
Math level	−0.61	−0.40	0.50	0.69	−0.17	−1.30***
Reading difference	0.01	−0.01	0.02	0.03	0.01	−0.02
Math difference	0.00	0.00	0.01	0.02	0.02	−0.02
Reading gain	−0.07	−0.03	0.07	0.12	−0.04	−0.19***
Math gain	−0.13	−0.03	0.03	0.04	0.00	−0.17***

19 Notice that using the means of the test-score levels, the corresponding number of schools that would be ranked in the top (bottom) decile for all four tests is 34 (29). Only 9 of these 34 schools are ranked in the top FE decile twice and only 13 of the 29 are ranked in the bottom FE decile twice. Thus, rankings based on raw test-score data will yield a very different set of schools classified as good and bad.

20 Note that we are not claiming that the differences reflect causal relationships. Here, we are examining the characteristics of schools across efficiency groups only.

Variable	Worst (N = 25)	Bad (N = 81)	Good (N = 76)	Best (N = 25)	Ugly (N = 28)	(Worst) (Best)
Grade 5:						
Reading level	−0.56	−0.36	0.45	0.65	−0.16	−1.21***
Math level	−0.64	−0.41	0.49	0.67	−0.18	−1.31***
Reading difference	−0.02	−0.01	0.01	0.01	0.03	−0.03
Math difference	0.01	−0.01	0.00	0.01	0.01	0.00
Reading gain	−0.04	−0.01	0.01	0.00	0.03	−0.04
Math gain	−0.03	−0.01	0.01	−0.01	0.01	−0.02
School characteristics and resources:						
Total enrollment as of 10/31	573.51	707.85	827.52	911.91	885.62	−338.40***
Grade 4 enrollment	75.85	89.82	126.71	135.98	134.38	−60.13***
Grade 5 enrollment	71.28	86.80	121.66	129.14	123.92	−57.86***
Terminal grade is fifth grade	0.24	0.31	0.79	0.64	0.64	−0.40***
Terminal grade is sixth grade	0.72	0.58	0.18	0.20	0.29	0.52***
Terminal grade is eighth grade	0.04	0.09	0.01	0.12	0.04	−0.08
Total expenditure per pupil in $1000 (ii)	10.49	9.26	7.59	7.23	7.93	3.26***
Nonteacher expenditure per pupil in $1000 (ii)	6.14	5.40	4.14	3.87	4.31	2.27***
Teacher–pupil ratio	0.08	0.07	0.06	0.06	0.07	0.02***
Percent teachers licensed/assigned	77.52	79.02	90.23	89.54	82.88	−12.02***
Percent teachers with >5 years of experience	59.12	58.50	65.03	64.18	61.40	−5.06**
Percent teachers >2 years in this school	61.66	63.64	73.47	71.80	70.81	−10.14***
Percent teachers with master's degree	77.97	77.37	84.92	84.96	80.62	−6.99***
Student characteristics:						
Percent full-time special education students	10.31	8.78	3.33	3.21	3.81	7.10***
Grade 5:						
Percent students having test scores	96.35	94.60	93.79	95.08	92.44	1.27
Percent females	50.85	51.65	49.91	51.12	50.97	−0.27
Percent free lunch	84.43	81.56	57.19	57.07	84.62	27.36***
Percent reduced-price lunch	2.59	4.62	8.81	9.07	5.88	−6.48***
Percent black students	64.29	48.91	25.62	30.70	35.47	33.59***

Measuring School Efficiency Using School Production Functions 63

Variable	Worst (N = 25)	Bad (N = 81)	Good (N = 76)	Best (N = 25)	Ugly (N = 28)	(Worst) (Best)
Percent Hispanic students	28.00	37.08	27.76	27.78	47.71	0.22
Percent Asians or others	2.04	4.71	17.43	14.05	8.59	−12.01***
Percent resource room students (iii)	10.22	10.31	9.54	7.26	8.88	2.96**
Percent recent immigrants (iv)	2.11	4.20	6.77	5.34	6.33	−3.23***

Notes:

i)   All values are four-year averages based on data from academic years 1996–1997 through 1999–2000.

ii) *Best* schools have efficiency measures from the FE model in the top 10% for both fourth and fifth grades. *Worst* schools are in the bottom 10% for both grades. *Good* schools are not in the top decile for both fourth and fifth grade but in one of the top three deciles for both grades. *Bad* schools are not in the bottom decile for both fourth and fifth grade but in bottom three deciles for both grades. *Ugly* schools are in the top three deciles for one grade and the bottom three for another.

ii) All expenditure figures are measured in 1997 dollars, deflated using the CPI.

iii) Resource room includes students receiving resource room, consultant teacher and related services.

iv) Recent immigrants are students who entered the U.S. school system within the last three years.

v)   * indicates that a mean difference is significant at the 10% level. ** indicates that a mean difference is significant at the 5% level. *** indicates that a mean difference is significant at the 1% level.

The pattern in many other characteristics is remarkably consistent, monotonically increasing or decreasing with quality, whereas the ugly set lies somewhere in the middle. For example, the best schools have a significantly lower share of special-education students and poor students than the worst. A larger share of the best schools terminates in grade 5. Whether this is because grades six up are disproportionately expensive, or older children distract the younger ones, or because a larger grade span presents managerial challenges is a worthwhile subject for future research.

Still it is interesting to note that good schools differ from bad schools in their resources. The best schools have fewer teachers per pupil and lower nonteacher expenditures. And teachers in good schools are more likely to have a master's degree, more than five years of experience, more than two years in the same school, and be licensed and permanently assigned to the school. Whether this reflects conscious resource allocation decisions or some other mechanism, the results suggest an important role for qualified teachers in school performance. Finally, the students differ significantly in their characteristics. Disappointingly, the worst schools are disproportionately black—the representation of blacks in the worst schools is more than double that in the best schools (64.3% versus 30.7%). The distribution of Asians runs dramatically in the opposite direction—the best schools have nearly seven times the representation of Asians than the worst. In comparison, the distribution of Hispanics is more even, ranging from 28%–48%. The most striking difference between the purported ugly schools and the others is in the representation of the Hispanic students. On average, nearly half of the students in this unusual group of schools is Hispanic; whether this reflects differential test-taking behavior or success because of English language proficiency programs is worthy of further consideration.

Implications and Lessons for Future Work

Estimating school efficiency using the econometric estimation of EPFs as outlined above, although appealing in many ways, is undoubtedly more difficult than the measures most commonly used to evaluate schools by school administrators, policymakers, and parents. The difficulty stems from two sources. First, measures constructed using regression analyses require more data and more data analysis compared to measuring efficiency using only test scores or changes in test scores. The former measures are also more difficult to interpret. Specifically, the efficiency measures need to be interpreted as measuring efficiency controlling for the set of regressors relative to the other schools in the sample. Thus, more effort is required to understand what has been estimated and to interpret the results.

Second, the estimation strategy that corrects for bias because of the correlation between the lagged test score and the error term is somewhat more difficult to implement, both because of the more significant data requirements and because of the statistical sophistication. Although the latter problem can be addressed with user-friendly statistical packages, the need for additional years of data presents a particular challenge if there is significant turnover in schools (because of some sort of reorganization), school personnel (especially principals and superintendents), or policies. If we need four years of data for the same school, how do we deal with schools that are changing? Although including only the stable schools solves the data problem, it poses potential problems if this means including only stagnant, less innovative schools and excluding dynamic, potentially more efficient, schools.

The main lesson from our analyses is that using raw test scores to rank schools will produce results that can be quite different from the rankings obtained from the school-efficiency measures based on the econometric estimation of education production functions and panel data. These differences arise because the raw test scores do not control for school inputs and student characteristics as do the EPF based school-efficiency measures. Although the raw test scores are highly correlated across tests and grades, the corresponding school-efficiency measures are not as highly correlated. Based on the raw test scores, it appears that there are many good schools that obtain high rankings across tests and grades. Once school inputs and student characteristics are accounted for, however, the number of consistently high ranking, or good schools, decreases markedly. The same is true when identifying bad schools. In the end, EPF-based efficiency measures distinguish between good schools and bad based on the contribution of the school and not just the quality of the students enrolling in September.

Further, our best estimates of the EPF indicate that the coefficient on the lagged test score is significantly different from both zero and one. This provides support for the fixed-effect model over the gain model and over the level model that excludes the lagged test score.

In addition, our results provide support for using school-efficiency measures based on the fixed-effect model as the best approach for evaluating school performance. This school-efficiency measure compares favorably with that from the difference model. Thus, although the difference model provides the best results from a statistical standpoint, the additional two years of data needed to estimate this model (compared to the fixed-effect model) means that the added benefits of this model are not likely to outweigh the extra costs. This is a particularly important lesson, given the difficulty of gathering and maintaining multiyear data sets.

Finally, it is important to note that even the unusually rich data assembled for this study were insufficient to fully explore school efficiency. Most notable is the inadequacy of the resource data—although detailed school-level expenditure data were available by object, no programmatic breakdowns were available, nor was there information on class size. Noninstructional expenditures and teacher–pupil ratio had to suffice. Similarly, the limited data on the characteristics and quality of the staff is unfortunate. The results are suggestive, but the importance of the issue suggests more detailed data and research are warranted. Whether measures based on superior data will yield significantly different insight into the efficiency of public schools is an empirical question, which can (and should) be addressed as we have done in this chapter—by constructing and comparing alternative measures of school efficiency.

This chapter has focused on constructing school-efficiency measures based on the estimation of school-level education production functions, following the theoretically appealing models developed for measuring efficiency of manufacturing firms. As described in Schwartz and Stiefel (2001), school-efficiency measures can also be constructed based on cost functions, using data envelopment analysis, or relying on the more widely used—and somewhat easier to construct—adjusted-performance measures. (See this volume for chapters on these techniques.) To what extent do the schools identified as good using the EPF approach also emerge as good using alternative measures? Adjusted-performance measures are of particular interest because they are, in some sense, viewed as the poor man's production function—a production function estimated with less sophisticated econometrics and fewer variables. In future work, we plan to explore the relationship between the EPF based efficiency measures and adjusted-performance measures, to gain insight into the value added by the EPF based measures.

References

Bartelsman, E. J., & Doms, M. (2000). Understanding productivity: Lessons from longitudinal microdata. *Journal of Economic Literature*, XXXVIII, 569–594.

Hsiao, C. (1986). *Analysis of panel data. Cambridge,* U.K.: Cambridge University Press.

Iatarola, P. (2002). Equity and distribution of resources and performance across elementary and middle schools with large urban school districts: Evidence from New York City. Unpublished Dissertation, New York University, New York.

Kane, T., & Staiger, D. (2002). The promise and pitfalls of using imprecise school accountability measures. *Journal of Economic Perspectives*, 16, 4.

Schwartz, A. E., & Stiefel, L. (2001). Measuring school efficiency: Lessons from economics, implications for practice. In D. Monk, H. Wahlberg, & M. Wang (Eds.), *Improving Educational Productivity: Lessons from Economics*, (pp. 115–137), Information Age Publishing.

Schwartz, A. E., & Zabel, J. (2002). Good schools, good students? Measuring school performance using education production functions, New York University, mimeo.

Stiefel, L., Schwartz, A. E., & Rubenstein, R. (1999). Measuring school efficiency using school-level data: Theory and practice. In M. E. Goertz & A. Odden (Eds.), *School-based financing*, Corwin Press, California.

Todd, P., & Wolpin, K. (2003). On the specification and estimation of the production function for cognitive achievement. *Economic Journal*, 113.

Zabel, J., Stiefel, L., & Schwartz, A. E. (2004) Student-level and school-level production functions: Effects of aggregation and sample composition on efficiency measures and coefficient estimates, Tufts University, mimeo.

4

Measuring School Performance Using Cost Functions

Amy Ellen Schwartz, Leanna Stiefel,
and Hella Bel Hadj Amor

Introduction

United States public schools in the first decade of the twenty-first century are faced with increasing demands for improving performance; simultaneously, government budgets are stagnant or shrinking. Thus it is particularly important to consider ways in which schools and school districts can use their resources effectively. Although much of the research linking resources and performance focuses on estimating a production function for education, using a cost-function framework holds considerable appeal for the investigation of school performance and efficiency. Perhaps most important is that cost functions can be specified to include multiple-output measures simultaneously, allowing us to estimate the efficiency of schools without having to assume that a single test score, or other measure, fully captures the product of a school, as production functions typically require. This chapter develops and explores the estimation of school efficiency using school-level cost functions. The aim is to identify ways to minimize the cost of schools, which implies identifying schools that can achieve their performance levels at lower costs.

Cost functions capture the minimum cost of producing a bundle of outputs, given prices of inputs and a technological process. As such, although they capture technological possibilities as fully as a production function does, their data requirements and econometric properties differ from those of production functions in useful ways. Most important is that cost functions allow the use of multiple output measures simultaneously, rather than relying on a single measure, as in a production function. Second, the data requirements differ—cost functions require data on school-level spending, outputs, and input prices, whereas production functions require data on the quantities and quality of inputs used. Third, the underlying assumptions differ—cost functions assume that input prices rather than quantities are exogenously determined at the school level, which may be a more apt description of school decision making.

This chapter develops and explores the use of school-level cost functions for estimating school efficiency and differentiating between more- and less-efficient schools. Using data for elementary and middle schools in the state of Ohio, we explore a range of specifications and the resulting efficiency measures. The next section presents an overview of the literature on education cost functions. In the third section we present the theory of cost functions, and in the fourth section we describe the data. The fifth section provides estimation results, and the chapter concludes in the fifth section with implications and lessons for future research.

Literature Review

Research on Costs and District Size

A vast literature on the relationship between school-district cost and size, measured by enrollment, developed before the attention of researchers turned to estimating cost functions per se. The goal of this literature is to explore economies of scale and determine the optimal size for school districts in an effort to guide policy on school-district consolidation. This literature is reviewed in Fox (1981) and Andrews, Duncombe, and Yinger (2002). In his classic review of studies of economies of size, Fox argues that substantial scale economies are present, and he puts forward optimal sizes of over 10,000 for school districts (and 1,000 to 2,000 pupils for high schools.) Andrews, Duncombe, and Yinger (2002) provide a review of the more recent literature and find that economies of scale obtain by moving from very small districts (up to 500 students) to districts with 2,000 to 4,000 students.

Research on the Cost of Education— the Cost of Increasing Output

More recently, the district-level literature has moved toward the estimation of cost functions, which include prices. This body of research focuses on adjusting costs for the presence of students with special needs with an eye toward a fairer distribution of state aid.

Some of the more recent papers, such as Reschovsky and Imazeki (2001) and Duncombe and Yinger (2000), aim to estimate a minimum cost of providing an adequate education. Districts are often instructed by state education departments to provide a given, adequate level of education for their students, which they fund with a combination of local resources and state aid. Cost research attempts to assess the minimum amount of money each school district must spend to provide its students with an adequate education. Once standards have been chosen, school districts require different amounts of money to meet them, because districts face different costs. Although some of these costs are under their control, others are not, and a well-designed formula for the distribution of state aid is expected to take these uncontrollable costs into account. Cost research aims to estimate cost indices that reflect these costs and that may be incorporated in the design of state aid schemes.

These studies usually use a single year of data, which preclude them from using fixed effects as efficiency measures; district (school) fixed effects capture the time-invariant characteristics of districts (schools), which affect costs. In other words, they are a measure of residual costs, costs that are not related to variables explicitly controlled in the cost regression. As such, fixed effects are an imperfect measure of inefficiency, among other costs, in as much as they are time invariant, or at least, slow to vary. Some cross-sectional studies, however, include (DEA-based) inefficiency measures to disentangle high costs from inefficiency (Reschovsky & Imazeki, 2001; Duncombe, Ruggiero, & Yinger, 1996; Duncombe & Yinger, 1998, 1997). Some develop weights for categories of students considered more costly to educate (Reschovsky & Imazeki, 1998).[1]

More specifically, the authors of these studies estimate regressions of expenditure per pupil on performance, input prices, and characteristics of the districts and their student population, using data on single states. Performance measures are usually represented by achievement on standardized tests (scores or pass rates), although dropout rates, graduation rates, and indicators of continuation to college are also employed. The specifications generally include lagged performance measures as well. Teacher salaries seem to be the most commonly available measure of input prices and, when possible, the authors construct a teacher-salary index that reflects only factors outside of school-district control (Reschovsky & Imazeki, 2001) and adjusts for teacher characteristics (Duncombe & Yinger, 1998). Some relevant factors are not included because of unavailable data (data on school facilities, for example) or multicollinearity (the salaries of administrators tend to be highly correlated with teacher salaries).[2] Characteristics of the districts and their student population that are believed to affect costs and to be outside the control of districts are the percentage of students in the district who are poor, disabled, in high school, and have limited English proficiency (LEP). Performance and input prices are generally treated as endogenous. Typical instruments for performance are variables that measure the demand for education, such as population characteristics that make them more or less likely to support educational spending as well as state and federal aid and variables that capture local wealth. Teacher cost indices are commonly used as instruments for salaries, which are generally the only or one of the few input prices available.

Usual findings include a positive effect of the current achievement measures and a negative effect of the lagged achievement measures, reflecting the higher cost of producing a higher current level of output and the lower cost of bringing up the performance of districts where students performed better previously.

---

1 Other authors construct cost indices based on expenditure functions. They control for performance indirectly, (Bradbury et al., 1984; Ratcliffe, Riddre, & Yinger, 1990), through the use of variables (outside school-district control) that reflect the demand for school quality and influence performance, such as income, tax price, intergovernmental aid, and voter characteristics. Cost and expenditure functions are used under different circumstances: The cost function requires that measures of outputs be available, whereas the expenditure function requires assumptions on the determination of government spending. Downes & Pogue (1994) find that the results of the two methods of estimation are quite close.

2 Duncombe & Yinger, 1999.

When significant, the coefficients on the input prices are positive, translating the increase in the price of a category of input that, to a large extent cannot be replaced, to expected increases in expenditure. Some categories of students do appear to be more costly to educate (the coefficient on the poverty variable tends to be positive), although the estimates vary for other characteristics (the coefficient on the LEP variable is positive, but not always significant), and others seem not to affect costs (the coefficient on the high school and disability variables are often insignificant, although the latter case may reflect the fact that the expenditure variable used does not include categories of expenditure related to disabled students). There is some evidence of economies of scale as the relationship between expenditure and enrollment is U-shaped. The efficiency measure shows that inefficiency increases cost.

In some recent work, the focus has shifted from adequacy to efficiency. As an example, Duncombe, Miner, and Ruggiero (1993) use data envelopment analysis to estimate the technical efficiency of New York State school districts, revealing that about half of them are relatively efficient. Astonishingly, they find that smaller, more advantaged districts tend to be more inefficient than others, such that inefficiency may not be the cause of lower student achievement in poorer districts. Ray and Mukherjee (1998) obtain a measure of organizational efficiency in 166 public-school districts in Connecticut for years 1980–1981 to 1983–1984, based on a method developed in Ray (1991). The authors use a cost function to explore the possibility of reducing costs by having several units of production generate smaller output quantities rather than having one unit turn out all the output, quality being held constant. They find that it is possible to cut costs in some urban school districts and in some wealthy suburban districts by reducing their size. This new focus follows a trend observed at the school level as well. Indeed, there is greater focus on the efficiency of schools, as states are introducing reforms based on school accountability.

School-Level Cost Studies

A small number of studies estimate school-level models with costs on the left-hand side. This has been difficult so far because of the dearth of spending data at the school level, but the increasing national focus on individual school performance and newly available school-level data have spawned several new studies. In addition, the efficiency of the schools in a district appears to be a requirement for the efficiency of that district.

Daneshvary and Clauretie (2001) assess the presence of economies of scale in Nevada schools, because of moving from a nine-month to a whole-year schedule. Per-pupil cost is regressed on attendance, change in enrollment, a performance measure, student characteristics (students in special education, LEP students, and gifted students—a poverty variable is removed because of high correlation with the performance variable), and a dummy variable for school schedule. The performance measure and the dummy are treated as endogenous and instrumental variables are used to correct for the endogeneity. The authors do find some evidence of economies of scale for schools with a year-round schedule. The coefficient on the performance measure is positive and sometimes significant, and so are the coefficients on the special education and LEP variables. The coefficient on the gifted variable is usually negative but never significant. The change in enrollment has a negative, sometimes significant coefficient.

Jimenez (1986) estimates economies of scale for primary and secondary schools in two Latin American countries, using a multiproduct specification (generalized translog). Cost is regressed on test scores and student inputs (ethnicity, parent education, and socioeconomic status, proxies for household wealth and ability). The author estimates the marginal cost of educating an additional student and assesses economies of scale. Transportation costs are taken into account through the time it takes students to go to school, and cost savings are weighed against this. He also studies the complementarities of outputs and finds some substitutability between labor and nonlabor inputs. There are some scale economies with respect to percentage changes in quality-adjusted enrollment.

The Theory of Measuring Efficiency: A Cost Function for Schools

Cost Functions

A *cost function* captures the minimum cost of producing output, given input prices. In its general form, it can be represented as:

$$E_s = C(W_1, \dots, W_M; Y_{Rs}) \tag{1}$$

where E_s is the amount spent on purchased inputs, $W_1, \dots, W_M$, are the prices of the M inputs to production and Y_{Rs} is a vector of the quantities of the R outputs produced by schools. $C()$ is the transformation linking prices, outputs, and costs.

In general, cost functions exhibit positive, increasing marginal costs. Costs should increase with factor prices—put simply, if the prices of purchased inputs go up, then the cost of production must go up. The relationship between costs and the overall price level is fixed: If factor prices double, costs double; if they triple, costs triple and so on. In addition, if output increases, costs go up. One attractive feature of a school-level cost function is that prices, which are district-level variables, are more likely to be exogenous than are school inputs in a school-production function.

This relationship can be statistically estimated given data on the prices of inputs, the quantities of outputs, and the costs incurred. Further, the results can be used to identify more- and less-efficient schools. Those schools that are found to spend fewer resources (that is, spend less money), given the level of outputs they produce and the prices of inputs they face, are deemed more efficient and those that spend more are deemed less efficient. Notice, however, that the results obtained from the estimation of a cost function and the interpretation of those results, are critically determined by the way in which, E_s, the W_{Ms} and Y_{Rs} are specified and by the level of aggregation of the data. For example, analyses based on school-level data will yield different results than analyses based on district-level data; efficiency measures will depend critically on the output measures used and, potentially, the specification of the functional form of the cost function. We discuss each of these in greater depth below.

Although equation (1) can be estimated using a single cross section of data on schools, panel data provides greater flexibility and power in estimating school efficiency. To be concrete, assuming a Cobb-Douglas or log-linear form for the cost function, we can write a cost function for education for school s in district d at time t as:

$$\ell n E_{sdt} = \ell n C_{sdt}(W_1, \ldots, W_M; Y_{Rs}) = \rho + \sum_{m=1}^{M} \beta_m \ell n W_{msdt} +$$
$$\sum_{r=1}^{R} \theta_r \ell n Y_{rsdt} + \sum_{p=1}^{P} \gamma_p SD_{psdt} + \sum_{s=1}^{S} \propto_s S_s + \sum_{t=1}^{T} \lambda_t YEAR_t + e_{sdt} \tag{2}$$

where β_m, θ_r, γ_p, $\propto_s$ and λ_t are parameters to be estimated, S_s is a dummy variable for school s (the school fixed effect), SD_{pdst} is a set of school and district characteristics—including socioeconomic or educational characteristics—that affect the cost of education, $YEAR_t$ is a year dummy, and e_{sdt} is an error term, which encompasses other unobserved cost factors assumed independent of the explanatory variables. M is the number of inputs, R is the number of outputs, P is the number of school and district characteristics, S is the number of schools, and T is the number of years.

Here, β_m, the coefficient on the price of input m, can be interpreted as an estimate of the elasticity of cost with respect to the price of m and the coefficients on the school fixed effects, $\propto_s$, capture the residual variation in the school costs unaccounted for by variation in the other included variables. Thus the $\propto_s$ can be viewed as measures of school efficiency—the school effects are measures of residual costs that are not explained by variables included in the model and, as such, can be thought to measure the relative *inefficiency* of schools.[3] Schools with a higher coefficient on the fixed effect have higher unexplained costs for that school, such that higher values are worse (more inefficient) and lower values are better (more efficient). Note, however, the $\propto_s$ in some sense represent measures of our ignorance about what explains differences in costs. Further, the inclusion of school-specific dummy variables precludes the inclusion of any time-invariant school-level variables—both those that are truly fixed, such as school location, and those that are slow to change, such as the physical capital. The implication is that the $\propto_s$ will reflect the impact of all the time-invariant, school-level variables that might have been included. (Note that it may be possible to purge the fixed effects of the contribution of the time invariant factors in a second regression analysis. This is discussed below.) Finally, the model includes a year dummy capturing the effects of common macroeconomic factors affecting costs such as inflation.

Student characteristics are included to capture any differences in the cost of educating students with different needs. Some groups of students are more costly to educate because they come to school with less preparation than others. Poor students may come from homes where parents are less educated and

---

3 Stiefel, Schwartz, & Rubenstein, 1999.

Measuring School Performance Using Cost Functions

unable to help them with homework, or homes where educational resources such as books or computers are unavailable. At the same time, students with disabilities may require separate classrooms and specialized instruction and teachers; students who do not speak English well may need bilingual teachers, teacher aides, or additional class time; students who have recently entered the school system from another country may encounter difficulties adapting to a new culture and require counseling services. Ignoring these factors will incorrectly attribute the added costs of educating these students to school inefficiency.

Besides the student characteristics, the cost function should include enrollment, to capture any economies of scale, and other time-variant features of the school, such as grade span.

The data required for estimating a cost function as in (2) is substantial. Ideally, a cost function includes the prices of all the inputs that enter the education production process: teachers and staff, physical plant, books, computers, laboratories, and so on. In practice, input price data are often unavailable (especially data on facilities), or may not be included because of high correlations among the variables (particularly, the salaries of various categories of personnel). This is less of a concern, however, when the object is to estimate the coefficients on the fixed effects. Further, estimating all the parameters in the equation requires data on the prices of inputs that vary across the schools in the sample. Thus, although there are a small number of school districts that pay different salaries for similarly qualified teachers in different schools, it will not, in general, be possible to estimate the β's using a sample of schools within a single school district.

Finally, consider the treatment of output in the cost function. A vector of R outputs, Y_{rsdt}, is explicitly written in equation (2), in which case the coefficients, θ_r's, capture the elasticity of costs with respect to output. A particularly attractive feature of a cost function is that it is possible to include multiple output measures. Multiple-output measures might be incorporated directly—including graduation rates, attendance, retention, or promotion, besides test scores—following the notion that schools produce multiple outputs. Alternatively, we might think of one or more of the outputs of the school, Y_{rsdt}, as a product with multiple characteristics, and specify a function linking these outputs to these characteristics, in the spirit of Lancaster (1971) or Schwartz (1997). Further, outputs might be specified in levels or gains, to create value-added cost functions.

Note that there are many alternative functional forms for the cost function that may be used instead of the log-linear or Cobb-Douglas form in (2). As discussed above, the Cobb-Douglas is a convenient formulation; the estimated parameters are relatively easy to interpret and, because the model is linear in the parameters, it is relatively easy to estimate.[4] Unfortunately, the price of the simplicity is that this form constrains the elasticity of substitution between two factors to be equal to one.

A common, more flexible form for cost functions is the translog cost function, which is also linear in the parameters, but allows the partial elasticities of substitutions between inputs to vary.[5] Although previous work in other public services, and to a much more limited degree in education, suggests that these elasticities are not one, exploratory work suggested the additional complexity added little to our analyses.

Cost Functions versus Production Functions

Although a production function provides a more direct representation of production possibilities, a cost function describes a firm's technology as fully as a production function. The intuition behind this follows from the recognition that cost minimization and output maximization are closely tied: If a firm chooses an input combination that minimizes costs, this input combination also maximizes output, and vice versa.

The underlying behavioral assumptions of the cost function model are that the school chooses inputs to minimize costs subject to output constraints and that it takes factor prices (e.g. teacher salaries) as given. The second assumption seems particularly apt at the school level, because salaries tend to be determined

---

4 Note that a Cobb-Douglas is said to be self-dual: the Cobb-Douglas cost function $\ell nC_{sdt} = \ell n\mu + \sum_{m=1}^{M}\beta_{m}\ell nW_{msdt} + \sum_{r=1}^{R}\theta_{r}\ell nY_{rsdt}$ is associated with a production function $\ell nY_{rsdt} = \ell nv + \sum_{i=1}^{N}\delta_{i}\ell nX_{irsdt}$ also of the Cobb Douglas form.

5 $\ell nC_{sdt}(W;Y_{rsdt}) = [\mu + \sum_{m=1}^{M}\beta_{m}\ell nW_{msdt} + \frac{1}{2}\sum_{i=1}^{M}\sum_{j=1}^{M}\phi_{ij}\ell nW_{isdt}\ell nW_{jsdt}]Y_{rsdt}$ where $\sum_{i=1}^{M}\beta_{i} = 1, \phi_{ij} = \phi_{ji}, \sum_{j=1}^{M}\phi_{ij} = 0$ for $i = 1,\ldots,n$ (see Varian, pp. 127–128). Note that a translog cost function becomes a Cobb Douglas function under certain restrictions: $C_{sdt}(W;Y_{rsdt}) = \mu\prod_{m=1}^{M}W_{msdti}^{\beta_{mi}}Y_{rsdt}$.

by negotiations between districts and unions.[6] Thus—and this is an important advantage of cost functions versus production functions in the measurement of efficiency—*input prices are more likely to be exogenous to schools than are input quantities* (the exogeneity of input quantities being an assumption of production functions).

Note that this exogeneity of factor prices to the *school's* decision makers is likely to hold even if prices are endogenous at the *district* level, as is likely. In contrast, much of the difficulty presented by estimating school production functions arises because of the potential endogeneity of the key independent variables—school resources. If factor prices are in fact exogenous, they will be uncorrelated with the error term, and ordinary least squares estimates of the parameters will be unbiased. Still, there may be nonzero correlation if included factor prices affect other factor prices or cost factors that are measured with error, or omitted from the model. As an example, if teacher salaries reflect the labor market in the area (wealthier, higher cost-of-living areas may offer higher salaries), they are likely to be correlated with excluded prices (or other cost factors) that are also related to income (construction prices or administrative salaries for example), which may affect the coefficients on other included variables.

As discussed above, cost functions also have the flexibility to include multiple output measures, rather than being limited to a single output measure as are production functions. Clearly, schools may be best viewed as producing an array of outputs, such as students who attend classes, students who obtain high test scores, students who graduate, students who are responsible citizens, or as producing a product with multiple characteristics. Ignoring these in evaluating efficiency, as in production function approaches, may introduce significant bias in the measurement of efficiency because any resource spent producing an omitted output will be counted as wasted.[7]

---

6 In states or districts without formal unions, there are still likely to be uniform salary schedules across schools, perhaps set at the state level, as has been reported to happen in Texas.

7 An index of outputs can be created to use in a production function but the weights in the index are arbitrary (or reflect values) and do not reflect, necessarily, school production behavior. It is also possible to estimate production functions for multiple outputs and constrain the school efficiency coefficients to be the same across equations.

Learning about Efficiency

In this chapter, we estimate school cost functions as described above in (2), which yield school efficiency measures, $\propto_s$, and use these $\propto_s$ to examine differences between efficient and inefficient schools. To be specific, we estimate efficiency measures using panel data on Ohio public schools serving grades four and/or six using four different specifications. The first uses four contemporaneous output measures—fourth-grade writing and math-test pass rates and sixth-grade writing and math-test pass rates.[8] A second specification includes the lagged values of these test scores. A third specification includes pass rates on three other tests administered in Ohio—in reading, citizenship, and science. For comparison purposes, we also estimate a model that excludes the salary variables. The resulting efficiency measures from this last estimate might be viewed as *adjusted cost measures*, capturing the differences in costs between schools, controlling for a variety of school and student characteristics, that are similar, in spirit, to the adjusted performance measures commonly used in modern accountability regimes (Ladd, 1999; Stiefel, Schwartz, Bel Hadj Amor, & Kim, 2003).

We compare the efficiency measures using simple correlation measures and then examine the mean differences between schools ranked as highly efficient and schools ranked as inefficient.

Data, Samples, and Measures

We use data for elementary and middle schools in the state of Ohio to estimate cost functions for education and investigate the efficiency of schools. The ODE provided data on test scores, demographics, teachers, and other characteristics of schools; and the Ohio Education Association (OHEA) provided salary data, as described below.[9]

We use a three-year panel of data (1996–1997 through 1998–1999) on 2,357 schools that have at least two years of data on the fourth-grade or sixth-grade reading and math performance measure and reliable expenditure data.[10] There are 611 districts in Ohio and 13% of the schools are in small town districts, whereas the rest of the sample is divided almost equally among rural, suburban, urban, and major urban districts (as classified by the state of Ohio).

---

8 Based on a conversation with Ohio Department of Education (ODE) personnel, each year ODE defines the cutoff point that determines who passes and attempts to equate levels of difficulty across years.

9 The ODE provides data from three sources: the Educational Management Information System (EMIS), the Expenditure Flow Model (EFM), and the Report Cards. See http://www.ode.state.oh.us/ for publicly available data.

10 Observations that are outliers with respect to expenditure per pupil (whose expenditure is less than 50% of the 5th percentile or more than 150% of the 95th percentile) are removed from the sample.

Measuring School Performance Using Cost Functions

Figure 4.1 presents descriptive statistics for 1998–1999. The schools in the sample spend an average of $5,720 per pupil, and there is a wide range of variation, with the lowest spending school spending as little as $1,509 and the highest spending school spending almost ten times as much ($13,560).

Figure 4.1. Descriptive Statistics
for Regression Sample, 1998–1999 N = 2,357

Variable	Mean	Std. Dev.	Minimum	Maximum
Total Expenditure per Pupil	5,720	1,074	1,509	13,560
Minimum Salary Teachers with a Bachelor's Degree	24,077	2,564	17,721	33,054
Maximum Salary Teachers with a Master's Degree	45,432	5,724	30,847	67,889
Enrollment	430	186	17	1,616
Percent Passing Grade 6 Math	51.57	21.18	2.10	100.00
Lagged Percent Passing Grade 6 Math	47.23	20.50	2.20	100.00
Percent Passing Grade 6 Writing	79.43	13.89	21.60	100.00
Lagged Percent Passing Grade 6 Writing	88.98	10.43	23.70	100.00
Percent Passing Grade 6 Reading	51.92	18.88	2.50	96.60
Lagged Percent Passing Grade 6 Reading	52.03	18.45	4.50	100.00
Percent Passing Grade 6 Citizenship	71.71	18.51	10.90	100.00
Lagged Percent Passing Grade 6 Citizenship	66.08	18.72	8.70	100.00
Percent Passing Grade 6 Science	45.99	19.74	1.00	97.20
Lagged Percent Passing Grade 6 Science	49.18	20.24	1.20	100.00
Percent Passing Grade 4 Math	49.09	20.14	1.20	100.00
Lagged Percent Passing Grade 4 Math	40.62	20.06	1.20	100.00
Percent Passing Grade 4 Writing	62.50	19.45	2.30	100.00
Lagged Percent Passing Grade 4 Writing	56.24	20.19	1.50	100.00
Percent Passing Grade 4 Reading	58.01	18.53	4.50	100.00
Lagged Percent Passing Grade 4 Reading	45.88	18.87	2.10	93.80
Percent Passing Grade 4 Citizenship	69.01	19.86	3.90	100.00
Lagged Percent Passing Grade 4 Citizenship	55.48	20.01	1.30	100.00
Percent Passing Grade 4 Science	51.33	19.85	2.00	100.00
Lagged Percent Passing Grade 4 Science	47.74	20.37	1.60	100.00
Percent Free Lunch Students	30.38	25.85	0.00	100.00
Percent Black Students	15.19	27.02	0.00	100.00
Percent Asian and Other Students	2.25	5.12	0.00	60.9
Dummy = 1 if Highest Grade is 5	0.36	0.48	0.00	1.00

The OHEA provides the minimum and maximum salaries for teachers holding bachelors and master's degrees for Ohio school districts.[11] Because of high correlation among these four variables (above 0.90), we use the two that are least correlated: the minimum salary for teachers holding bachelor's degrees and the maximum salary for teachers holding a master's degree.[12] Teachers with a bachelor's degree start at a salary of about $18,000 on average, whereas teachers with a master's degree earn up to $68,000 on average, and the variation is much higher for the latter category.

Ohio elementary and middle schools enroll an average of 430 students and a total of almost a million students. Some schools are much larger, with over a thousand students, and one has fewer than 20 pupils. The vast majority of students are white (81%), although some schools have an all-black population. The representation of nonblack minorities is very small, about 2% on average. About one-third of the students in the average school are poor, as represented by the percentage of children receiving a free lunch. Some schools have no poor students at all, whereas in others all the children are poor. There is a lot of variation in student performance, with schools where all the students are performing very poorly (2% or less of the students pass the math and writing tests), and others where all the students pass the tests. On average, more students pass the writing tests (79% in the sixth grade and 63% in the fourth grade) than the math tests (52% in the sixth grade and 49% in the fourth grade).

Results

Figure 4.2 shows the parameter estimates from various specifications of the cost function regressions. The simplest regression (column 1) includes two teacher salaries, output as captured by performance measures and enrollment, and student characteristics as proxies for cost factors. This regression includes only math and writing test scores because there is substantial collinearity between the scores. Thus we include the least correlated subjects, which are math and writing.[13]

---

11 Because of missing data, the salary variables are corrected using an algorithm developed by Evans, Murray, and Schwab (1997).

12 Including these district-level variables in the school-level models is appropriate because all schools within a district face the salary scale prevalent in the district.

13 Correlations range from 0.75 to 0.91 in fourth grade, and from 0.61 to 0.90 in sixth grade.

Measuring School Performance Using Cost Functions

Figure 4.2. Regression Results and Correlations of Efficiency Measures: Dependent Variable is the Logarithm of Total Expenditure per Pupil

Independent Variables	(1) Levels	(2) Levels + Lags	(3) Levels + Lags + More Subjects	(4) Adjusted Cost Measures
Log Minimum Salary Teachers with a Bachelor's Degree	−0.0112 (0.1171)	−0.0102 (0.1167)	−0.0005 (0.1170)	
Log Maximum Salary Teachers with a Master's Degree	0.1791* (0.0934)	0.1769* (0.0931)	0.1872** (0.0932)	
Log Enrollment	0.9003*** (0.1314)	0.8806*** (0.1311)	0.8971*** (0.1316)	0.8922*** (0.1307)
Log Enrollment Squared	−0.1022*** (0.0117)	−0.1009*** (0.0117)	−0.1025*** (0.0117)	−0.1018*** (0.0117)
Percent Passing Grade 6 Math	−0.0001 (0.0002)	−0.0001 (0.0002)	−0.0002 (0.0003)	−0.0001 (0.0002)
Lagged Percent Passing Grade 6 Math		0.0001 (0.0002)	−0.0002 (0.0003)	0.0001 (0.0002)
Percent Passing Grade 6 Writing	0.0002 (0.0002)	0.0002 (0.0002)	0.0002 (0.0002)	0.0002 (0.0002)
Lagged Percent Passing Grade 6 Writing		0.0002 (0.0001)	0.0001 (0.0002)	0.0002 (0.0001)
Percent Passing Grade 6 Reading			0.0000 (0.0003)	
Lagged Percent Passing Grade 6 Reading			0.0001 (0.0003)	
Percent Passing Grade 6 Citizenship			0.0001 (0.0003)	
Lagged Percent Passing Grade 6 Citizenship			0.0004 (0.0003)	
Percent Passing Grade 6 Science			−0.0001 (0.0003)	
Lagged Percent Passing Grade 6 Science			0.0001 (0.0003)	
Percent Passing Grade 4 Math	−0.0001 (0.0002)	−0.0001 (0.0002)	−0.0002 (0.0002)	−0.0001 (0.0002)
Lagged Percent Passing Grade 4 Math		−0.0001 (0.0002)	0.0001 (0.0002)	−0.0001 (0.0002)
Percent Passing Grade 4 Writing	0.0002 (0.0001)	0.0002 (0.0001)	0.0002 (0.0001)	0.0002 (0.0001)
Lagged Percent Passing Grade 4 Writing		−0.0000 (0.0001)	0.0001 (0.0001)	−0.0000 (0.0001)
Percent Passing Grade 4 Reading			0.0002 (0.0002)	
Lagged Percent Passing Grade 4 Reading			−0.0001 (0.0002)	

Independent Variables	(1) Levels	(2) Levels + Lags	(3) Levels + Lags + More Subjects	(4) Adjusted Cost Measures
Percent Passing Grade 4 Citizenship			0.0002 (0.0002)	
Lagged Percent Passing Grade 4 Citizenship			-0.0001 (0.0002)	
Percent Passing Grade 4 Science			-0.0001 (0.0002)	
Lagged Percent Passing Grade 4 Science			-0.0003 (0.0002)	
Percent Free Lunch Students	-0.0001 (0.0002)	-0.0001 (0.0002)	-0.0001 (0.0002)	-0.0002 (0.0002)
Percent Black Students	-0.0012 (0.0008)	-0.0012 (0.0008)	-0.0012 (0.0008)	-0.0013 (0.0008)
Percent Asian and Other Students	-0.0016 (0.0010)	-0.0015 (0.0010)	-0.0015 (0.0010)	-0.0015 (0.0010)
Dummy = 1 if Highest Grade is 5	0.0158 (0.0105)	0.0175* (0.0105)	0.0168 (0.0105)	0.0156 (0.0105)
Constant	6.8422*** (0.3718)	6.8683*** (0.3714)	6.8231*** (0.3730)	6.8040*** (0.3698)
Observations	6,963	6,963	6,963	6,963
Number of Schools	2,357	2,357	2,357	2,357
R-squared	0.30	0.31	0.32	0.31

Pearson Correlation Coefficients for Efficiency Measures

	(1)	(2)	(3)	(4)
(1)	1.0000			
(2)	0.9922	1.0000		
(3)	0.9898	0.9995	1.0000	
(4)	0.9869	0.9966	0.9956	1.0000

Notes:

1) The sample is schools that have a sixth and/or a fourth grade between 1996–1997 and 1998–1999.

2) All models include school effects, year dummies, and missing dummies.

3) * indicates significance at the 10% level.
** indicates significance at the 5% level.
*** indicates significance at the 1% level.

4) Standard errors are reported in parentheses.

The next step is to add lagged performance measures, a proxy for past school characteristics and unmeasured inputs (column 2). Because multicollinearity is not a primary concern when the aim is to estimate the coefficients on the fixed effects, next we estimate a fuller set (column 3), which includes all five subjects to minimize the potential for bias in the efficiency measures. Finally, to assess the contribution of the price variables, we estimate a set of adjusted cost measures (column 4), where the salary variables are removed. Because of some missing

Measuring School Performance Using Cost Functions 81

data on performance, teacher variables, student characteristics, and enrollment, a number of variables were recoded; that is, a zero replaced the missing values, and a missing dummy was included in the model.[14]

All of these models are estimated with school fixed effects, which are used as measures of efficiency (or rather, *in*efficiency). Correlations for efficiency measures are presented at the bottom of Figure 4.2.

Results across the four specifications are strikingly similar. The expected positive relationship between costs and input prices obtains. Indeed, although the coefficient on the minimum salary of teachers with a bachelor's degree is insignificant, the coefficient on the maximum salary of teachers with a master's degree is positive and significant. A 1% increase in this variable raises costs by about 0.2%. The relationship between enrollment and costs is contrary to usual research findings: It has the shape of an upside-down U. Algebraic calculations show that the maximum is attained for a school of about 90 students, such that the vast majority of schools are on the decreasing portion of the curve. The relationship between performance and costs is perhaps the most surprising: regardless of whether lags are included or whether additional subjects are included, the coefficients on these variables are always insignificant. This suggests that raising performance does not raise costs once the characteristics of students and the schools are held constant. This stresses the importance of breaking down the black box of the fixed effects to better understand the areas in which cost cutting is possible.[15] Characteristics of the student population do not appear to place a burden on school costs: The coefficients on the percentages of students who are receiving a free lunch and the percentage of students who are ethnic minorities are insignificant. There is very weak evidence that schools with a highest grade of 5 are more expensive than other schools: The coefficient on this variable is small (about 0.02), significant in one case (column 2), and marginally significant in the other cases.

All in all then, it appears that costs are driven by enrollment and the school fixed effects, which are highly significant in all cases, as well as the salaries, which are significant although not always as highly. It appears that a large fraction of the variation in costs is explained by school factors that are unobservable.

The school fixed effects capture unexplained costs of which inefficiency is an element. As such, they are a measure of school efficiency with larger (smaller) fixed effects indicating lower (higher) efficiency, that is higher (lower) *in*efficiency. The fixed effects for each model are saved and used as measures of the efficiency of schools. As mentioned previously, all four models yield very similar results, and accordingly, the Pearson correlations across the four efficiency mea-

---

[14] The coefficients on the dummy variables for missing data are not reported.

[15] F tests of the joint significance of performance measures never even come close to significance.

sures are very high (close to or above 0.99).[16] Thus it appears that the inclusion of lags, additional subjects, or even prices will leave school rankings virtually unchanged.

Given that further comparisons across efficiency measures seem unwarranted because of high similarities, we choose to explore patterns in the efficiency measures. We pick the efficiency measures from the most comprehensive model, in Figure 4.2, column 3, where more performance variables are controlled and consequently not included in the fixed effects. These provide one potential set of measures. Alternatives involve further purging of these fixed effects, which can be done in a number of ways, all requiring a regression of these fixed effects on other variables. First, the fixed effects can be regressed on a set of district dummies in a procedure that is akin to a hierarchical linear model. In this case, the efficient and inefficient schools will be those that deviate from their district averages. Perhaps more meaningful in the Ohio context is to group the districts according to their location—rural, small town, suburban, urban, and major urban—as the ODE groups them. A third alternative is to use the location groups along with averages of the nearly time-invariant sociodemographic characteristics of the schools, which may not be fully controlled for in the first set of regressions because they vary so little over the three years. These variables include free-lunch and race/ethnicity percentages. A fourth option is to include averages of all the independent variables from the first stage—free lunch, race/ethnicity, enrollment, and test scores. Here we show the second (districts by type) and last options (both district type and averages of all control variables are included).

The results of the purged fixed-effects regression are presented in columns 1 and 2 of Figure 4.3. Starting with those purged simply of time-invariant district types, it appears that rural districts, the category left-out, are most efficient. (Recall that a positive coefficient means higher costs.) Small towns are second best, with a difference of only about 0.08. Urban districts have slightly lower efficiency (the coefficient on this variable is 0.14). The coefficient on the suburban category is almost twice as high (0.26) and major urban districts are least efficient (0.36). This latter finding is not surprising; large urban districts are often considered to be very inefficient because they tend to be characterized by high spending and low performance, and the only real control for demographic characteristics is the percentage of students receiving free lunches. Thus the district dummies are likely correlated with omitted variables (i.e. student characteristics) that are not part of school efficiency, and next we reduce omitted variable bias. The pattern changes somewhat, however, when we control for average enrollment, performance, and student characteristics. In column 2, we add the average values of the school-level time-variant variables used in the original regressions. Control-

16 Spearman correlations were also very high, above 0.98. We also used the four sets of efficiency measures to rank the schools and constructed cross-tabulations for the 10th, 50th, and 90th percentiles. It appears that fewer than 5% of the schools move from one of these percentiles to another when a different efficiency measure is used. The high similarity in rankings is expected, following regression results and correlations. Results are available on request.

Measuring School Performance Using Cost Functions

ling for these additional factors erases the differences in efficiency between rural and small town districts.[17] Urban and major urban districts have somewhat lower efficiency (0.06 and 0.08 respectively); but the difference is much smaller than in the previous model (0.02 versus 0.22), and major urban districts are no longer the least-efficient ones. Indeed, suburban districts seem to have the lowest efficiency (0.13) or at least the highest unexplained costs. This could be because of the ability of those districts, which are generally wealthier, to spend funds on things that are not necessarily directly related to performance, such as art classes, field trips or more luxurious school grounds.

Figure 4.3. Regressions of Efficiency Measures on Time-Invariant Variables and Average Values of Time-Variant Variables

Dependent Variable is the Fixed Effect from the Regression in Figure 4.2, Column 3

Independent Variables	(1)	(2)
Small Town District Dummy (a)	0.0784***(0.0171)	0.0105(0.0156)
Suburban District Dummy	0.2571***(0.0214)	0.1253***(0.0181)
Urban District Dummy	0.1359***(0.0174)	0.0546***(0.0143)
Major Urban District Dummy	0.3587***(0.0382)	0.0762***(0.0272)
Unknown Type District Dummy	0.1257***(0.0433)	−0.0090(0.0284)
Log of Average Enrollment		−0.9253***(0.1603)
Log of Average Enrollment Squared		0.0983***(0.0135)
Percent Passing Grade 6 Math		0.0002(0.0012)
Lagged Percent Passing Grade 6 Math		0.0005(0.0013)
Percent Passing Grade 6 Writing		−0.0002(0.0008)
Lagged Percent Passing Grade 6 Writing		0.0001(0.0008)
Percent Passing Grade 6 Reading		0.0005(0.0016)
Lagged Percent Passing Grade 6 Reading		0.0002(0.0016)
Percent Passing Grade 6 Citizenship		−0.0013(0.0012)
Lagged Percent Passing Grade 6 Citizenship		−0.0003(0.0013)
Percent Passing Grade 6 Science		−0.0003(0.0014)

---

17 Note that the coefficient on districts of unknown type becomes insignificant as well. Descriptive statistics for these districts are quite similar to those of small towns (results not reported).

Independent Variables	(1)	(2)
Lagged Percent Passing Grade 6 Science		0.0002(0.0014)
Percent Passing Grade 4 Math		0.0019**(0.0009)
Lagged Percent Passing Grade 4 Math		−0.0023***(0.0009)
Percent Passing Grade 4 Writing		−0.0015*(0.0008)
Lagged Percent Passing Grade 4 Writing		0.0005(0.0009)
Percent Passing Grade 4 Reading		0.0024**(0.0010)
Lagged Percent Passing Grade 4 Reading		−0.0005(0.0010)
Percent Passing Grade 4 Citizenship		−0.0008(0.0006)
Lagged Percent Passing Grade 4 Citizenship		0.0005(0.0009)
Percent Passing Grade 4 Science		0.0004(0.0010)
Lagged Percent Passing Grade 4 Science		0.0011(0.0011)
Average Percent of Free Lunch Students		0.0011***(0.0004)
Average Percent Black Students		0.0029***(0.0004)
Average Percent Asian and Other Students		0.0064***(0.0010)
Average Share of Schools where Highest Grade is 5		−0.0578***(0.0174)
Constant	−0.1692***(0.0096)	2.0014***(0.4758)
Observations	2,357	2,357
R-squared	0.28	0.63

Notes:
1) The sample is schools that have a sixth and/or a fourth grade.
2) Model (2) includes missing dummies.
3) * indicates significance at the 10% level.
  ** indicates significance at the 10% level.
  *** indicates significance at the 10% level.
4) Robust standard errors are reported in parentheses.
a) The category left out is rural districts.

The relationship between unexplained costs and enrollment does have the traditional U-shape, and the presence of poor, black, and other minority students raises these costs (the coefficients on these variables are positive and significant, 0.001, 0.003, and 0.006 respectively). As before, most performance measures (both current and lagged) have insignificant coefficients; but fourth-grade math and reading have a small positive effect on the dependent variable (about 0.002), whereas writing has a surprisingly negative effect that is almost as large. Lagged grade 4 math performance has a negative coefficient, which may reflect the lower costs associated with the education of students who have a more solid background in that subject. Overall (and this is confirmed by joint F tests), unexplained costs are affected by performance in the fourth grade, although performance in the sixth grade does not appear to play a role.

We collect the residuals from these two models (columns 1 and 2 in Figure 4.3) and use them as additional sets of efficiency measures, purged of the effect of the added variables. How closely related are these purged efficiency measures to the nonpurged ones (or school fixed effects from the previous regressions, as in column 3 in Figure 4.2)? Does the choice of measure affect the ranking of schools? The Pearson correlations between the three measures are nowhere near as high as the correlations we observed previously. The correlation between the nonpurged measure and the measure purged of the district variables is only 0.85, the correlation between the nonpurged measure and the measure purged of the district and average variables is 0.61, and the correlation between the two purged measures is 0.72.[18] Cross-tabulations for the 10th, 50th, and 90th percentiles show that between 15% and 23% of the schools are ranked differently by these three measures of efficiency.

We use these three sets of efficiency measures to investigate differences between schools at the top and bottom of the efficiency distribution. Descriptive statistics for the 10% most and least-efficient schools in 1998–1999 are presented in Figure 4.4. Columns 1 and 2 refer to the nonpurged efficiency measures. As expected, the most-efficient schools spend less ($4,504 on average, column 1) than the least-efficient schools do ($7,135, column 2), yet their pass rates are consistently higher (the difference is anywhere between 8% and almost 20% percent). Some difference appears between the share of spending allocated to instructional (0.68 versus 0.63) and noninstructional (0.32 versus 0.37) expenditure. The most-efficient schools are much smaller (270 versus 646 students on average, although there is some overlap), and they face lower teacher salary scales (about $22,000 and $41,000 for teachers with a BA and an MA respectively, versus $27,000 and $52,000) than the least-efficient schools do. About half of the most-efficient schools are located in rural districts and most of the rest are in small towns and urban areas. Conversely, about half of the least-efficient schools are located in major urban districts and another third in suburbs. The student population in the most-efficient schools is characterized by students who are usually considered to be easier to educate and who come to school better prepared than others. Less than a quarter of the students are poor, and most of the students are white. In the least-efficient schools, about half of the students are poor and about half are black.

---

18 The corresponding Spearman correlations are a bit lower, 0.80, 0.52, and 0.64 respectively.

Figure 4.4. Descriptive Statistics for the Most and Least Efficient Schools According to Three Efficiency Measures, 1998–1999

	Nonpurged		Purged			
			Urban Only		Urban + Averages	
	Most (1)	Least (2)	Most (3)	Least (4)	Most (5)	Least (6)
Total Expenditure per Pupil	4,504 (740)	7,135 (1,148)	4,664 (938)	6,889 (1,387)	4,366 (758)	7,226 (1,222)
Percent Instructional Expenditure	67.76 (10.90)	63.28 (6.00)	69.74 (12.13)	62.68 (5.64)	72.14 (12.41)	62.56 (6.15)
Percent Noninstructional Expenditure	32.24 (10.90)	36.72 (6.00)	30.26 (12.13)	37.32 (5.64)	27.86 (12.41)	37.44 (6.15)
Minimum Salary Teachers with a Bachelor's Degree	22,191 (1,625)	26,930 (1,940)	23,397 (2,409)	25,622 (2,583)	23,344 (2,259)	25,185 (2,847)
Maximum Salary Teachers with a Master's Degree	41,140 (3,958)	51,960 (4,662)	43,980 (5,059)	49,571 (6,566)	43,835 (4,925)	48,569 (7,331)
Enrollment	270 (123)	646 (212)	309 (133)	652 (238)	416 (186)	409 (180)
Percent Passing Grade 6 Math	56.46 (18.37)	39.66 (26.35)	55.84 (19.37)	45.52 (24.22)	53.53 (19.99)	55.93 (19.46)
Lagged Percent Passing Grade 6 Math	51.35 (17.44)	34.97 (24.64)	52.27 (18.29)	40.30 (22.74)	48.56 (18.74)	50.99 (19.94)
Percent Passing Grade 6 Writing	81.74 (12.24)	73.03 (17.68)	82.12 (12.36)	75.63 (16.68)	79.18 (11.90)	82.38 (11.74)
Lagged Percent Passing Grade 6 Writing	91.40 (7.83)	80.40 (16.28)	91.62 (7.58)	83.68 (15.84)	89.66 (10.14)	90.37 (9.87)
Percent Passing Grade 6 Reading	57.53 (16.10)	41.84 (23.88)	56.84 (16.39)	46.82 (21.75)	54.05 (16.81)	56.20 (17.52)
Lagged Percent Passing Grade 6 Reading	55.23 (13.98)	41.40 (23.72)	57.00 (14.36)	46.60 (21.91)	53.51 (16.00)	55.40 (18.11)
Percent Passing Grade 6 Citizenship	76.32 (13.64)	58.16 (24.51)	76.45 (15.57)	64.87 (22.94)	73.82 (15.39)	75.46 (15.74)
Lagged Percent Passing Grade 6 Citizenship	70.80 (14.06)	53.17 (24.62)	72.17 (14.51)	58.81 (23.42)	68.09 (15.93)	69.87 (18.04)
Percent Passing Grade 6 Science	51.01 (15.20)	35.21 (24.47)	50.01 (16.81)	40.88 (22.07)	48.83 (17.36)	50.30 (17.85)
Lagged Percent Passing Grade 6 Science	53.71 (14.96)	36.23 (25.43)	53.71 (15.84)	42.91 (23.69)	51.55 (17.37)	52.44 (19.05)
Percent Passing Grade 4 Math	52.04 (17.31)	39.32 (25.04)	51.90 (18.56)	49.32 (23.92)	50.18 (19.16)	51.77 (20.36)
Math Grade 4: Percent Passing Previous Year	43.83 (18.02)	30.45 (22.60)	41.96 (18.90)	40.61 (22.15)	42.90 (19.83)	42.66 (21.19)
Lagged Percent Passing Grade 4 Math	64.93 (18.23)	52.30 (23.35)	64.47 (18.36)	62.16 (21.51)	63.82 (19.17)	65.18 (19.88)

Measuring School Performance Using Cost Functions

	Nonpurged		Purged			
			Urban Only		Urban + Averages	
	Most (1)	Least (2)	Most (3)	Least (4)	Most (5)	Least (6)
Percent Passing Grade 4 Writing	57.51 (18.51)	47.42 (22.75)	56.94 (19.15)	56.02 (21.56)	57.75 (19.64)	57.29 (21.74)
Lagged Percent Passing Grade 4 Writing	61.61 (15.92)	46.78 (22.52)	60.27 (16.98)	57.44 (21.07)	59.02 (18.28)	60.78 (18.44)
Percent Passing Grade 4 Reading	49.66 (16.39)	33.63 (22.20)	48.45 (16.72)	45.19 (21.98)	47.55 (18.06)	48.67 (19.35)
Lagged Percent Passing Grade 4 Reading	74.02 (15.41)	54.68 (24.42)	72.25 (16.76)	65.81 (22.87)	70.85 (18.75)	71.13 (19.30)
Percent Passing Grade 4 Citizenship	59.10 (16.99)	42.69 (23.12)	56.95 (18.19)	53.87 (22.14)	56.74 (19.57)	58.15 (21.15)
Lagged Percent Passing Grade 4 Citizenship	55.07 (16.20)	38.90 (24.10)	53.83 (17.91)	49.32 (22.90)	52.50 (19.06)	53.06 (19.67)
Percent Passing Grade 4 Science	51.34 (16.79)	34.95 (23.22)	49.71 (18.22)	45.95 (23.37)	48.99 (19.68)	50.56 (20.11)
Percent of Free Lunch Students	21.27 (15.45)	48.32 (33.90)	23.99 (18.25)	34.24 (30.80)	24.72 (21.01)	26.67 (24.79)
Dummy = 1 if School has Highest Grade 5	2.05 (7.22)	46.41 (36.31)	0.44 (0.50)	0.19 (0.39)	0.36 (0.48)	0.36 (0.48)
Percent Black Students	0.55 (2.00)	4.57 (8.35)	6.28 (14.00)	28.29 (34.55)	11.04 (21.68)	13.86 (23.26)
Percent Asian and Other Students	0.34 (0.47)	0.24 (0.43)	0.73 (2.03)	3.48 (6.20)	2.25 (6.05)	2.29 (3.37)
Rural District Dummy	0.46 (0.50)	0.00 (0.07)	0.14 (0.35)	0.09 (0.29)	0.20 (0.40)	0.16 (0.37)
Small Town District Dummy	0.17 (0.38)	0.01 (0.09)	0.10 (0.31)	0.12 (0.33)	0.12 (0.32)	0.11 (0.32)
Suburban District Dummy	0.04 (0.19)	0.30 (0.46)	0.26 (0.44)	0.25 (0.43)	0.28 (0.45)	0.30 (0.46)
Urban District Dummy	0.18 (0.38)	0.12 (0.32)	0.18 (0.39)	0.20 (0.40)	0.20 (0.40)	0.19 (0.39)
Major Urban District Dummy	0.03 (0.18)	0.52 (0.50)	0.20 (0.40)	0.21 (0.41)	0.11 (0.31)	0.11 (0.32)
Unknown Type District Dummy	0.11 (0.32)	0.05 (0.21)	0.10 (0.31)	0.12 (0.33)	0.10 (0.30)	0.12 (0.33)

Notes:

1) Most and least refer to the bottom and top 10% (229 schools) of a distribution of the schools according to the relevant efficiency measure.

2) The table shows standard deviations in parentheses.

Most of this pattern is observed when the comparison is made based on the first purged efficiency measure (columns 3 and 4), although the difference in spending is a little smaller and the proportion of poor and black students in the least-efficient schools is lower (34% and 28% respectively). The main dissimilarity is in the fact that the distribution of schools across district types is about the same whether the schools are in the most- or least-efficient group. About a quarter of the schools in each group are in suburbs, and the rest of the schools are divided almost equally between urban districts, major urban districts, and small town or miscellaneous-type districts. This reflects the fact that the efficiency measures are deviations from district means. Interestingly, it appears then that major urban, urban and suburban districts are a combination of very efficient and very inefficient schools, as well as schools in between.[19]

Comparing the most- and least-efficient schools based on the third efficiency measure (columns 5 and 6) leads to a very different pattern. The least-efficient schools perform better, on average, on all tests, although the difference between the two groups is smaller than they were in the previous comparisons (less than 3%). However, spending in the least-efficient districts is much higher. Indeed the difference between the two groups is $2,860 (it was $2,225 in the previous comparison and $2,631 when using the nonpurged measure for comparison). Average spending in this most-efficient group ($4,363) is lower than in the most-efficient groups as defined by the other efficiency measures ($4,664 and $4,504), and average spending in this least-efficient group ($7,226) is higher than in the most-efficient groups as defined by the other efficiency measures ($6,889 and $7,135). There is also more of a difference in how money is spent: In the most-efficient schools, 72% of spending is on instruction and 28% on other items, whereas in the least-efficient schools, 63% of spending is on instruction and 37% on other items. By design, the schools across the two groups do not differ much in terms of variables that are controlled when generating the efficiency measures. Enrollment is 416 in the most-efficient schools and 409 in the least efficient on average, and although the least-efficient schools serve more poor and black students, the differences are small (under 3%). The distribution of schools across district types is once again similar between the two groups. Although rural areas account for somewhat more most-efficient (20%) than least-efficient (16%) schools, a little under a third of the schools in each group are in suburbs, about 20% are in urban areas, and the rest are divided equally between the other district types.

Implications and Lessons for Future Work

To be considered a cost model, a regression must have costs (or their best approximation) on the left-hand side and outputs, input prices, and possibly other cost factors on the right-hand side. Within those guidelines, choices are made that depend on data availability, ease of understanding for potential users (policymakers, educators, etc.), and the intended use of the results. In this chap-

---

[19] This may have something to do with the fact that major urban and suburban districts tend to be the largest.

ter, the concern is with the estimation of efficiency measures that will be employed to compare how schools are ranked based on different models. Thus, obtaining unbiased efficiency measures is more important than, for instance, analyzing the effect of specific variables on the dependent variable. In this light, various specifications were estimated. First, the best possible cost models according to the theory were designed and estimated, and then additional models were run with the specific objective of deriving efficiency measures from them. The cost models perform well in the sense that the estimated signs of coefficients are the ones expected. In addition, differences in the exact variables included in equations make little difference to efficiency ratings.

Although coefficients on fixed effects are conceptually a good measure of efficiency if they are estimated from a well-specified cost model with good data on needed variables, it is still possible that the fixed effects include variables unrelated to efficiency, especially time-invariant ones that could not be included in the panel data estimations. To pursue even better efficiency measures, we purged the original fixed effects of control variables that do not vary, or vary very slowly, over time. The new purged measures, in comparison to the original fixed effects, are not extremely correlated. To see the differences across the nonpurged and purged efficiency measures, we compared the characteristics of the most- and least-efficient (top and bottom 10 percent) schools according to three different measures. One of the most persistent findings across all three is that the most-efficient schools spend a larger proportion of their expenditures on instruction; one of the least-persistent findings is that major urban districts are inefficient. The more the efficiency measures are purged, the less this latter finding holds. Sending more money to the classroom is one of the mantras of school reform, and this result showing that efficient schools spend larger proportions on instruction is certainly consistent. At the same time, this is a reflection of the fact that the output measures that are included in these models, and more generally the output measures commonly available, are test scores or similar measures of performance. Results suggest that the share of instructional spending in the least-efficient schools is smaller than it is in other schools. These are suburban schools that are likely to allocate higher shares of their spending on subjects that are not tested (or for which tests cores are not commonly available in administrative data) such as art, as well as field trips or other facilities. This only makes them less efficient in relation to the outputs measured here. This stresses the importance of more varied data on school outputs.

Cost functions hold promise for helping to identify efficient schools while including a multitude of outputs. As more states and districts begin to produce school-level resource data, such models should become part of the arsenal of accountability measures at the disposal of policymakers. Their results should also be compared to those derived from other methods such as production functions, improvement scores, and DEA indices.

References

Andrews, M., Duncombe, W., & Yinger, J. (2002). Revisiting economies of size in education: Are we any closer to a consensus? *Economics of Education, Review*, 21(3), 245–62.

Bradbury, K., Ladd, H. F., Penault, M., Reschovsky, A., & Yingu, J. (1984). State aid to offset fiscal disparities across communities. *The National Jorrnal*, 37(3), 151–70.

Daneshvary, N., & Clauretie, T. M. (2001). Efficiency and costs in education: Year-round versus traditional schedules. *Economics of Education Review*, 20, 279–87.

Downes, T. A., & Figlio, D. N. (1999). Do tax and expenditure limits provide a free lunch? Evidence on the link between limits and public sector service quality. *The National Tax Journal, LII*, 1, 113–28.

Downes, T. A., & Pogue, T. F. (1994). Adjusting school aid formulas for the higher cost of educating disadvantaged students. *The National Tax Journal*, 47(1), 89–110.

Duncombe, W. D. (1992). Costs and factor substitution in the provision of local fire services. *Review of Economics and Statistics*, 74(1) 180–84.

Duncombe, W. D., Miner, J., & Ruggiero, J. (1993). Scale economies and technical efficiency in New Yoirk public schools. Metropolitan Studies Program Occasional Paper No. 163. Syracuse, NY: Syracuse University, Center for Policy Research, the Maxwell School.

Duncombe, W., Ruggerio, J., & Yinger, J. (1996). Alternate approaches to measuring the cost of education. In H. F. Ladd (Ed.), *Holding schools accountable* (pp. 327–356). Washington, D. C., Brookings Instition.

Duncombe, W., & Yinger, J. (1997). Why is it so hard to help central city schools? *Journal of Policy Analysis and Management*, 16(1), 85–113.

Duncombe, W., & Yinger, J. (1998). School finance reform: Aid formulas and equity objectives. *The National Tax Journal*, 51(2), 239–62.

Duncombe, W., & Yinger, J. (1999). Performance standards and educational cost issues: You can't have one without the other. In H. F. Ladd, Chalk, & J. S. Hansen (Eds.) *Equity and adequacy in education finance* (pp. 260–97). Washington, D. C, National Academy Press.

Evans, W. N., Murray, S. E., & Schwab, R. M. (1997). Schoolhouses, courthouses, and statehouses after Serrano. *Journal of Policy Analysis and Management*, 16(1), 10–31.

Fox, W. (1981). Reviewing economics of size in education. *Journal of Education Finance*, 6(3), 273–96.

Jimenez, E. (1986). The structure of education cost: Multiproduct cost functions for primary and secondary schools in Latin America. *Economics of Education Review*, 5(1), 25–39.

Ladd, H. F. (1999). The Dallas school accountability and incentive program: An evaluation of its impacts on student outcomes. *Economics of Education Review*, 18(1) 1–16.

Lancaster, K. J. (1971). *Consumer demand: A new approach.* (Columbia Studies in Economics 5). New York: Columbia University Press.

Ratcliffe, K., Riddre, B. & Yinger, J. (1990). The fiscal condition of school districts in Nebraska: Is small beautiful? *Economics of Education Review*, 9, 81–99.

Ray, S. C. (1991). Resource-use efficiency in public schools: A study of Connecticut data. *Management Science*, 37(12), 1620–28.

Ray, S. C., & Mukherjee, K. (1998). Quantity, quality, and efficiency for a partially super-additive cost function: Connecticut public schools revisited. *Journal of Productivity Analysis*, 10(1), 47–62.

Reschovsky, H. R. & Imazeki, J. (2001). Achieving educational adequacy through school finance reform. *The National Tax Journal. 26(2), 373–96.*

Schwartz, A. E. (1997, March). Public characteristics and expenditures on public services: An empirical analysis. *Public Finance Review*, 25(2), 163–81.

Stiefel, L., Schwartz, A. E. Bel Hadj Amor, H., & Kim, D. Y. (2003). Measuring school performance using adjusted performance measures. Unpublished working paper.

Stiefel, L., Schwartz, A. E., & Rubenstein, R. (1999). Conceptual and empirical issues in the measurement of school efficiency. *Proceedings of the 91st Annual Conference on Taxation.* Washington, D.C.: National Tax Association.

Varian, H. R. (1992). *Microeconomic analysis,* New York: W.W. Norton & Company.

5

The Reliability of School Efficiency Measures Using Data Envelopment Analysis

Ross Rubenstein

Introduction

The measurement of performance and efficiency in educational organizations has long been plagued by the complexity of accounting for schools' multiple missions and outputs. In economic terms, schools are multiproduct firms, producing a variety of outputs and outcomes. Moreover, schools may have different objective functions depending on their missions and students. For example, although some schools may focus on producing the highest possible test scores, others may seek to maximize graduation rates, whereas still others may stress less readily observable student outcomes such as socialization and future aspirations. An inherent limitation in most regression-based techniques is that they focus on a single output. Although the results of these models may be combined in a variety of ways to assess overall performance, the techniques do not explicitly adjust for specialization or varying missions across organizations.

One technique that holds promise for addressing these limitations is data envelopment analysis (DEA), a nonstochastic method for assessing relative technical efficiency across organizations.[1] More specifically, it is a linear programming technique that involves the construction of a nonparametric efficiency frontier that envelops all the units in the sample. That is, all decision-making units (DMUs) lie either on the frontier or below it. Each unit's efficiency index is calculated as 100 minus its aggregate distance from the efficiency frontier, resulting in an efficiency rating that varies from 100 (on the frontier) to 0 (farthest distance

---

1 Extensions of the model can also account for allocative efficiency, but the basic model does not.

possible from the frontier).[2] In a case with multiple outputs, the frontier will be a multidimensional "virtual frontier."

The DEA concept is distinct from regression-based techniques in several ways. First, DEA assesses efficiency in relation to the *best* results actually achieved by units in the sample, rather than the *average* results achieved. Second, DEA can include both multiple inputs *and* multiple outputs. Finally, the DEA procedure seeks to maximize each unit's efficiency rating by assigning unit-specific weights in the optimization program. Therefore, units can achieve efficiency through specialization as well as through high performance across multiple measures.

The next section of this paper outlines the concepts underlying the DEA procedure. It is followed by discussions of practical issues surrounding the choice of data and the procedure itself. Empirical examples using data from New York City and Ohio follow, and the chapter concludes with a discussion of DEA's implications for the analysis of school efficiency.

Conceptual Basis

DEA assumes that efficiency can be defined as the ratio of outputs to inputs. In the case of a single output or single input, measuring relative technical efficiency is simple and the efficiency frontier can be constructed by plotting the units with the highest ratios of outputs to inputs. Consider the following Figure 5.1 of a school with one input (per pupil spending) and two outputs (average reading scores and average math scores):

Figure 5.1. DEA Analysis Based on Reading and Math Scores

School	Per Pupil Spending	Reading Score	Math Score	Cost per Reading Point	Cost per Math Point
A	$3,500	80	60	$44	$58
B	$4,000	70	60	$57	$67
C	$6,000	95	80	$63	$75
D	$5,000	75	92	$67	$54
E	$5,500	60	60	$92	$92

If reading scores were the only output and spending the only input, the schools could easily be easily ranked by their cost per point of reading score, with school A achieving the lowest unit cost and therefore the highest efficiency. When examining cost per math point rather than reading point, however, school D is the most efficient. To assess these multiple output/input ratios, an efficiency frontier could be constructed as in Figure 5.2:

---

2 The index may alternatively be scaled from zero to one.

Figure 5.2. Input Minimization Efficiency Frontier

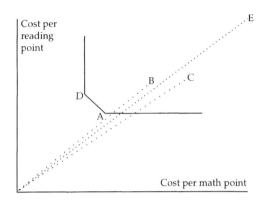

The efficiency frontier is constructed by joining the two schools with the most efficient ratios (A and D) on each of the two measures. Units B, C, and E are each enveloped by the frontier and therefore deemed to be inefficient to some degree. The efficiency rating for unit E in the above example is calculated as the ratio of its distance from the origin to the efficiency frontier over the distance from the origin to point E. Examining the length of the line segments between each inefficient unit and the frontier suggests that school B would have the highest efficiency score among the inefficient units, whereas school E would have the lowest score. Note that this example assumes that units are trying to minimize their cost per unit of output. An equally plausible assumption is that schools attempt to maximize outputs given a fixed-budget constraint. In such a case, the efficiency frontier would be convex rather than concave. This process is more complicated (and no longer two-dimensional) when using multiple inputs and outputs.

The distance between each inefficient unit and the efficiency frontier can be interpreted as the unit's *slack*. In the case of input minimization, this would tell us by how much a DMU can reduce inputs without affecting outputs. In the output-maximization case, the slacks would be indicated by how much the DMU can increase outputs without using more inputs. Although the slack values indicate potential output increases or input decreases, it offers little guidance as to how these increases or decreases can be achieved. For example, suppose the analysis finds slack spending of $500 per pupil in school A, indicating that the school could reduce expenditures by 10% without adversely affecting student performance. Clearly, all budget reductions are not created equal. If the outputs used in the analysis consist of math and reading test scores, then cutting $500 per pupil from reading programs likely will reduce those outputs whereas cutting $500 from physical education programs may not. To some extent, this black box problem can be reduced by employing better and more detailed spending data. Thus finding slack in aggregate per-pupil spending may offer little guidance for school administrators, but finding slack in third-grade mathematics teaching supplies, for example, might provide useful information to guide resource allocation decisions.

An advantage of DEA over regression-based techniques is that it provides an intuitive method for identifying the most efficient units. Because DEA places each unit either on or below the efficiency frontier, there is no need to define an arbitrary cutoff for efficiency. However, because all efficient units receive the same efficiency score, the technique provides little guidance for differentiating the most efficient from among the efficient. Therefore, all the units on the frontier will typically receive the same ranking. Modifications to the DEA procedure that allow ranking among efficient units have been suggested to overcome this drawback (see Lovell et al., 1994).

Measuring Outputs

The mix of outputs will be a critical determinant of each school's efficiency score, particularly because units are able to achieve efficiency by specializing. That is, a unit may be on its efficiency frontier despite producing an extremely low level of one or more outputs. If it is possible to place a unit on the efficiency frontier, DEA will do so even if the unit produces a mix of outputs that most analysts would deem to be unacceptable. In theory, this may mean that schools specializing in lower-quality or cheaper outputs may appear to be more efficient than those producing more expensive outputs. Suppose, for example, that schools are judged on two outputs: the percentage of students over the national median on a nationally normed reading test and graduation rates. Further suppose that cheap technologies exist to quickly boost test scores for those students just below the median to just above the median, but increasing graduation rates requires intensive and individualized work with students at risk of dropping out. The data envelopment analysis is likely to recognize those schools that use their resources to boost test scores over the median, whereas schools that focus resources on keeping students in school will be deemed inefficient. In short, DEA assesses only technical efficiency, not social well-being. This shortcoming can be addressed by assigning weights to each of the outputs. For example, if both outputs are equally important, a restriction can be introduced so that each output receives the same weight (Sexton et al., 1986). This restricts the flexibility of the linear program, however, and requires strong theoretical or practical justification for the selection of the weights.

Measuring Inputs

Extensions to the original DEA models have allowed analysts to designate inputs as either controllable (discretionary) or uncontrollable (nondiscretionary). Controllable inputs are those for which DMU managers and administrators can affect the level and/or quality, whereas uncontrollable inputs are those over which managers do not have discretion. This distinction is crucial from a managerial perspective because finding slack in uncontrollable inputs (for example, client characteristics) offers no guidance for action and risks holding organizations accountable for factors over which they have no control. Conceptually, if there are uncontrollable inputs in the model, DEA will project inefficient units to the point on the efficiency frontier at which they can produce more of the output, using less of the controllable inputs but the same level of the uncontrollable inputs. The nondiscretionary inputs are not used directly to estimate the efficiency score and slacks, but they are used to choose the reference set for construction of the efficiency frontier (Charnes et al., 1994; Cooper et al., 2000). Certain models will calculate slack values for the nondiscretionary inputs on the assumption that the inputs may be controllable at a higher management level, but these slacks are not directly used in estimating each unit's efficiency.[3]

In the case of schools, defining inputs as controllable and uncontrollable can be problematic. Often, one or more measures of expenditures per pupil will be used as controllable inputs (see empirical example below). As has been well established in the educational literature, however, schools themselves often have very little control over budgetary decisions, with most resources allocated on the basis of formulas, grant restrictions, or district-level decisions (Stiefel, Rubenstein, & Berne 1998). Moreover, the *level* of resources may also be largely determined by factors outside the control of schools, such as the salaries of teachers working in the school and the number of students with special needs that generate additional categorical funding. Therefore, the analysis could be biased in favor of schools receiving lower funding, assuming they are able to achieve a minimal level of output. Conversely, schools with higher levels of resources are likely to be deemed inefficient, particularly if they spend their additional resource to achieve more expensive outputs.

Technical Issues

The more inputs and outputs included in the model, the greater the likelihood that the program can find a set of weights for each unit that places it on the efficiency frontier. All extreme units (those with the highest ratio of a given output to a given input) will be placed on the frontier, and thus the more inputs and outputs in the model, the greater the number of units that will be deemed efficient. Also, as more inputs and outputs are added, the efficiency scores of inefficient units will increase, and a greater number of units will be deemed efficient. This suggests that considerable attention should be paid to selection of the appropriate input and output variables. Including several highly correlated inputs, for example, may substantially increase the number of units rated efficient without adding substantially more useful information to the analysis.[4] Moreover, comparisons of average efficiency across years or across samples may not be valid if different inputs and outputs are used in the models.

DEA is sensitive not only to the *number* of inputs and outputs included but also to the *choice* of the inputs and outputs. Unlike regression-based methods, DEA does not provide any goodness-of-fit measures to compare different specifications and variable sets. The linear program will produce a set of efficient units and efficiency scores regardless of the choice of variables, but it provides no guidance for choosing among specifications; therefore the choice of an appropriate model must be guided by strong theory. One option sometimes considered is to first conduct a regression or correlation analysis to assess which inputs have a significant relationship with outputs and the direction of the effect (Bessent et al.,

---

3 The software program Frontier Analyst, used in the DEA calculations presented below, operates in this way.

4 Charnes et al., (1989) suggest that the number of DMUs should be at least three times the product of inputs/outputs.

1982; Sexton 1986). Inputs with insignificant coefficients are excluded from the DEA. Regardless of whether the relationship is significant, if the variable is included in the DEA, it will be used to construct the efficiency frontier.

DEA is similarly sensitive to the values of individual units' inputs and outputs; therefore, errors in the data can—potentially—drastically change the results of the analysis. In the presence of measurement error, the efficiency frontier may be constructed with observations containing error and thus may overestimate inefficiency. The measurement error problem tends to increase with sample size (Bifulco & Bretschneider 2001). The effect will depend on whether the error places the unit on the efficiency frontier. Data errors or deletion of units below the frontier affect only the results for that unit. However, incorrect data for units on the frontier will alter the results for all other units in the sample. Sexton et al., (1986) test the sensitivity of DEA results to one coding error in a sample of 49 Project Follow Through sites and report that the miscoding of one output for one unit resulted in an overall change in average efficiency scores of 12%, and that 7 of the 16 efficient units were no longer efficient once the coding error was corrected.

Empirical Results

Using school-level data for New York City (NYC) elementary schools for the 1999–2000 school year, I conduct 11 data envelopment analyses using a variety of specifications of the DEA model with the same data set. To compare results using a single district to those encompassing an entire state, I also use school-level data on Ohio elementary schools for the 1998–1999 school year and run an additional six DEA models using the same variables. Only schools with valid data for each of the inputs and outputs are included in the dataset.[5] The models use either a value added or a lagged test score approach to measuring outputs (test scores). The value-added specifications use the *change* in the percentage of students passing the previous year's reading and math tests from the previous grade as output variables, with no prior test-score data used as inputs. The lagged specifications use the percentage of students passing the reading and math tests as output variables with the lagged values from the previous year included as inputs. Both approaches approximate a cohort measure, but to the extent that there is migration into and out of the school, the change between grades will not measure identical groups of students. Additional models use fourth-grade scores from consecutive years rather than the change between fourth and fifth grades. Figure 5.3 displays the list of New York City models; those marked with a *no* indicate that the DEA software could not solve the linear program for those models. All specifications also include the following variables:

Controllable inputs:

♦ Expenditures on classroom teachers per pupil

♦ Expenditures on non-classroom teachers per pupil

---

5 As noted, the DEA program cannot run with missing data.

The Reliability of School Efficiency Measures Using Data Envelopment Analysis   99

Uncontrollable inputs:

♦ Percentage of students who are not free-lunch eligible

♦ Percentage of students who are not black

♦ Percentage of students who are not Hispanic

♦ Percentage of students who are white

♦ Percentage of students who are Asian

♦ School enrollment[6]

Several of these variables are constructed in nontraditional ways because of data constraints in the data envelopment analysis program. First, variables can contain only positive numbers. Therefore, a constant is added to several of the variables (such as the change in pass rates) to produce positive values.[7] Adding a constant does not change the calculation of the efficiency frontier or scores, although it must be removed to facilitate interpretation. Also, all inputs are assumed to have a positive effect on outputs. Therefore, variables that are negatively correlated with outputs (such as percentage of free-lunch eligible students) are subtracted from 100. One variable with a negative correlation, school enrollment, is not a percentage and is specified as its inverse to create a positive correlation.

Figure 5.3. List of NYC DEA Models

	Input Minimization	*Output Maximization*
Constant Returns	Yes	Yes
Variable Returns	Yes	No
Output = Value-added, fifth-grade reading and math scores minus lagged fourth-grade scores		
Constant Returns	Yes	Yes
Variable Returns	No	Yes
Output = School improvement, fourth-grade reading and math scores with lagged fourth grade		
Constant Returns	Yes	Yes
Variable Returns	No	Yes
Output = Fourth-grade reading and math scores minus lagged fourth-grade scores		
Constant Returns	Yes	Yes
Variable Returns	No	No
Output = Value-added, fifth-grade reading and math scores with lagged fourth grade		

6 Because the input must have a positive relationship with outputs, I specify it as 1/enrollment, implying that smaller schools have better outputs.

7 Many schools exhibit lower pass rates in fifth grade than in fourth grade, resulting in a negative value added.

New York City Results

Figure 5.4 displays descriptive statistics for each of the NYC DEA models. The models using fifth-grade scores as outputs include 603 schools reporting fifth-grade scores, whereas the models using fourth-grade scores include 628 schools. Mean efficiency scores range from 74.36 (input minimization, constant returns, and lagged test scores with fifth-grade scores) to 90.36 (input maximization, variable returns, and lagged fourth-grade scores with fifth-grade scores). The latter model also has the largest number of efficient units (236), whereas the models using fifth-grade scores in a value-added specification with constant returns (both minimization and maximization) have the fewest number (90) of efficient schools. Comparing the minimization and maximization specifications shows that changing this assumption alone has no effect on the number of units rated efficient. It does change the mean and range of the efficiency scores, demonstrating that conclusions about the overall level of efficiency in a sample can vary depending on the assumptions used, even when the data and DMUs are identical.

Figure 5.5 displays the Pearson correlation coefficients comparing the results of each model. As shown, the correlations between the results vary widely. For example, the first row indicates that the correlation between the models using input minimization/constant returns and input minimization/variable returns (both using fifth-grade scores and the value-added specification) is 0.936, the highest correlation between any two models. At the other end of the scale, the correlation between the model using minimization/constant returns/lagged test score with fifth-grade scores and the one using maximization/variable returns/value-added with fourth-grade scores (which might be thought of as opposite models) is only 0.184.[8] In general, the models tend to be more correlated with the other models using the same grade level as outputs than with the models using the different grade level, suggesting, as one might expect, more consistency across models within grades than across grades. This result could be caused, in part, by differences in the students across grades. The inconsistencies across grades are not uniform, however. For example, the correlation between the fifth-grade model using minimization/constant returns/value added and the fourth-grade model using the same specification is 0.845. This correlation is higher than many of those between models using the same grade level but different specifications of the DEA model.

---

8 All correlation coefficients are significant at $p<.01$.

Figure 5.4. Descriptive Statistics, NYC DEA Efficiency Scores

Variable Name	Variable Description	N	Mean	Minimum	Number Efficient
Outputs = Fifth-grade scores					
mncrva45	Input Minimum, Constant Returns, Value Added	603	79.67	35.65	90
mxcrva45	Output Maximum, Constant Returns, Value Added	603	84.37	50.48	90
mnvrva45	Input Minimum, Variable Returns, Value Added	603	83.95	37.46	112
mncrlg45	Input Minimum, Constant Returns, Lagged Score	603	74.36	7.9	144
mxcrlg45	Output Maximum, Constant Returns, Lagged Score	603	86.63	19.07	144
mxvrlg45	Output Maximum, Variable Returns, Lagged Score	603	90.63	20.61	236
Outputs = Fourth-grade scores					
mncrva44	Input Minimum, Constant Returns, Value added	628	78.92	35.96	115
mxcrva44	Output Maximum, Constant Returns, Value added	628	84.36	45.81	115
mxvrva44	Output Maximum, Variable Returns, Value added	628	87.75	51.96	137
mncrlg44	Input Minimum, Constant Returns, Lagged score	628	74.97	16.36	150
mxcrlg44	Output Maximum, Constant Returns, Lagged score	628	86.11	22.15	150

Figure 5.5. NYC DEA Efficiency Scores Correlation Coefficients

	mncr va45	mxcr va45	mnvr va45	mncrl g45	mxcrl g45	mxvrl g45	mncr va44	mxvr va44	mxcr va44	mncrl g44	mxcrl g44
mncrva45	1.00	0.881	0.936	0.563	0.560	0.547	0.845	0.727	0.645	0.468	0.458
mxcrva45		1.00	0.798	0.383	0.449	0.445	0.758	0.831	0.694	0.293	0.363
mnvrva45			1.00	0.512	0.444	0.429	0.858	0.724	0.622	0.460	0.429
mncrlg45				1.00	0.919	0.718	0.348	0.188	0.184	0.633	0.537
mxcrlg45					1.00	0.838	0.328	0.217	0.220	0.564	0.542
mxvrlg45						1.00	0.342	0.235	0.291	0.459	0.456
mncrva44							1.00	0.903	0.862	0.575	0.600
mxcrva44								1.00	0.931	0.451	0.556
mxvrva44									1.00	0.501	0.622
mncrlg44										1.00	0.918
mxcrlg44											1.00

The correlations between the models using the value-added specification and those using the lagged test scores as inputs tend to be lowest among all the models. Only one correlation between a value-added model and a lagged test-score model is over 0.60 and most are below 0.50. These results suggest that models using changes in outputs tend to produce very different efficiency results as compared to those that use the levels of outputs with prior results as inputs. Because the models use the same sets of inputs, this result suggests that whereas certain schools may be able to efficiently produce high test scores, these schools may not be equally successful at producing increases in test scores, perhaps because it is may be easier to produce large gains from low starting levels as compared to high starting levels.

Figure 5.6 presents an illustrative example comparing the characteristics of schools judged efficient and inefficient for the variables included in the model as well as several others. For illustrative purposes, the figure uses the results from the input minimization/constant returns/value-added model with the change from fourth to fifth grade as the outputs. As expected, the efficient schools tend to have better performance changes between fourth and fifth grades while spending less per pupil. For reading scores, however, both groups actually lost ground, on average, between the two years, although the decline was smaller in the efficient group.

Figure 5.6. Difference of Means, NYC Efficient and Inefficient Schools

(model = minimization, constant returns, value added)			
Variable	*Efficient*	*Inefficient*	*Difference*
Included in model			
Change in pct passing reading, fourth to fifth	−2.10	−5.92	3.82**
Change in pct passing math, fourth to fifth	4.15	−1.54	5.68**
Classroom teacher expenditures per pupil	3,515	3,763	−248**
Nonclassroom teacher expenditures per pupil	4,269	4,514	−245*
Pct white	2.87	20.58	−17.70**
Pct Asian	3.46	11.92	−8.46**
Pct Black	43.36	34.24	9.12**
Pct Hispanic	50.30	33.27	17.03**
Pct free lunch	91.67	72.50	19.17**
Enrollment	947	769	178**
Other variables			
Pct passing, fifth-grade reading, 2000	39.31	49.90	−10.59**
Pct passing, fifth-grade math, 2000	54.95	64.38	−9.44**
Lagged fourth-grade reading, 1999	41.41	55.82	−14.41**
Lagged fourth-grade math, 1999	50.80	65.92	−15.12**
Pct LEP	21.50	15.00	6.50**
Schoolwide project	0.46	0.37	0.09
Pupil teacher ratio	16.16	16.05	0.12
Attendance	90.59	91.20	−0.61*
Pct teachers with master's degree	72.46	77.44	−4.98**
Pct teachers fully licensed	79.91	85.44	−5.53**
Pct teachers > 5 years of experience	57.08	62.91	−5.83**
Average teacher salary	40,943	43,530	−2,587**
** Significant at $p<.01$ * Significant at $p<.05$ Note: t-test assumes unequal variances			

The efficient schools also have significantly lower proportions of white and Asian students as well as significantly higher percentages of black and Hispanic students and students eligible for free and reduced-price lunch. This pattern is a result of the specification of the DEA model. By construction, the efficient schools tend to have larger test gains (or smaller declines) despite spending less money and working with higher proportions of black, Hispanic, and poor students.

The remaining variables in the figure are not included in the DEA model.[9] Examining the level (rather than value-added) test scores shows that the inefficient schools tend to have higher fourth- and fifth-grade test scores than do the efficient schools. Thus it appears that the efficient schools were able to produce better value-added results by starting with a lower percentage of students passing as compared to the inefficient schools. Although the efficient schools start lower and gain more, they do not reach the average fifth-grade scores of the inefficient schools.

Results using the same specification with lagged test scores (Figure 5.7) provide an interesting counterpoint to the value-added results. In the lagged model, the schools are almost identical in their previous year's fourth-grade scores, but the efficient schools have significantly higher percentages of students passing in the fifth grade. The change between the two years is similar to the change using the value-added specification. Both the efficient and inefficient schools lost ground in reading between fourth and fifth grade, but the loss is larger for the inefficient schools. In math, the efficient schools gained almost four percentage points, whereas the inefficient schools lost over two points. Thus the lagged model identifies a group of schools with a significantly higher level of absolute performance in fifth grade as well higher gains, while serving comparable proportions of students with special needs and spending slightly less per pupil. Because the model adds two additional input variables (prior scores), it also increases the number of schools rated as efficient (from 90 to 144).

---

9 Several of the variables are correlated with variables in the model, such as classroom teacher expenditures and average teacher salary.

Figure 5.7. Difference of Means, NYC Efficient and Inefficient Schools

(model = minimization, constant returns, lagged test scores)			
Variable	Efficient	Inefficient	Difference
Included in model			
Pct passing, fifth-grade reading, 2000	51.83	47.35	4.48*
Pct passing, fifth-grade math, 2000	67.82	61.61	6.22**
Lagged fourth-grade reading, 1999	53.30	53.89	−0.59
Lagged fourth-grade math, 1999	63.93	63.70	0.23
Classroom teacher expenditures per pupil	3,584	3,769	−185
Nonclassroom teacher expenditures per pupil	4,239	4,550	−311
Pct white	13.98	19.25	−5.27
Pct Asian	8.90	11.24	−2.34
Pct black	37.25	35.04	2.21
Pct Hispanic	39.87	34.48	5.39
Pct free lunch	78.34	74.32	4.02
Enrollment	861	774	87
Other variables			
Change in pct passing reading, fourth to fifth	−1.47	−6.54	5.07
Change in pct passing math, fourth to fifth	3.89	−2.09	5.99
Pct LEP	17.47	15.48	1.99
Schoolwide project	41.67	36.98	4.69
Pupil teacher ratio	16.55	15.92	0.63
Attendance	91.44	91.02	0.42
Pct teachers with master's degree	77.42	76.52	0.90
Pct teachers fully licensed	84.75	84.62	0.13
Pct teachers > 5 years of experience	61.04	59.65	−1.40
Average teacher salary	42,761	43,277	−516
** Significant at p<.01 * Significant at p<.05 Note: t-test assumes unequal variances			

The Reliability of School Efficiency Measures Using Data Envelopment Analysis   107

Figures 5.8 to 5.11 examine the stability of the DEA rankings across models by comparing quartile rankings from several of the models.[10] Figure 5.8 compares the quartile rankings from a model using input minimization to a model using output maximization (both with constant returns to scale, and using value-added pass rates between fourth and fifth grades). The first quartile contains schools with the highest efficiency scores (including those rated efficient) and the fourth quartile contains schools with the lowest efficiency ratings. Looking across the diagonal from the upper left to lower right, we see that 390 of the 603 schools (64.7%) are in the same quartile using both assumptions. Only one school switches from the first to fourth quartile, 198 schools move one quartile, and 14 move two quartiles. Thus it appears that changing the DEA assumption from input minimization to output maximization does change the relative ranking of schools, although the changes are not dramatic. Schools deemed efficient would be efficient under both assumptions and the relative performance of inefficient schools is similar under both assumptions.

Figure 5.8. NYC DEA Results, Constant Returns, Value added

| | | *Maximization* | | | | |
		1	**2**	**3**	**4**	**Total**
	1	128	22	0	0	150
		21.2%	3.7%	0.0%	0.0%	24.9%
	2	20	86	45	0	151
		3.3%	14.3%	7.5%	0.0%	25.0%
Minimization	3	1	30	73	48	152
		0.2%	5.0%	12.1%	8.0%	25.2%
	4	1	13	33	103	150
		0.2%	2.2%	5.5%	17.1%	24.9%
	Total	150	151	151	151	603
		24.9%	25.0%	25.0%	25.0%	100.0%

Figure 5.9 compares two models with the same DEA assumptions (input minimization, constant returns) but different grade levels as outputs. One model uses the change in the percent passing between fourth grade in 1999 and fifth grade in 2000, whereas the other uses the change from fourth grade in 1999 to fourth grade in 2000. Again, the rankings are relatively consistent, with 376

---

10 Although a more disaggregated ranking may be preferable, over one-fifth of the schools in some models are rated efficient. Therefore, classifying schools into quintiles or deciles would result in disproportionate numbers of schools in the top category.

schools (62.4%) appearing in the same quartile in both models. In this specification, two schools move three quartiles, 200 move one quartile, and 25 move two quartiles.

Figure 5.9. NYC DEA Results, Input Minimum, Constant Returns, Value added

		Value Added, fourth to fifth				
		1	**2**	**3**	**4**	Total
	1	116	25	8	1	150
		19.2%	4.2%	1.3%	0.2%	24.9%
	2	18	81	49	3	151
Value Added, fourth to fourth		3.0%	13.4%	8.1%	0.5%	25.0%
	3	7	40	68	37	152
		1.2%	6.6%	11.3%	6.1%	25.2%
	4	1	7	31	111	150
		0.2%	1.2%	5.1%	18.4%	24.9%
	Total	142	153	156	152	603
		23.6%	25.4%	25.9%	25.2%	100.0%

Figure 5.10 examines the effect of changing from the constant returns to the variable returns assumption and reports results similar to the previous two comparisons. The schools on the diagonal comprise over three-quarters of the schools (460), whereas again two schools move between the first and fourth quartiles. Only four schools move two quartiles and 137 move one quartile.

Figure 5.10. NYC DEA Results, Input Minimum, Value added

		Variable Returns				
		1	**2**	**3**	**4**	Total
	1	130	20	0	0	150
		21.6%	3.3%	0.0%	0.0%	24.9%
	2	16	100	35	0	151
Constant Returns		2.7%	16.6%	5.8%	0.0%	25.0%
	3	2	29	100	21	152
		0.3%	4.8%	16.6%	3.5%	25.2%
	4	2	2	16	130	150
		0.3%	0.3%	2.7%	21.6%	24.9%
	Total	150	151	151	151	603
		24.9%	25.0%	25.0%	25.0%	100.0%

The Reliability of School Efficiency Measures Using Data Envelopment Analysis 109

Figure 5.11 examines the effect of changing from the value-added output to one with a lagged input. The school rankings are more inconsistent than in the previous tables. Only 268 schools (44.4 percent) are in the same quartile under both methods, whereas a much larger number of schools than in the previous comparisons move three quartiles (14 schools). The remaining schools move one quartile (243) or two quartiles (78). In sum, the results indicate that changing the assumptions under which the DEA model operates can change the relative efficiency ranking of schools, but the effect is much smaller than is changing from a lagged to a value-added specification. This difference could be partially because of the fact that the lagged specification changes the number of input variables, whereas changing the DEA assumptions does not. With more variables in the model, as in the lagged specification, more schools can be placed on the efficiency frontier. Thus many schools deemed inefficient under the value-added approach may be deemed efficient under the lagged approach, and many inefficient schools would be closer to the frontier.

Figure 5.11. NYC DEA Results, Input Minimum, Constant Returns

			Lagged Fourth Grade				
			1	**2**	**3**	**4**	**Total**
Value Added, fourth to fifth		1	95	29	15	11	150
			15.8%	4.8%	2.5%	1.8%	24.9%
		2	39	48	33	31	151
			6.5%	8.0%	5.5%	5.1%	25.0%
		3	13	55	50	34	152
			2.2%	9.1%	8.3%	5.6%	25.2%
		4	3	19	53	75	150
			0.5%	3.2%	8.8%	12.4%	24.9%
	Total		150	151	151	151	603
			24.9%	25.0%	25.0%	25.0%	100.0%

To test the sensitivity of the results to the choice of input and output variables, I compare the results from a model using two outputs, two controllable inputs, and eight uncontrollable inputs to a model using only one controllable input. Both models use the minimization constraint and constant returns to scale. The model with the two controllable inputs produces efficiency scores ranging from 7.9 to 100, with 154 efficient units. When the controllable input is removed, the scores range from 7.8 to 100, with 127 efficient units. The correlation of efficiency scores between the two models is .960, suggesting the results are largely the same but not identical.

I also test the sensitivity of the results to deletion of one efficient unit using the input minimization constraint and constant returns to scale, with two outputs, two controllable inputs, and four uncontrollable inputs. Using the full sample, efficiency scores range from 35.96 to 100, with 74 efficient units. After deleting a single efficient unit from the sample and running the DEA again, the analysis produces 75 efficient units with the same range of scores. The correlation between the efficiency scores from the first and second examples is .999, suggesting that in large samples small changes in the sample will not have a large impact on the results.

Ohio Results

To test the robustness of the results to an entirely different sample of schools from a different jurisdiction, I compare the New York City DEA results to those using elementary school data from the state of Ohio. Unlike the New York City data, the Ohio sample includes schools from across the state rather than from a single city. For comparability, the models use the same variables included in the New York City analysis, with one major exception. Students in Ohio are tested in reading and math in fourth grade but not in fifth grade. Therefore, student performance cannot be measured as the change in reading for a cohort of students between fourth and fifth grade. Instead, the models presented here use 1998 fourth-grade scores as inputs in models using 1999 fourth-grade scores as outputs, or use the change in fourth-grade scores between the two years as outputs. To the extent that the characteristics of fourth-grade students vary little from year to year, this method provides a reasonable measure of school improvement. It does not, however, measure changes in individual students. (See Stiefel, Rubenstein, & Schwartz 1999 for further discussion of this approach in the context of adjusted performance measures.)

Figure 5.12 displays descriptive statistics for the six Ohio models.[11] The number of schools without missing data is 1,724 from across the state. As shown, the mean efficiency scores are generally lower than in New York City, and the range of scores also tends to be much larger, perhaps because of the greater heterogeneity in the sample. In the New York sample, only one model produced a minimum efficiency score below 10, whereas in the Ohio sample three of the six have a minimum score below 10, and one has a score below 1.0. Two models, both using input minimization and variable returns to scale, also identify over half of the schools as efficient, whereas each of the other models has fewer than 10% efficient schools.

---

[11] Because there are no fifth-grade scores, eight variations are possible. Two of the eight did not converge, leaving the six models presented here.

The Reliability of School Efficiency Measures Using Data Envelopment Analysis

Figure 5.12. Descriptive Statistics, Ohio DEA Efficiency Scores

Variable Name	Variable Description	N	Mean	St. Dev.	Minimum	Number Efficient
Outputs = fourth-grade scores, with lagged fourth-grade scores						
mxcrva44	Output Maximum, Constant Returns, Value Added	1,724	76.16	11.07	0.93	65
mxvrva44	Output Maximum, Variable Returns, Value Added	1,724	77.23	10.49	39.14	91
mnvrva44	Input Minimum, Variable Returns, Value Added	1,724	81.70	22.76	32.29	1,035
mncrlg44	Input Minimum, Constant Returns, Lagged Scores	1,724	56.28	21.56	4.89	90
mxcrlg44	Output Maximum, Constant Returns, Lagged Scores	1,724	66.31	18.54	7.06	90
mnvrlg44	Input Minimum, Variable returns, Lagged Scores	1,724	94.22	12.95	45.76	1,428

Figure 5.13 displays the Pearson correlation coefficients for the efficiency scores produced by the six models. They vary considerably more than do the scores produced in the New York City analysis. For example, two of the correlation coefficients are actually negative, whereas all were positive (although sometimes small) in the New York City data. As in the New York City analysis, the lowest coefficients are between the models using the lagged scores as inputs and those using the value-added specification. The correlation coefficients between the lagged and the value-added models range from 0.431 to 0.113, suggesting that the models produce very different efficiency scores. The correlation coefficients between the lagged specifications range from 0.054 to 0.943, whereas the coefficients between the value-added specifications range from 0.236 to 0.843, indicating a great deal of variability in efficiency scores even within models using the same variables but different DEA specifications.

Figure 5.13. Ohio Efficiency Score Correlation Coefficients

	mxcrva44	mnvrva44	mxvrva44	mncrlg44	mxcrlg44	mnvrlg44
mxcrva44	1.00	0.231	0.832	0.183	0.308	0.139
mnvrva44		1.00	0.236	−0.113	−0.076	0.293
mxvrva44			1.00	0.310	0.431	0.115
mncrlg44				1.00	0.943	0.067
mxcrlg44					1.00	0.054
mnvrlg44						1.00

As in the previous analyses, the correlation coefficients may overstate the variability of the results from a practical perspective if the various models all produce the same list of high-performing and low-performing schools. In other words, the correlation coefficients may identify small differences in efficiency scores although schools remain in the same aggregate performance group. Figures 5.14 and 5.15 each compare the quartile rankings generated by two different models.[12] Figure 5.14 compares a lagged model to a value-added model, each using output maximization and constant returns to scale. Approximately 37% of the schools remain in the same quartile for both models, whereas the same proportion of schools moves one quartile. Six percent of schools (103 of 1,724) move between the highest and lowest quartiles, and 20% move two quartiles. Not surprisingly, the rankings produced by the two value-added models are much more consistent. Almost 88% of the quartile rankings are the same across the two models. Only 1% of schools switch from the highest to lowest quartile, and the remaining schools move one or two quartiles. The patterns from both models suggest that changing DEA assumptions has some effect on school rankings, although the effect is typically not large. Changing the data used in the analysis, however, can cause substantial changes in the rankings, even causing a large number of schools to move from the highest to lowest quartiles and vice versa.

Figure 5.14. Ohio DEA Results, Output Maximum, Constant Returns

		Lagged fourth grade				
		1	2	3	4	Total
Value-added, fourth to fourth	1	194	104	82	51	431
		11.25%	6.03%	4.76%	2.96%	25%
	2	97	133	105	96	431
		5.63%	7.71%	6.09%	5.57%	25%
	3	88	114	127	102	431
		5.10%	6.61%	7.37%	5.92%	25%
	4	52	80	117	182	431
		3.02%	4.64%	6.79%	10.56%	25%
	Total	431	431	431	431	1,724
		25%	25%	25%	25%	100%

---

[12] Note that these tables do not include the two specifications that produced over 1,000 efficient schools because it is not possible to divide the rankings into quartiles.

The Reliability of School Efficiency Measures Using Data Envelopment Analysis 113

Figure 5.15. Ohio DEA Results, Output Maximum, Value Added

		Variable Returns				
		1	2	3	4	Total
	1	398	33	0	0	431
		23.09%	1.91%	0%	0%	25%
	2	15	363	53	0	431
		0.87%	21.06%	3.07%	0%	25%
Constant Returns	3	1	29	391	40	431
		0.06%	1.68%	20.94%	2.32%	25%
	4	17	5	19	390	431
		0.99%	0.29%	1.10%	22.62%	25%
	Total	431	430	433	430	1,724
		25%	24.94%	25.12%	24.94%	100%

Stability Across Years

Assessing the stability across years of rankings derived from DEA is somewhat more complicated than assessing the cross-sectional stability across models. Differences in efficiency rankings and scores across different models within the same year are due entirely to the changes in the specification and/or variables used in the models. Changes across years, however, may be because of changes in student population, the models and specifications, or actual changes in school efficiency. It may be particularly difficult for schools to maintain test score gains, as opposed to levels, for multiple years. This section uses a consistent set of 637 urban schools across years for Ohio to examine the stability of efficiency rankings across years and across models. Figure 5.16 compares quartile rankings for Ohio schools for 1997 and 1999. The models for both years use the controllable and uncontrollable variables described earlier, change in test scores as the output variables, and input minimization/constant returns to scale in the model. For 1997 the efficiency scores range from 54.5 to 100 with 101 efficient schools. For 1999 the scores range from 59.37 to 100, with 91 efficient schools. The Spearman rank correlation across the two years is 0.460, suggesting a mid-range level of stability across years. As shown in Figure 5.16, 47.5% of schools remain in the same quartile for both years, whereas 25 schools (3.9%) move from the highest to lowest or lowest to highest. Given that the models use the same variables and DEA assumptions, the large changes in rankings across the two years reflect changes in the values of both the input and output variables. That is, schools could move from below the efficiency frontier to the efficiency frontier by reducing their controllable inputs, increasing their outputs, or through a combination of the two. Fewer than half of schools (37.6%) register the same efficiency quartile across the two years, and only 43 schools (6.7%) are able to maintain an efficient level of production in both years.

Figure 5.16. Ohio DEA Results, Input Minimization, Constant Returns, Value Added

Quartile		1999				
		1	2	3	4	Total
	1	71	42	32	14	159
		11.2%	6.6%	5.0%	2.2%	25.0%
	2	51	41	44	24	160
		8.0%	6.4%	6.9%	3.8%	25.0%
1997	3	26	39	50	44	159
		4.1%	6.1%	7.9%	6.9%	25.0%
	4	11	37	34	77	159
		1.7%	5.8%	5.3%	12.1%	25.0%
	Total	159	159	160	159	637
		25.0%	25.0%	25.0%	25.0%	100.0%

The results in Figure 5.17 examine whether results using test-score levels rather than changes are more stable across years. The analyses use the absolute level of school-level mean test scores for 1997 and 1999 as the outputs rather than the change in mean test scores between 1997 and 1999. One might assume, a priori, that such a model would produce more consistent efficiency rankings across years because mean test scores and resource use would not be expected to change appreciably across a two-year time span. In fact, the results are approximately the same as those using the value-added scores as outputs. The Spearman rank correlation between 1997 and 1999 efficiency rankings is 0.459 and 41.8% of the schools remain in the same quartile for both years, whereas 5.2% moved between the highest and lowest quartiles. The low correlation across years may be caused, in large part, by the low correlation of mean test scores across years. Although math scores have a Spearman rank correlation coefficient of 0.721 across years, the mean writing scores are correlated at only 0.521. Thus it is likely that most efficiency or performance measures using these pass rates as outputs would have a relatively low level of stability across years.

The Reliability of School Efficiency Measures Using Data Envelopment Analysis

Figure 5.17. Ohio DEA Results, Input Minimization, Constant Returns, Level Scores

Quartile		1999				
		1	2	3	4	Total
1997	1	86	38	17	18	159
		13.5%	6.0%	2.7%	2.8%	24.7%
	2	37	50	46	26	159
		5.8%	7.9%	7.2%	4.1%	25.0%
	3	21	42	56	41	160
		3.3%	6.6%	8.8%	6.4%	25.1%
	4	15	30	40	74	159
		2.4%	4.7%	6.3%	11.6%	25.0%
	Total	159	160	159	159	637
		25.0%	25.1%	25.0%	25.0%	100.0%

Figure 5.18 compares specifications using mean school pass rates as outputs and lagged mean pass rates as uncontrollable input variables. The cross-year correlation is a very low 0.324, although 42.4 percent of schools are in the same quartile for each year. This is due, in part, to the relatively large number of schools rated efficient using this model (over 41% of schools).[13] Not surprisingly given previous analyses, this model appears to produce the most inconsistent school rankings across years.

---

[13] The lagged specification adds four additional input variables to the model, as compared to the value-added and level specifications. Recall that the higher the number of input variables, the larger the number of schools rated efficient.

Figure 5.18. Ohio DEA Results, Input minimization, Constant Returns, Lagged Scores

Quartile		1999				
		1	2	3	4	Total
1997	1	154	24	53	39	270
		24.2%	3.8%	8.3%	6.1%	42.4%
	2	23	2	18	5	48
		3.6%	0.3%	2.8%	0.8%	7.5%
	3	49	16	47	48	160
		7.7%	2.5%	7.4%	7.5%	25.1%
	4	39	12	41	67	159
		6.1%	1.9%	6.4%	10.5%	25.0%
	Total	265	54	159	159	637
		41.6%	8.5%	25.0%	25.0%	100.0%

Conclusions

The preceding discussions and empirical examples provide insight on the usefulness of data envelopment analysis in assessing school productivity. Clearly, considerable caution is warranted in using DEA to rank schools, particularly for the purpose of distributing rewards or sanctions. The underlying linear mathematical computations are, perhaps, even more complex and less-easily understood than many other quantitative methods to assess performance and efficiency; and they are considerably more complex than a simple list or ranking of school test scores. Therefore unless school personnel understand the ways in which they can affect their school's ranking, the DEA results may be of limited use in providing incentives for more productive behavior.

Despite these caveats, and those raised earlier, DEA does hold the promise of providing useful information for educators and policymakers. In particular, the method's ability to simultaneously incorporate multiple outputs is extremely useful for analyzing public sector organizations. It may not be surprising, therefore, that DEA was first developed to analyze the performance of educational organizations participating in Project Follow Through in the 1960s (Rhodes, 1978), and it continues to be used with some frequency in educational contexts. DEA may be most useful, however, as an additional tool for assessing school performance rather than as a stand-alone technique, particularly for purposes of ranking and grading individual schools.

The empirical examples also provide some insight on issues likely to arise in the use of DEA to measure school efficiency. One of the most important issues is the specification of the output variables. Although level test scores or pass rates are often seen as inferior to valued-added measures because of level scores' high correlations with student demographics, the use of level pass rates in DEA

The Reliability of School Efficiency Measures Using Data Envelopment Analysis 117

appears superior in many ways to value-added scores. For example, in the Ohio analyses, the models using level scores as outputs with lagged test scores as inputs produced a set of efficient schools with higher test scores in all grades and larger increases across years, as compared to the inefficient schools. Conversely, the value-added measure produced the somewhat counterintuitive result of efficient schools with lower pass rates than inefficient schools (but larger gains). Although the pattern was relatively consistent in the data and models used here, further analysis is needed to determine whether this result will hold across multiple-data sets. Because DEA can accommodate multiple test scores in the model, it is also possible to simultaneously include multiple subjects and grade levels, thereby providing a multidimensional measure of school performance and perhaps lessening concerns over the use of simple-level scores.

The analyses also identified groups of schools that appeared to be achieving higher pass rates despite serving more students with special needs *and* generally using lower levels of resources. Further study of these schools could present important opportunities for identifying best practices and effective pedagogical strategies. Although it is likely that some of the schools on the efficiency frontier could turn out to be less-than-exemplary (for example, schools with extremely high scores on one measure but not others), the use of DEA could provide useful data on the ways in which some schools appear to be performing well. At the least, DEA can provide another tool in the ongoing search for effective ways to measure school performance.

References

Bessent, A., Bessent, W., Kennington, J., & Reagan, B. (1982). An application of mathematical programming to assess productivity in the Houston Independent School District. *Management Science, 28*(12), 1355–1367.

Bifulco, R. & Bretschneider, S. (2001). Estimating school efficiency: A comparison of methods using simulated data. *Economics of Education Review, 20,* 417–429.

Charnes, A., Cooper, W. W., Lewin, A. Y., & Seiford, L. M. (1994). Extensions to DEA models. In Charnes, A., Cooper, W. W., Lewin, A. Y., & Seiford, L. M. (Eds.). *Data envelopment analysis: Theory, methodology and application* (pp. 23–48). (Boston: Kluwer Academic Publishers).

Charnes, Charnes, A., Cooper, W. W., Lewin, A. Y., & Seiford, L. M. (1994). The DEA process, usages and interpretations. In Charnes, A., Cooper, W. W., Lewin, A. Y., & Seiford, L. M. (Eds.) *Data envelopment analysis: Theory, methodology and application* (425–435). (Boston: Kluwer Academic Publishers).

Cooper, W.W., Seiford, L.M., & Tone, K. (2000). *Data envelopment analysis: A comprehensive text with models, applications, references and DEA-solver software.* Boston: Kluwer Academic Publishers.

Rhodes, E. (1978). Data envelopment analysis and approaches for measuring the efficiency of decision making units with an application to program follow through in U.S. education. Unpublished doctoral dissertation, Carnegie Mellon University, Pittsburgh, PA.

Sexton, T. R. (1986). The methodology of data envelopment analysis. *New Directions for Program Evaluation, 32,* 7–30.

Sexton, T. R., Silkman, R.H., & Hogan, A.J. (1986). Data envelopment analysis: critique and extensions. *New Directions for Program Evaluation, 32,* 73–106.

Stiefel, L., Rubenstein, R., & Berne, R. (1998). Intra-district equity in four large cities: Methods, data and results," *Journal of Education Finance* , 23(4): 447–467.

Stiefel, L., Rubenstein, R., & Schwartz, A.E. (1999). Using adjusted performance measures for evaluating resource use. *Public Budgeting and Finance,* 19(3), 67–87.

6

Measuring School Performance: Promises and Pitfalls

David Figlio

Introduction

With the passage of the No Child Left Behind Act (NCLB) of 2001, school accountability is now federal law, and every state in the United States is obligated to assess students in grades 3–8 in reading and mathematics and in three grades in science. Additionally, they are required to evaluate schools on the basis of their aggregate performance on these examinations. In the federal law, schools are evaluated based on whether the school makes adequate yearly progress in a given year. Adequate yearly progress is defined recursively: Every student is expected to be proficient by 2013–2014, which sets an ultimate performance target for that year. Meeting this proficiency target, however, is not sufficient to make adequate yearly progress; schools must meet proficiency targets for each subgroup represented in the school, in each subject tested. Schools that persistently fail to meet these targets are sanctioned, with students offered increased school choice and federal education aid rerouted to other purposes. Eventually, these schools may experience closure or major governance changes.

This law has proven to be quite controversial, with educators and policymakers deeply divided about the conduct and use of these examinations. Although it is too early to measure the effects of the NCLB Act, the early evidence on state-level school accountability suggests that placing high stakes for schools based on student test scores improves student performance. For example, Jacob (2002), Figlio and Rouse (2004), and Deere and Strayer (2001) all find evidence that test scores on high-stakes tests increase with high-stakes accountability. Carnoy and Loeb (2002) and Hanushek and Raymond (2004), comparing states' aggregate performance on the National Assessment of Educational Progress, find evidence that stronger accountability systems seem to have larger positive results on test scores. That said, states face many choices when adopting school accountability initiatives and implementing the federal policy, and these choices may have substantial repercussions.

The purpose of this chapter is to outline a number of the key decisions that a state faces in its implementation of a school accountability system and to detail some of the implications of the various decisions that a state could make. I then describe how these decisions could influence the intended and unintended consequences of school accountability initiatives, and how they could affect school finance.

In the first section, I describe three aggregation decisions that states must make when designing accountability systems—are test scores aggregated across time, across subjects, and across subgroups? In the second section, I consider the implications of determining the scope of measurement, across grades and subjects. In the third section, I discuss the relative virtues of measuring schools based on level test performance versus value added. In the fourth section, I address issues surrounding the composition of the test pool. In the fifth section, I briefly describe fiscal implications of school accountability initiatives.

Aggregation Issues in Accountability Systems

Although the NCLB Act dictates many features of a federal accountability system, states have considerable flexibility in how they both implement the federal system as well as, of course, how they implement and design their own systems of accountability. One area of particular flexibility involves how test scores are aggregated for the purposes of accountability. There are several key aggregation issues—aggregation across time, aggregation across subjects, and aggregation across groups of students. This first section addresses these aggregation issues in turn.

Aggregation Across Time

One basic aggregation issue for states to consider involves aggregation across time—should schools be held accountable for any given year's performance, or should their scores be aggregated across several years? In different settings and different contexts, Kane and Staiger (2002) and Figlio (2002a) demonstrate how unstable school rankings based on test performance are from one year to the next. The basic problem here involves measurement error: Tests have large stochastic components to them, and schools deemed improving at one point in time could (almost necessarily) be found to be declining at another point. This measurement error has implications for rewards and sanctions in state aid systems and school accountability systems: Should schools be punished or rewarded on the basis of a single good draw or bad draw? These problems are particularly exacerbated when performance is measured by changes in proficiency from one year to the next across different cohorts (as is the case in many state accountability systems.) When two successive years' average test scores are each measured with error (not least because the classroom compositions change dramatically, although this is not the only reason), it is unclear what, if anything, is being uncovered by an accountability system that rewards (penalizes) improvements (fallbacks) in fractions of students passing the exam from one cohort to the next. Both Kane and Staiger (2002) and Figlio (2002a) illustrate that taking multiyear moving averages considerably reduces (although it remains a problem) the likelihood that measurement error will lead to dramatic instability in measured school performance.

States that assess schools solely on the basis of a single year of student performance make it more difficult for schools that are sanctioned to leave their sanctioned state, thereby increasing the fiscal costs borne by states and sanctioned school districts under the NCLB Act. Assessing schools on the basis of a single year of performance at a time could increase the probability that previously unsanctioned schools would be sanctioned in any given year, but this likelihood is far lower. The reason for this nonlinearity stems from the fact that schools that are below performance targets may still avoid NCLB sanctions by making year-to-year improvements toward their performance goals. Allowing schools to aggregate across cohorts over time thereby is less likely to punish improving schools that are still below performance targets in one or all subgroups than would a system that requires year-to-year improvements without permitting cross-cohort averaging.

To get some bearing on this and other design issues, I employ performance data from 1998–1999 through 2001–2002 on the Florida Comprehensive Assessment Test, the standards-based assessment test that Florida is using to comply with the requirements of the federal accountability law. These simulations cover all 1,688 elementary schools in the state of Florida, with schools averaging 45% of the student body who are free-lunch eligible, 28% of students who are black, and 15% of students who are Hispanic. I limit my analyses to the elementary-school-tested grades used throughout the entire time period—fourth grade for reading and fifth grade for mathematics. I simulate the attributes of the schools that are likely to be sanctioned under various permutations of the federal law. Although it is now possible to actually observe which schools were labeled as failing to make adequate yearly progress under the NCLB Act, I opt for simulations because this permits me to make forecasts of what might have occurred under different assumptions. I should point out, however, that the correlation between the schools that I predicted to be sanctioned and the schools that ultimately were sanctioned is very high. For the purposes of simulating the effects of the federal law, I assume that the first year of testing counted for the purposes of accountability was given in the 1998–1999 school year, so that four years of testing would have been conducted by the end of the time period employed in my data set. Hence, I can identify which schools might have been in the third year of improvement after the 2001–2002 school year and can also attempt to gauge the effects of the first federally mandated increase in proficiency targets on the distribution of sanctioned schools.

Of course, this exercise assumes that schools do not respond to the federal accountability system in manners that would affect student test performance. This is a major weakness of this type of projection because this is, of course, the purpose of enhanced school accountability. That said, these projections can be thought of as a first approximation of what might have happened. Moreover, 1998–1999's test scores were the first year of Florida's new accountability system, Governor Jeb Bush's A+ Plan for Education, which imposed potentially harsher sanctions and enhanced rewards based on student test performance. This makes Florida an ideal place to make projections about the potential effects of a national system of school accountability on the distribution of sanctions.

Although Florida's experience with an accountability system similar in nature to the federal system now being implemented makes Florida a desirable place to address this question along many dimensions, Florida is imperfect in other ways. For one, Florida districts rely less on federal education aid than do comparable school districts in much of the rest of the country. More important, schools in Florida districts tend to be more racially and ethnically heterogeneous than in the United States in general. However, patterns of test performance in Florida match those in other states, such as California, North Carolina, and Texas, suggesting that Florida data are usable for the present purposes. Because Florida districts tend to rely less on federal aid than do similar districts elsewhere in the country, one consequence of using Florida data for the present study is that the magnitudes of the forecast effects of the federal accountability system are likely to be understated. In Florida, under conservative assumptions, within three years many school districts would lose as much as 1% or more of their current expenditure as a result of federally mandated sanctions, and in other parts of the United States, where schools are more reliant on federal aid, similar school districts may lose as much as 2% of current expenditures. I should point out, however, that these are merely back-of-the-envelope projections, because most of the factors that would ultimately determine the incidence of the federally mandated sanctions have yet to be fully decided.

Using these Florida data, I simulate the effects of aggregation over time on the set of schools likely to be sanctioned under the NCLB Act. I estimate that time aggregation has very substantial implications for the rate of negative sanction among schools: The fraction of schools sanctioned under a system without time aggregation is approximately one-fifth higher than would be the fraction of schools sanctioned under a system with three-year time aggregation. Moreover, I estimate that the importance of time aggregation is particularly large for schools that are highly racially heterogeneous. Among schools where no racial or ethnic subgroup has a clear majority, the rate of predicted sanction is one-quarter higher without time aggregation as compared to the state of the world with three-year time aggregation. For schools without countably significant subgroups, this difference is only about 10%. The reason for these differences is that schools fail under the federal accountability system when they do not make adequate yearly progress in every category; small sample sizes exacerbate the noise problem highlighted by Kane and Staiger (2002). Over time, aggregation reduces this noise problem and allows for a more accurate picture of trends in student performance within a student category. The downside of longer time aggregation, however, is that schools that make pronounced year-to-year progress are punished by earlier low test scores for a longer period.

Aggregation Across Subjects Tested

A second aggregation issue involves aggregation across types of tests (or other performance indicators). Although mathematics and reading tests, for example, tend to trend together within a school, Figlio (2002a) shows that the correlation between changes from one year to the next in one test relative to another test is quite weak. Therefore, performance standards that require meeting particular criteria on multiple outputs may be overly difficult to attain (if the standards are set appropriately high) and those that require cross-cohort improvements in these criteria along multiple dimensions may merely reward schools with good luck and punish those with bad luck. This is clearly an issue for the federal accountability law, where annual yearly progress must be met in both reading and mathematics. However, in the federal law, only the proficiency target for schools moves over time, rather than the *change in* proficiency target, making this less of an issue in the federal case than it may be in individual state cases. Potential fixes to this problem include aggregating multiple outcomes into a single indicator (such as the approach described by Duncombe and Yinger [1998]) or evaluating schools on multiple criteria separately without requiring standards to be met (or improvements to be realized) in every year.

The introduction of science testing mandated by NCLB for 2007–2008 raises new questions for accountability. Unlike for reading and mathematics, there is no federal obligation to include science testing in accountability systems, nor is there an obligation to test students at every grade level. Rather, science tests must be administered only once per school level. How science tests are incorporated into an accountability system could make a significant difference in the treatment of science and schools.

The inclusion of science in an accountability system is likely to lead to an increased emphasis on science education in the classroom, with special attention paid to the specific skills and subject material explicitly examined. Therefore, the choice of the testing instrument and the alignment of this assessment to state science standards—not just with regard to content matter, but also with respect to methods of scientific inquiry—are crucial. If science test scores are included in accountability systems as an additional hurdle to overcome, this may exacerbate the issues already described above. On the other hand, if science tests are aggregated together with other examinations for the purpose of accountability, less emphasis may be placed on science than would otherwise occur, particularly in states that choose to minimally comply with the federal law and only assess science in three grades.

Aggregation Across Student Subgroups

A third aggregation issue to consider involves how multiple subgroups in a school should be considered. Disaggregating students into subgroups (such as along racial, ethnic, or socioeconomic lines, or based on prior performance levels) exacerbates the measurement error problems described in the preceding paragraphs and is required by the federal accountability law. On the other hand for normative reasons, one may wish to pay special attention to the performance of certain subgroups, and indeed, many equity and adequacy discussions (as well as the rationale for the name of the NCLB Act itself) have centered on the performance of minorities, low-income students, and low-achievers. The prescriptions for improvement of measurement described above are particularly relevant when students are divided up. Kane and Staiger (2002) demonstrate that measurement error problems are most acute for small schools; the same is true for smaller subgroups within schools.

States have the ability under NCLB to set the size that a subgroup must be before it gets counted in a school's accountability grade. There is a strong correlation between the minimum size of a subgroup and the likelihood that schools will fail to make adequate yearly progress. The rationale behind why a large minimum subgroup size translates into an increased likelihood of success under the federal accountability system is that any negative stochastic shock in any subgroup is sufficient to lead to a negative rating for a school. The higher the subgroup size threshold, the fewer opportunities there are for this negative shock to occur. With small subgroup size thresholds, more heterogeneous schools face greater risks of low accountability ratings than do more homogeneous schools. Cecilia Rouse and I have found that, among Florida schools rated by the state as A in 2004, schools with small numbers of measured subgroups were half as likely to receive negative federal accountability ratings as were schools with larger numbers of measured subgroups.

The Scope of Measurement

A related issue to the aggregation issues described above involves the scope of measurement—that is, which tests should be included in a school accountability system and which grades should be tested. The available evidence on school responses to accountability systems (see the preceding section) suggests that schools are highly responsive to the design of the accountability system and could reasonably be expected to tend to concentrate their energies on the subjects tested and the grades that have high-stakes examinations. This tendency to respond to incentives (or to *game the system*) indicates that school accountability systems should have broad coverage, in terms of students and subject matter, to minimize the potential for strategic behavior on the part of school administrators.

This push for increased scope of measurement is tempered by logistical and pedagogical considerations, however. Increasing the number of grades tested (although now federal law for grades 3–8 in the case of reading and mathematics) and increasing the number of subjects tested increases the coverage of testing and accountability and reduces incentives for game playing; but at the same time, it increases the costs to states for administering, grading, and designing state assessments. The design of assessments is particularly important. Although testing companies offer off-the-shelf examinations in many subjects and at all grade levels, these tests are not necessarily well aligned to state standards in the subjects, and if teachers and school administrators tend to teach to the test (as is evidenced by many authors, including Figlio and Rouse [2004] and Jacob [2002]) then a poorly aligned standardized examination used for accountability may actually undermine instruction in these added subject matter areas. Therefore the decision to increase the scope of measurement, although desirable from a coverage and strategic perspective, should be accompanied by considerable efforts to design new assessments that are instructionally supportive and that reflect state standards for content and methods.

Although the emphasis of NCLB and most existing state accountability systems is on student test performance, it is also possible to design accountability systems that incorporate or focus on different measures of school progress. Hanushek and Raymond (2002) construct a hierarchy of nontest indicators of school performance, ranked on the basis of their relevance and likely alignment to objective measures of school progress. For example, they argue that certain variables, such as the drop-out rate, graduation rate, number of students in advanced courses, percent of students passing end-of-course exams, retention rate, student mobility, and suspension rate are more closely related to student achievement for the purposes of accountability, whereas other variables, such as college entrance exam scores, course offerings, number of computers, number of noncredentialed teachers, parental satisfaction, school crime rate, principal mobility, or teacher mobility are only weakly related to student achievement. The goals of the accountability system should dictate which, if any, nontest-based measures are incorporated into school rankings.

Evaluating Schools Based on Value Added

The federal accountability law sets proficiency targets for schools and designates a school as successful if it brings a certain fraction of students (and eventually, all students) up to the minimum acceptable proficiency level. The normative argument behind this approach is clear: All students should be expected to achieve at least some reasonable level of academic success, and schools are delinquent in their duties if they do not bring students to at least this level. In this view, making progress toward proficiency but not achieving proficiency is not acceptable. But many economists and educators call instead for evaluating schools based on a measure of value added, where schools are rated on how much they improve individual students' performance from one year to the next. There are several approaches to measuring a school's value added. One approach is regression based, and involves using a previous year's test score as a control variable, whereas a special case of this approach is to consider schools' gain scores—the average difference in test scores from one year to the next. The gain score approach is equivalent to the more general value-added approach with the coefficient on the lagged test score constrained to equal one.

The rationale behind value-added approaches is that schools with large numbers of children prone to academic success would achieve proficiency goals—even in the federal program, at least in the early years—regardless of whether they are truly mediocre; and schools serving impoverished populations might fail to meet proficiency targets even though they may be excellent in bringing students to basic-proficiency levels from their very low starting points. Figlio and Page (2002), among others, show that levels-based methods of evaluating schools tend to lead to rankings of schools that are nearly completely unrelated to value-added-based methods. The implication of this finding is that many schools that are sanctioned under a levels-based system of school accountability may actually have quite high value added and should likely be rewarded rather than punished. The lack of concordance between state and federal accountability systems, also described by Kane and Staiger (2002), may also tend to undermine the credibility of one, or both, of the systems in the eyes of the general population.

Another benefit of value-added-type systems is that they are more difficult to game. There is reason to believe that schools and school districts do respond strategically to accountability pressures. The most studied response has to do with test exclusions and special-education placement—many studies (Cullen &

Reback, 2002; Figlio & Getzler, 2002; Jacob, 2002) show that schools tend to classify low achievers as learning disabled in the wake of accountability systems. It is debatable whether this is a strategic response to accountability pressure or a desired outcome of increased test-based scrutiny of student progress, but in either case, this result raises the possibility that the testing pool may be manipulated for the purposes of school accountability. In a related study, Figlio (2002b) shows that schools change their discipline patterns in an apparent response to accountability pressures, further suggesting that the test pool may change as a result of accountability systems. And Figlio and Winicki (2004) demonstrate that schools change their meals programs in an apparent attempt to raise performance on high-stakes examinations. The net message of this literature is that schools respond to incentives to raise performance in both academically supportive and other ways, and accountability systems should ideally take these responses into account in their design and implementation. It is considerably more difficult for these types of behavior to occur in value-added accountability systems than in levels-based accountability systems.

Despite their popularity among economists, there exists debate whether value-added measures of school performance are really to be preferred to raw levels of performance. The normative argument presented above, that schools and students should be held accountable to a given standard, regardless of background characteristics or starting values, is compelling to many. This argument has appeal because it does not prescribe different standards for different groups of students (or schools), but given the high correlation between test performance and background characteristics, especially in aggregate, evaluating schools solely on performance levels, with rewards and sanctions associated with said performance, does not seem fair to schools with large numbers of students predicted to perform poorly based on background characteristics. Although it may be the case that some of these correlations are explainable by factors within the control of the school system (e.g., different expectations for low-income and minority students than for higher-income and white students) it still defies reason to suggest that all of these differences are because of controllable factors, suggesting that equity concerns with evaluating schools solely on the basis of level test performance are valid.

There are, however, other reasons to believe that value-added measures of evaluating schools may not be a panacea. Gains in test scores within a cohort may reflect school contributions, but may also reflect unmeasured student and family characteristics. Student-background characteristics are often found to be correlated with gains in test scores as well as test-score levels, although this is not a universal finding, and it is not necessarily the case that schools that have high starting values also experience high gains. Still, these correlations may be because of differential school selection by families of different types, but they could also point to different family inputs, either independently of or jointly with the school's efforts. They may also indicate that schools serving high-socioeconomic-status families may be better able to find resources to boost instruction and outcomes in tested subjects. These correlations suggest that value-added measures of school productivity should be taken with a grain of salt. Moreover, the Kane and Staiger (2002) argument mentioned above on measurement error, and their finding that schools showing poor gains in one year tend to show high gains the next, suggests that measurement error may be a bigger problem in accurately assessing schools based on value added than based on absolute test-score levels. In sum, although value-added systems of measuring school performance are likely better than most systems, they are no silver bullet.

But even were a state to introduce a system of value added based school accountability, how exactly to quantify a school's value added is up to debate. However, at the very least, accounting for value added requires some control for circumstances such as student and family background characteristics. Typically, however, student background characteristics (or more specifically, the background characteristics available in administrative data) explain only a small portion of the observed variation in individual test scores. (Student information aggregated to the school level does a better job in explaining aggregate test scores, although this, too, is extremely incomplete.) Therefore, it seems important to go beyond observed background attributes when measuring value added.

Measures that aggregate changes in student test scores from year to year are arguably closer indicators of a school's contribution to student outcomes than are those that consider only a level test score. These measures range in complexity from the extremely simple and transparent (for example, simply averaging year-to-year test-score gains) to very complicated models that impose considerable structure on the relationships between inputs and outputs. All models of value added require annual (or at least extremely frequent) testing of students, using tests that can be vertically equated—that is, the test scores for one grade can be compared to those of the next, and tests administered uniformly across schools. Moreover, and even more fundamentally, the administrative data system must be able to reliably follow students from year to year.

As mentioned above, value-added measures of school performance, regardless of how they are measured, are still imperfect indicators of a school's contribution to student gains. Given the correlations often found in the data between student test-score gains and background characteristics, it may be that a further correction for student body attributes is warranted. However, this decision is not obvious and depends in part on what the accountability system seeks to measure.

The choice of measuring school performance using levels rather than value-added approaches has fiscal implications as well. In the out years, it will become progressively more difficult to meet accountability goals under NCLB than would occur under a value-added approach, because the ultimate goal is 100% proficiency under the levels-based federal law. Gaming along the lines mentioned above is likely more simple when using a levels-based system of school-performance measurement than when value-added measures are used, implying that levels-based systems may generate greater indirect fiscal costs for states and school districts than might value-added-based systems of school accountability.

Who Should Be in the Test Pool?

All measures of school performance based on standardized tests must also address the question of which students should be included in the test pool for the purposes of standards and accountability. This is inherently a normative and political question, rather than a scientific one, although it derives from a positive debate. Key decisions must be made with regard to whether mobile populations are counted in the accountability testing pool, as well as whether disabled students should be considered for school reporting purposes. The state of Florida, for example, has taken two very different tacks with regard to student mobility. In the first iteration of the A+ Plan for Education, Governor Jeb Bush's education reform enacted in 1999, school evaluations were based not only on stable students but also students who recently arrived in the school. But the next year, school grades were based only on students present in the school for the entire school year up to the testing date. These rule changes had substantial implications for schools and students, and the sets of schools identified as low quality or high quality changed considerably when only the more stable set of students were included. The federal accountability system limits students counted for a school's proficiency goals to those spending the full academic year in the evaluated school, but mobile students still count for district proficiency goals.

Although the federal accountability law mandates that disabled students be included in calculations of a school's adequate yearly progress, states also vary with respect to which disabled students should remain in the test pool for the purposes of constructing performance measures. Although Florida, for example, excludes all disabled students, even test-taking students, from the school-level aggregates used to measure productivity, Virginia goes to the other extreme, including all disabled students in the accountability pool, except for the rather small fraction who are explicitly excluded from testing in their Individualized Education Plans. The federal accountability system, in this regard, is much closer to the Virginia approach to counting disabled students than the Florida system, and in fact requires schools to meet proficiency goals for disabled students (except the most seriously disabled populations) as a listed subgroup.

These issues pose substantial tradeoffs to policymakers seeking to develop accountability and state aid systems. A policymaker deciding whether to include or exclude mobile students or disabled students, for example, may wish to exclude these students from the pool for the purposes of gauging school performance, out of a concern for fairness: Schools with large fractions of mobile and disabled students could argue, with validity, that they are being judged on factors well outside their control. On the other hand, excluding students on the basis of *classification* provides schools with the incentive to selectively reclassify or move students to look better against performance metrics. The case of special education is a margin that may be worked for these purposes. Cullen (2002) and Cullen and Figlio (1998) have demonstrated that schools tend to reclassify students along the special-education margin in response to *fiscal* incentives, and Garing (2002) demonstrates that schools' classifications of students are responsive to *parental* fiscal incentives as well. And as mentioned previously, Cullen and Reback (2002), Figlio and Getzler (2002) and Jacob (2002) show that special-education classification responds to *accountability* incentives, too. Although the federal accountability law will only present limited incentives to reclassify low-performing students as disabled to evade inclusion in the school's test pool, state accountability systems may still provide these incentives. And the federal accountability system, by naming disabled populations as a subgroup with its own proficiency goals, may actually present incentives for school districts to overclassify potentially high-performing students as disabled to yield improvements in the disabled group's proficiency levels. These incentives, of course, also have a different form of implications for school finance, as the increased classification of marginal students as special-education students increases total education costs for school districts and states.

The same types of tradeoffs are relevant with the decision to move from levels-based assessment of schools for accountability and school finance to a more value-added based assessment. The argument for value added is very much the same as the argument for excluding disabled and mobile students from the high-stakes (for schools) testing pool: Schools with certain populations that tend to fare worse on standardized examinations argue that their quality is masked by the poor outcomes of students starting at a low level. On the other hand, introducing value added (or even controlling for background factors) raises political concerns, both because it becomes more difficult for the lay public to interpret the assessment of schools; and (popular as an argument currently) explicitly controlling for different student composition is seen by some as making excuses for poor performance, or alternatively, holding different types of students (and hence, schools) to different standards. It is possible that including background characteristics as part of a cost correction, á la Duncombe and Yinger (1999), might be a politically palatable way to control in part for student attributes in an environment where it would be difficult to do so otherwise.

School accountability and school-finance systems may provide different incentives for schools to reclassify, move, or hold back students. Although school accountability systems tend to encourage schools to classify students as disabled, for example, school-finance systems may either encourage or discourage this practice, depending on the financial incentive structure. For example, some states compensate school districts for disabled students on the basis of predicted disability caseloads, rather than actual disability counts. In such a case, reclassifying a student as disabled to avoid that student being counted in an accountability system will be costly to the district that must now provide special services for the student without additional compensation from the state. On the other hand, other states provide compensation to districts that for marginal students exceeds the excess cost necessary to educate them if classified as disabled. In these states, school accountability incentives may exacerbate the incentives to overclassify students provided by the finance system. Similarly, moving students from school to school across the years may lead to increased costs to school districts, but school accountability systems that exclude mobile students may provide sufficient incentives to make these moves worthwhile for school districts.

Fiscal Implications of School Accountability

School accountability systems in general and the NCLB Act in particular have both direct and indirect implications for school finance. The direct effects of school accountability initiatives are straightforward. In the case of the federal system, for example, school districts that are sanctioned stand to lose a considerable fraction of their Federal Title I aid. Although Title I aid comprises only a small fraction of the total revenues received by school districts, in many cases these funds represent a nontrivial fraction of a school district's discretionary budget. In 2002, Title I grants per pupil averaged $198 (weighted by total district student membership) or $940 per low-income student. But these averages mask considerable heterogeneity in the magnitude of the grants. Nearly 10% of school districts, representing 11% of the student population in the United States, average more than $400 per student, and just over 2% of school districts, representing one-half of one percent of the student population, average more than $700 per student. One-third of school districts, representing 32% of the low-income student population, receive over $1,000 in Title I grants per disadvantaged student, and almost 5% of school districts, representing one-half of one percent of the low-income student population, receive over $1,500 per disadvantaged student.

School districts have considerable latitude in determining the use of Title I funds. Although these funds are dedicated to improving the academic outcomes of low-performing disadvantaged children, the mechanisms through which these funds are expendable are plentiful, and if sufficiently large numbers of targeted students are present in a school, the funds can be used for schoolwide programs. Of course, to the degree to which money is fungible, in essence these funds could almost be considered grants for schoolwide programs, and Gordon (2001) shows that states and localities adjust downward their funding of schools as Title I grants increase. This is directly relevant for the present chapter, as federal and state requirements for districts to use a large fraction (or, perhaps, all) of the Title I funds for noninstructional purposes (e.g., school choice-related transportation or privately provided supplemental services) may lead to significant reductions in instructional spending in affected districts.

Using the simulations of sanctions that I describe above, I have estimated which schools are most likely to be sanctioned under school accountability systems based on the provisions of NCLB under various scenarios. I find that the schools that are heavily minority and particularly low income are considerably more likely to be sanctioned than are Title I schools in general. This tendency is apparent regardless of whether I employ a relatively low or high level of performance standard for students to attain, but is particularly pronounced as the performance standard level increases. However, the inclusion of a subgroup performance requirement such as that included within the NCLB Act serves as an equalizer; when every measurable subgroup within a school is required to make adequate yearly progress, the relationship between probability that a school will be sanctioned and its racial, ethnic, and socioeconomic composition is weaker. These simulation results are described in detail in Figlio (2003).

There are both social and fiscal reasons to care about the demographic characteristics of the schools likely to be sanctioned under the federal accountability

Measuring School Performance: Promises and Pitfalls   131

laws. The social reasons stem from the basic purposes of the accountability law—to improve the quality of education for students trapped in chronically low-performing schools. Although accountability pressures may induce schools to improve, removing finances from these same schools (which may actually provide high value added even if overall proficiency levels remain low) could reduce school quality for the students most in need of school improvement or remediation. The benefits of providing a within-district exit option are weakened if district-level sanctions affect all schools in a district. From a fiscal perspective, low-socioeconomic-status schools could be expected to have a harder time raising the funds to replace lost federal aid, and are also precisely the schools that many states have reformed their school-finance systems to help. The withdrawal of federal aid from these districts may place state school-finance systems out of compliance with court orders in some states, requiring a change in the level or distribution of state aid. At the same time, if states changed their school-finance systems to compensate school districts for the loss of federal revenues resulting from sanctions, such a move would undermine the incentive effects of the introduction of a school accountability system.

Because the overwhelming incidence of the direct fiscal impacts of the federal accountability reforms will likely be borne by districts serving large numbers of low-income students, these reforms will likely work to offset some of the school-finance equalizations put forward by state legislatures or often ordered by state supreme courts. (Incidentally, this disequalization also counteracts one of the goals of the Federal Title I program itself, which provides additional Title I aid to schools in states that have more equalized school-finance systems.) As described above, the school districts with the highest fractions of minority and low income, precisely the districts typically supported in school-finance-equalization scenarios, are the schools projected to lose the most under the federal accountability rules. To the extent to which this triggers further equalization aid from the state, this will lead to increased fiscal responsibility from the state. (On the other hand, this state bail out would undermine the goals of the federal accountability system.) Alternatively, districts would either have less revenue with which to work, or would need to raise revenues to replace the lost Title I grants.

This highlights an interesting tension between school-equity and school-accountability objectives. One of the principal arguments for school accountability programs is, in essence, an equity argument: The schools that may be most in need of accountability pressure are the schools that face the least competition or parental oversight. Presumably, these schools are those that serve families that are either liquidity constrained or minority. Given that these types of schools generally constitute the bottom of the equity distribution, so to speak, accountability systems could lead to differential improvements in the performance of these schools, which may in turn narrow the gap between the richest and poorest schools, or members of society. On the other hand, it need not be this way: If schools serving low-socioeconomic-status students are better able to game the system because they lack parental oversight, accountability systems could lead to no change in the distribution of school performance, or perhaps even a widening of the gap between the haves and have-nots. Moreover, if school accountability systems base financial rewards and punishments on student test performance, then these gaps could grow as well. School accountability systems that base rewards and sanctions on the levels of test performance, such as those mandated by the NCLB Act, are particularly vulnerable to this (unless corrections are made, such as in California and South Carolina, for family background characteristics), although even accountability systems that base rewards and sanctions on value-added measures of student performance may be vulnerable if these measures of value added, or student test-score gains in general, are correlated with socioeconomic or other student background characteristics.

Besides the direct fiscal consequences put in place in both the federal accountability system and potentially as part of state accountability systems, there are a number of indirect fiscal consequences likely under the imposition of an accountability program. The largest potential indirect fiscal consequence involves special-education placement. As mentioned earlier in this chapter, schools have the apparent tendency to attempt to improve their state-assigned grade or classification by taking their poorest performing students out of the testing pool by classifying them into the special-education categories exempt from taking the tests, or by refraining from classifying better-performing students into the special-education categories exempt from taking the tests (Cullen & Reback, 2002; Figlio & Getzler, 2002; Jacob, 2002). Student classification as disabled, even in the most moderate disability categories, introduces large incremental costs to school districts and states, as the Individuals with Disabilities Education Act requires that all disabled students receive special services and an educational environment appropriate for their educational needs. State school-finance systems increase state payments to school districts by an average of 40% when classifying a student as learning disabled. As Cullen and Figlio (1998) point out, in some states this incremental revenue exceeds the likely cost of reclassifying a student and in other states it may not. In most states, the additional costs would be shared (to different degrees, depending on the system, as depending on the degree to which reclassification truly generates substantial marginal costs to the school district) between the state and the school district. But in a growing number of states, the state allocation to districts for special-education finance is based not on actual special-education counts but rather on predicted special-education counts; in these states, the full fiscal burden of reclassification is borne by the school district, implying that school districts in these states have mixed incentives to reclassify students as disabled in response to accountability systems.

As Jacob (2002) shows, schools have the same incentives to retain low-performing students in-grade as they do to reclassify students as disabled (except in the terminal grades at a given school; then, they have an incentive under the federal accountability system at least to promote low-performing students to the next grade.) Therefore, there are potential fiscal consequences associated with student grade retention as well. And unlike the case of special-education placement, where in some states school districts would bear the full fiscal cost of reclassifying a student as disabled in response to accountability pressures, in the case of student retentions in-grade states always bear part of the costs of school district responses to the accountability system.

The historical experience with *fiscal* accountability suggests that input prices may change as well with increased *academic performance* accountability. As one example, Figlio and Rueben (2001) show that one consequence of the so-called tax revolt of the late 1970s and 1980s was that many higher-quality potential teachers selected out of the teaching force and tended to be replaced by lower-quality teachers (where quality is measured by potential teachers' test scores.) Interestingly, they find that much of this response was not because of actual changes in resources, but rather, apparently, to changes in perceptions. Early evidence from Florida's experience with school accountability suggests that teachers, when they perceive that school grading is arbitrary or biased against their schools, are likely to contemplate leaving their schools. This may be one of the reasons why Downes and Figlio (1998) and Figlio (1997) find evidence of much larger effects of tax limits than would be predicted by looking at the changes in actual school revenues and spending. These pieces of evidence indicate that teacher input costs may increase with school accountability, and that the increases may be differentially borne by low socioeconomic-status school districts, precisely the districts that already face inflated teacher costs for any given unit of teacher quality. Although this last point is speculative, it does suggest that hasty design of a school accountability system or performance standards embedded within a state aid system might have unintended consequences that work at cross purposes to the goals of the accountability system.

Conclusion

The accountability movement is clearly affecting the ways in which American schools in the 21st century are doing business. The available evidence suggests that test scores seem to be rising as a direct result of the increased focus on these tests, but the available evidence also indicates that some of these apparent test-score gains may be because of other factors besides increased focus and efficiency in education. These two points are not conflicting; rather, they highlight the importance of design issues in the development and implementation of accountability systems.

This chapter highlights an additional issue with regard to accountability systems. The fiscal implications for schools and school districts—both direct and indirect—may have significant implications for school finance. Changing costs of education, such as input prices and increased special-education placements, may have adequacy implications for states in their school-finance systems. And the differential impacts of these systems across a wide range of aspects may create new equity issues or exacerbate existing uncorrected inequities. The design of school accountability and school-finance systems are likely to be indelibly intertwined.

References

Carnoy, M., & Loeb, S. (2001). Does external accountability affect student outcomes? *Educational evaluation and policy analysis.*

Cullen, J. (in press). Impact of fiscal incentives on student disability rates. *Journal of Public Economics.*

Cullen, J., & Figlio, D. (1998). *How effective are intergovernmental incentives?* (Working paper). Gainesville: University of Florida.

Cullen, J., & Reback, R. (2002). *Tinkering toward accolades: School gaming under a performance accountability system.* (Working paper). Ann Arbor: University of Michigan.

Deere, D., & Strayer, W. (2002). *Putting schools to the test: School accountability, incentives, and behavior* (working paper). College Station; Texas A&M University.

Downes, T., & Figlio, D. (1998). *School finance reforms, tax limits, and student performance: Do reforms level up or dumb down?* (Working paper). Boston, MA: Tufts University.

Duncombe, W., & Yinger, J. (1999). Performance standards and education cost indices: You can't have one without the other. In H. Ladd, Chalk, R., & Hanses, J. (Eds.) *Equity and adequacy in education finance: Issues and perspectives,* Washington, D.C.: National Academy Press, 260–297.

Figlio, D. (1997). Did the 'tax revolt' reduce school performance? *Journal of Public Economics,* 245–269.

Figlio, D. (2002a). Aggregation and accountability. In C. Finn, (Ed.) *No child left behind: What will it take?* Washington, D.C.: Thomas B. Fordham Foundation.

Figlio, D. (2002b). *Testing, crime and punishment.* (Working paper). Gainesville: University of Florida.

Figlio, D. (2003). Fiscal implications of school accountability initiatives. *Tax policy and the economy.* (17).

Figlio, D., & Getzler, L. (2002). *Accountability, ability and disability: Gaming the system?* (Working paper). Cambridge, MA: National Bureau of Economic Research.

Figlio, D., & Page, M. (2003). Can school choice and school accountability successfully coexist? In C. Hoxby (Ed.) *Economic analysis of school choice,* University of Chicago Press.

Figlio, D., & Rouse, C. (2004). *Do accountability and voucher threats improve low-performing schools?* (Working paper). Cambridge, MA: National Bureau of Economic Research.

Figlio, D., & Rueben, K. (2001). Tax limits and the qualifications of new teachers. *Journal of Public Economics,* 49–71.

Figlio, D., & Winicki, J. (forthcoming). Food for thought? The effects of school accountability plans on school nutrition. *Journal of Public Economics.*

Gordon, N, (2004). Do federal funds boost school spending? Evidence from Title I. *Journal of Public Econonics,* 88(9–10), 1771–1792.

Hanushek, E., & Raymond, M. (2002). *Improving educational quality: How best to evaluate our schools.* (Working paper). Stanford, CA: Hoover Institution.

Hanushek, E. & Raymond, M. (2004).Does school accountability lead to improved student performance? *Journal of Policy Analysis and Management.*

Jacob, B. (2002). *Accountability, incentives and behavior: The impact of high-stakes testing in the Chicago public schools.* (Working paper 8968). Cambridge, MA: National Bureau of Economic Research.

Kane, T., & Staiger, D. (2002). *Improving school accountability measures.* (Working paper). Los Angeles, CA: University of California Los Angeles.

Knapp, C. G. (2003). *Essays on the Personal Responsibility and Work Opportunity Reconciliation Act and Disabled Children.* (PhD dissertation). Gainsville: University of Florida.

7

Teacher Accountability Measures and Links to Learning

Anthony T. Milanowski,
Steven M. Kimball, and Allan Odden

Introduction

The level of educational productivity, like other types of productivity, depends on how well inputs are turned into outputs by the behaviors or processes of individuals and organizations. Teacher accountability can also be conceptualized in these terms. Teachers and schools can be held accountable for inputs such as the use of funds as budgeted or for hiring only licensed teachers, for practices or behaviors such as adopting specified curricula or maintaining an orderly classroom, or for outputs such as student learning or outcomes such as student achievement on state or district tests. Now, teacher accountability is mostly thought of in terms of measuring student achievement using test scores. Although this thinking is in part a healthy reaction against previous overemphasis on inputs, test-based measures of student achievement have some disadvantages as the sole basis for teacher accountability systems. On the technical side, these include limitations on any test's representation of the subject domain (e.g. by having too few or no questions on some important material), misalignment of tests and curricula, imprecision of average school, or classroom scores because of small class or school sizes, the potential for score inflation, and narrowing of the curriculum. (See Koretz, 2002, for more on these issues.) In addition, many teachers teach in subjects for which only teacher-made tests are available to measure learning, and in urban districts, high student mobility results in many students having more than one teacher or school during any one year. These problems make it difficult to attribute achievement to a specific teacher or school.

Besides these technical difficulties, outcome-based accountability provides little guidance to teachers or schools about how to improve performance. Many teachers and schools do not seem to have the ability to take test results and infer what changes in teaching processes are needed to improve performance. As Fuhrman (2003) concludes from her review of research on accountability systems, they do little to mobilize capacity to improve the outcomes for which teachers and schools are held accountable. Another potential problem area is teacher acceptance. Although test-based accountability systems get teachers' attention, many teachers continue to feel that student achievement is not totally within their control (Kelley, Heneman, & Milanowski, 2001). Add to this a limited understanding of how complex accountability measures are calculated and perceptions that the tests are not aligned with the curriculum taught, and it is easy to see why teachers often have concerns about the fairness of test-based accountability. Even in systems that hold schools—rather than individual teachers—accountable for test performance, fairness concerns can reduce acceptance and lower the motivational potential of incentives (Kelley and Milanowski, 2001). One of the few recent attempts to hold individual teachers accountable for the performance of their own students, in Colonial, Pennsylvania, caused strong resistance and was quickly dropped.

Instead of—or perhaps in addition to—holding teachers directly accountable for student achievement, it might make sense to hold them accountable for teaching behaviors or competencies that are causally related to student achievement. If we believe that quality of instruction makes a difference, it would be sensible to pay more to those teachers who deliver better-quality instruction. But this requires an accurate and reliable system of measuring instructional behavior; and evidence that the behavior we are holding teachers accountable for, and perhaps rewarding, is causally related to student learning.

One existing form of behavior-based accountability is teacher performance evaluation. Accountability has traditionally been a major purpose of teacher evaluation, and some states (e.g. Alabama, Nevada, Tennessee, and Texas) have state evaluation systems and/or legal requirements aimed at ensuring that districts hold teachers accountable for behaviors. However, few take very seriously teacher evaluation systems as accountability measures because of perceived poor validity (Peterson, 2000). There has been little evidence that teacher evaluation ratings are related to student achievement. In their classic paper, Medley and Coker (1987) reviewed studies relating teacher ratings and student achievement from the 1950s to the 1970s, concluding that most correlations were near zero. Their own study found correlations between principal performance ratings and learning gains of 0.10 to 0.23. More recently, Fritsche, Weerasinghe, and Babu (2003) reported correlations between total teacher evaluation scores and a measure of adjusted test score gains of 0.17 and 0.24 in the Dallas school district. Although these studies showed that there are some positive relationships, the magnitudes are relatively small.

Standards-Based Teacher Evaluation Systems

Recent developments in teacher evaluation hold out some hope that evaluation systems could focus on teacher behaviors that affect student learning. Developers of teacher evaluation systems have attempted to reflect the more complex conception of teaching and learning that has been the impetus for performance-based assessment for teacher licensing and certification (Porter, Youngs, & Odden, 2001), to go beyond ensuring minimally effective behavior (Danielson, 1996), and to provide more assistance to teachers in improving their practice (Stronge, 1997). One approach that has emerged is known as standards-based evaluation. Standards-based teacher evaluation is both analogous to standards for students and is its logical complement. The standards provide a comprehensive description of desired teacher performance, a competency model that describes what teachers should know and be able to do to facilitate student achievement.

Instead of comparing teachers to one another, these systems compare multiple forms of evidence on teacher performance to a set of detailed rating scales based on the standards that describe several levels of teacher performance. These rating scales, typically called rubrics, provide guidance to evaluators in making judgments, lessen subjectivity, and provide a common criterion reference for ratings. The standards and rubrics also provide guidance to teachers on what behaviors and skills are expected. Standards-based evaluation systems typically require more extensive collection of evidence about teachers' practices, including frequent observations of classroom behavior, and a review of artifacts such as lesson plans and samples of student work. They also require more extensive rater training to develop a common framework for applying the standards. Danielson and McGreal (2000) described a comprehensive approach to standards-based evaluation. Writings by Ellett, with and without his colleagues Annunziata and Schiavone (1997, 2002), are other sources of information about the design of standards-based evaluation.

The use of relatively detailed rating scales (rubrics), multiple sources of evidence (observations and artifacts), and rater training should provide more reliable and valid assessment of teacher behavior than the relatively unsystematic evaluation practices used in many districts (sometimes characterized as drive-by evaluation). Well-designed standards-based systems should also provide better signals for teachers seeking to improve their performance, because of the comprehensive coverage of the standards and the detail in the rubrics. These systems have the potential, and many have an explicit goal, to help improve teacher capacity in schools operating under the kinds of outcome-based accountability systems Fuhrman (2003) discussed. By providing a model of effective teacher behaviors and diagnostic tools to assess current practice, standards-based teacher evaluations could be one powerful way to influence instruction, which is likely to be the strongest means under a school's control to pursue the end of higher student achievement.

These evaluation systems could also contribute to a greater sense of internal accountability in the form of a shared conception of good teaching. The standards provide a clear set of expectations and a vocabulary to discuss instruction. To the extent that recruitment, selection, clinical supervision, compensation, and professional development programs, along with evaluation, are aligned with this competency model (Heneman & Milanowski, 2004), the organization communicates a normative vision of quality instruction that could counteract the fragmentation of teachers' personal notions of accountability found by Abelmann et. al (1999).

All of this presupposes, however, that there is some substantial relationship between standards-based evaluation ratings and important outcomes such as student achievement. For many, student achievement is still the ultimate accountability criterion. The public as well as the policy community want to see evidence that teachers' evaluation ratings are related to the performance of their students to continue to support these more expensive evaluation systems and any incentives such as pay for performance that might be attached to them.

This chapter describes evidence for a relationship between standards-based teacher evaluation ratings and student achievement collected from four sites. In each site, we have two years of evaluation and student achievement data and have been conducting case study research at three of the four for three or more years. After describing the standard-based evaluation systems at these sites, we summarize results on the relationship between teacher evaluation ratings and student achievement, briefly review some of our research on teachers' reactions to these systems, discuss the implications of this research for using teacher evaluation systems for accountability and teacher rewards, and make suggestions for improving teacher evaluation systems as accountability systems.

Sites and Systems

We conducted empirical work in four sites: Cincinnati (Ohio), the Vaughn Charter School in Los Angeles, Washoe County (Reno, Nevada), and Coventry (Rhode Island). In the first three sites, we collected data on system design and implementation and teacher reactions over multiple years, as well as data on evaluation ratings and student achievement. In Coventry, we collected only data on test scores and evaluation ratings. The sites were chosen because they are pioneers in implementing standards-based evaluation and represent a contrast in use, with two sites using or originally intending to use the evaluation results for pay differentiation (Cincinnati and Vaughn), while the other two (Coventry and Washoe) using the results for more traditional accountability and developmental purposes. A brief overview of the sites and their teacher evaluation systems is provided below and summarized in Figure 7.1.

Teacher Accountability Measures and Links to Learning 141

Figure 7.1. Summary of District Characteristics and Evaluation Procedures

District	Cincinnati	Washoe	Coventry	Vaughn
Location	Midwest, urban	Southwest, urban-suburban-rural	Northeast, suburban	Southwest, urban
Students	40,000	60,000	6,000	1,200
Race/ethnicity	Predominantly African American	Majority white, large Hispanic minority	Predominantly white	Predominantly Hispanic
Family income	Low SES	Mixed SES	High SES	Low SES
Teachers	2,500	3,300	475	40 pre-K through 5
Schools	81	88	9	1 Charter School
Year First Implemented	2000–2001	2000–2001	1998–1999	2000–2001
Standards	Streamlined version of Danielson Framework; 4 domains, 16 standards	Minor modifications to Danielson Framework; 4 domains, 23 components, 68 elements	Slightly streamlined version of Danielson Framework; 3 domains, 18 components, 56 elements	2 domains, modeled on Danielson Framework; 12 other content-specific domains developed locally
Procedures	Comprehensive evaluation on all domains for new teachers and some veterans. All others undergo less rigorous annual evaluation on one domain	Nontenured teachers evaluated on all domains/elements. Tenured evaluated on 1 domain (minor) or 2 domains (major) over 3-year cycle	Nontenured teachers evaluated on subset of standards each year for 3 years. Tenured evaluated on all domains every 2, 3, or 4 years depending on prior rating level	All teachers evaluated annually, with two ratings per year on selected domains. All rated on 5 core domains and selected content-relevant domains
Evaluators	Teacher evaluators, principals and assistant principals	Principals and assistant principals	Principals and department heads	Self, peer, and assistant principals

Cincinnati Public Schools

Cincinnati Public Schools (CPS) is a large urban district with 81 schools and programs enrolling about 40,000 students and employing over 2,500 teachers. It has low student achievement relative to surrounding suburban districts and a high proportion of African-American students and students eligible for free or reduced-price lunch. A state accountability program and public expectations put pressure on the district to raise average levels of student test scores. (In 1999, the district developed a new teacher evaluation system based on the Framework for Teaching, [Danielson, 1996]). The Framework for Teaching is a description of teaching practice consisting of 22 components within four domains: planning and preparation, creating an environment for learning, teaching for learning, and professionalism. Each component (e.g. selecting instructional goals, communicating with families) is further subdivided into elements describing specific behaviors or competencies. Four levels of competence are defined for each element. In adapting the framework, CPS reduced the number of components from 22 to 16, renamed them standards, and modified some of the level descriptions for the elements. The system called for teachers to receive comprehensive evaluations in their first and third years, and every fifth year thereafter. The comprehensive evaluation involved an assessment by a teacher from outside the school as well as a building administrator. In interim years, teachers were to receive a less rigorous assessment from a building administrator (principal or assistant principal). The evaluation system was initially designed to serve as the basis for a performance pay plan as well as for formative and professional development purposes. For the period under study, however, the evaluation system has not been used for pay purposes, and has been applied primarily to less experienced teachers.

In Cincinnati, teachers undergoing the comprehensive evaluation received a score on each of the four domains based on scores on the dimensions (standards) within the domains. For each standard, raters applied a four-level rating scale or rubric defining unsatisfactory, basic, proficient, and distinguished performance. For two domains (environment for learning and teaching for learning) teacher performance was evaluated based on six classroom observations. Four of these were made by a teacher evaluator from outside the school who had subject-matter and grade-level expertise similar to that of the teacher being evaluated. Building administrators (principals and assistant principals) did the other two observations. Based on summaries of the six observations, teacher evaluators made a final summative rating on each of the standards in these domains. Administrators, based on a portfolio including lesson and unit plans, attendance records, student work, family contact logs, and documentation of professional development activities, rated teachers on the standards in the planning and professionalism domains. Standard-level scores were then aggregated to a domain level score for each of the four domains using tables provided by the district.

Coventry, Rhode Island

The Coventry (Rhode Island) School District serves around 6,000 students in nine schools. The student population is 97% white, with 13% of students eligible for free or reduced-price lunch, according to 2003 data. There is a wide range of student achievement in the district, with three schools classified as high performing on the state report card, three others classified as moderate performers and two identified as in need of improvement and making insufficient progress. The district is growing rapidly and recently opened a new middle school.

The teacher evaluation system in Coventry is also based on Danielson's Framework for Teaching. The four domains and associated rubrics are very similar to those developed by Danielson. In Coventry, all the domains are used each time teachers are evaluated. Evaluations consist of teacher observations, preobservation and postobservation conferences, dialogue with the teacher, and a review of a portfolio put together by the teacher and containing artifacts relevant to each teacher's performance. Nontenured teachers are observed by the principal or department head at least twice annually, while tenured teachers are observed by the principal at least once. Teachers are classified as unsatisfactory, basic, proficient, or distinguished based on their performance as compared to the district's evaluation rubrics. The most frequently observed performance level across all standards becomes the teacher's overall performance rating. The performance rating in turn determines the timing of subsequent evaluations. Tenured teachers previously classified as basic are evaluated every two years, while those previously classified as proficient are evaluated every three years, and those previously classified as distinguished are evaluated every four years. Tenured teachers classified as unsatisfactory are assigned a mentor and evaluated the next year. Nontenured teachers are evaluated annually, based on at least two observations, for their first three years, but only limited subsets of key instructional standards are used during the first and second year, to ease teachers into the system. Evaluations do not affect teachers' pay in Coventry.

Vaughn Charter School

Vaughn Next Century Learning Center is a public charter school in San Fernando, California. Previously a public school in the Los Angeles Unified School District, the school converted to charter status in July 1993. From 1999 to 2002, the school served about 1,200 students in pre-K through grade 5. The student population was 94% Hispanic, and most students were not considered to be English proficient. Almost all students were eligible for free or reduced-price lunch. Vaughn had more than 70 staff, of which about 40 teach grades 1–5. Vaughn began developing its evaluation system during the 1997–1998 school year, and implemented it for volunteers in the 1998–1999 school year. The school began to use the system for all teachers the next year. Teachers are evaluated two times per year, and the evaluation results are used as the basis for a pay for performance system, as well as for developmental and accountability purposes.

At Vaughn, the teacher evaluation system included 13 domains: lesson planning and classroom management, plus subject-specific domains covering literacy, language development, mathematics, special education, history and social science, science, instruction in primary language for English learners, arts, technology, physical education, and teaming. Vaughn teachers are assessed using a four-level rating scale with unsatisfactory, basic, proficient, and distinguished levels. An administrator, a peer, and the individual teacher rate on the applicable domains based on classroom observations, discussions, and review of artifacts. Because not all the domains apply to all teachers, some are rated only on a subset of the domains, although all are rated on five core domains: lesson planning, classroom management, literacy, language development, and mathematics. Observations are conducted as many times as is necessary over a two-week period each semester. The average for the two semesters is used as the evaluation score for each domain. Along with the use of subject-specific domains, another feature of the Vaughn system that differs from those of the other three sites is the inclusion of teachers' self evaluation in the final ratings.

Washoe County School District

Washoe County School District is a large western district that includes the cities of Reno and Sparks, Nevada, and surrounding communities. There are 88 schools, over 60,000 students, and about 3,300 teachers in the district. After a two-year field test, the district began using a standards-based teacher evaluation system adapted from Danielson's Framework for Teaching in 2000. According to state law, teachers must undergo a performance evaluation each year. Teachers are evaluated annually in Washoe County on different performance domains depending on their stage in the evaluation cycle that begins in their first year. Teachers in their first and second year of probation (pretenure) are evaluated on all four performance domains. Postprobationary teachers are evaluated on one or two domains, depending on whether they are in a minor or major evaluation year. The evaluation process was designed to provide a common framework for evaluation discussions, promote teacher performance improvement through formative feedback, and encourage teachers to regularly reflect on their practice. Evaluation decisions have no direct bearing on salary, but they do serve as the basis for summative evaluation decisions, such as contract renewal and tenure.

In Washoe, the four Framework domains of planning and preparation, classroom environment, instruction, and professional responsibilities are the basis for the system. Each domain contains multiple elements that are rated by principals or assistant principals, using rubrics closely based on those in Danielson's 1996 book. Evidence may include a teacher self-assessment, a preobservation data sheet (lesson plan), classroom and nonclassroom observations with preobservation and postobservation conferences, instructional artifacts (e.g., assignments and student work), a reflection form, a three-week unit plan, and logs of professional activities and parent contacts. The system provides for three types of evaluation: probationary, postprobationary major, and postprobationary minor. Teachers new to the district are considered probationary and are evaluated on all four of the performance domains, where they must meet at least level 1 (target for growth) scores on all 68 elements. Probationary teachers are observed at least nine times during the year. Teachers in postprobationary status undergo a major evaluation on two performance domains. They are formally observed three times over the course of the year. In the next two years, they receive minor evaluations, focusing on one domain and involving at least one observation during the year. Over the course of the three-year major-minor cycle, teachers are evaluated on all four domains, but most are not evaluated on all domains each year. If a teacher is not evaluated on the instruction domain, however, he or she is evaluated using a supplemental evaluation form with four dimensions consisting of selected components and elements from the planning and preparation and instruction domains. Evaluators rate these dimensions using four performance designations (i.e., unsatisfactory, target for growth, proficient, and area of strength).[1]

Are Standards-Based Evaluations Related to Student Achievement?

Analytic Approach

To assess the relationship between the ratings teachers received under these standards-based evaluation systems and student achievement, we did two kinds of analyses. First, we derived an estimate of the classroom average achievement of the students of each teacher in the evaluation year using the following two level hierarchical linear model:

$$\text{Current year test score}_{ij} = \beta_{0j} + \beta_{1j} \text{prior year test score}_i$$
$$+ \beta_{2j} X_{2,ij} + \ldots + \beta_{nj} X_{n,ij} + R_{ij}$$

where $X_{2,ij} \ldots X_{n,ij}$ represent various student characteristics such as gender, ethnicity, or free and reduced-price lunch status for the ith student in the classroom of the jth teacher. (Different control variables were available and appropriate at each site.) All level 1 predictors were grand-mean centered. The level 2 model was:

$$\beta_{0j} = \gamma_{00} + U_{0j}$$

At level two, the U_{0j} represented the teacher (classroom)-specific differences from the average of the group intercepts. The slopes for all level 1 variables were treated as fixed. From this model, the empirical Bayes (*EB*) intercept residuals[2] were obtained. These residuals were taken as the measure of the average student performance relevant to each teacher. Given the grand mean centering, the *EB* intercept residuals represent the difference for the average student: average in prior-year test score and other characteristics at level 1. We then correlated the *EB* residuals with the teachers' evaluation ratings to provide a measure of the relationship between evaluation ratings and student achievement that was comparable across sites and with results reported by other researchers on teacher evaluation. Correlations are combined across grades to obtain a summary estimate of the relationship between evaluation scores and student achievement. Each grade

---

1 Further information about these sites can be found on our project's Web site, www.wcer.wisc.edu/cpre.

2 Empirical Bayes intercept residuals are the deviations of the intercepts representing the average achievement of a teacher's students from the average for all teachers. The *EB* residual is a weighted average of the classroom specific intercept and the average intercept, with weights reflecting the reliability of each. These reliabilities are a function of the variance within and between classrooms and the number of students. See Snijders & Bosker (1999, pp. 58–60).

within a subject is treated as a separate study and the correlations combined using the meta-analysis formulas for a random effects treatment.[3] Upper and lower bounds for the 95% confidence intervals were also calculated.

We also wanted to get an estimate of the effect of a change in a teacher's evaluated performance on student achievement. To do so, we also estimated models that included evaluation the teacher's rating as a level two predictor of the random intercepts, namely:

$$\beta_{ij} = \gamma_{01} \text{ evaluation score}_j + U_{0j}$$

The level 1 model remained as above. The coefficient for evaluation score estimates the effect in test score points of variations in rated teacher performance. We also estimated the effect, controlling for teacher experience, using the level 2 model:

$$\beta_{0j} = \gamma_{00} + \gamma_{01} \text{ evaluation score}_j + \gamma_{02} \text{ experience}_j + U_{0j}$$

In both variations, the slopes for all level 1 variables were again treated as fixed. (See Rowen, Correnti, & Miller, 2002, for more on this method of analyzing teacher effects.)

Test Scores

Student achievement was operationalized in terms of student test scores on reading, mathematics, and other tests at some sites. Scores on a variety of tests were used, based on data available. In most cases, the tests used closed-ended-response formats, but in some cases also included open-response items. The value-added models required test scores for a teacher's students in the year the teacher was evaluated and in the prior year. Because none of the sites tested in all grades, we were limited in the number of teachers for whom student achievement could be related to evaluation ratings. We were also limited to analyzing data from students and teachers in the elementary grades in all sites except Cincinnati. In Cincinnati, scores on a mixture of state and district criterion-referenced tests, as well as the TerraNova test, were available for grades 3–8. In Coventry, scores on the Stanford 9 test and the New Standards tests were available for grades 2, 3, 4, and 6. At Vaughn, the Stanford 9 scores were available for grades 2–5. In Washoe, state and district criterion-referenced test scores, and scores on the TerraNova test, were available for grades 3, 4, and 5 for 2001–2002, and 4, 5, and 6 for 2002–2003. The tests used for each site and grade are listed in the Appendix to this chapter. These data were provided by the districts or the test publishers.

---

3 An r to z transformation was done and a weighted average of the z's was calculated with the inverse of the variances as weights. Standard errors were calculated for this average, and 95% confidence intervals. These values were then transformed back into correlation coefficients. See Shadish & Haddock (1994) for a description of the details of these calculations.

It should be noted that at three of the four sites, a substantial proportion of students enrolled in each grade could not be included in the analyses. The most common reason for losing students from the analyses was missing scores on the current or prior year tests. Some students also were lost because we were unable to match them with teachers, even if test scores for both years were available. This appears mostly to be because of clerical errors in the student data system. In addition, a relatively small number of students was excluded from the analyses because their current or prior year scores were extreme outliers. Almost one-third of the students on the roster in Cincinnati and Coventry were lost, about a quarter at Vaughn, and around half at Washoe. It was particularly difficult to link Washoe student records across time and to link students with teachers, because of limitations in the district's information systems.

Teacher Evaluation Ratings

For all sites, the teacher evaluation scores were obtained from the district or school. For Cincinnati, scores on the four domains were added to yield a composite evaluation score, which was taken as an overall indicator of teacher performance. Because of the design of the Cincinnati system, which does not require a comprehensive evaluation every year, evaluation scores were not available for all teachers. Although scores for over 300 teachers were available in each year, much smaller numbers of teachers were included in the analyses, because most teachers taught subjects or grades for which no state or district standardized tests were given. This restricted our sample to 180 for 2001–2002 and 131 for 2002–2003. At Coventry, only the overall cross-domain ratings were available, and almost all teachers were rated either proficient or distinguished. Concentrating on these teachers, we were able to include 68 or 70 teachers in the analysis. At Vaughn, we averaged the ratings on the five core domains of planning, classroom management, literacy instruction, mathematics instruction, and language arts instruction. Although all teachers are evaluated on these domains each year, some teachers did not teach tested grades and subjects. We were able to include 34 teachers evaluated in 2000–2001 and 35 evaluated in 2001–2002 in our analyses. At Washoe, all teachers are not evaluated on all four domains each year, although if a teacher is not evaluated on the instruction domain, they are evaluated using a supplemental evaluation form with four dimensions consisting of selected elements from the planning and preparation and instruction domains. Because these dimension ratings were available for almost all teachers, they were used as the measure of teacher performance in our analyses. The scores on the four performance dimensions were averaged to derive a single indicator of teacher performance. Given the testing data we had available, we were able to include 330 teachers evaluated in 2001–2002 and 397 teachers evaluated in 2002–2003 in our analyses.

More detailed descriptions of our data and analyses can be found in papers by Milanowski, Kimball, and White (2004); Milanowski (2004); White (2004); Gallagher (2004, in press); Milanowski, (2004, in press); and Kimball, White, Milanowski, and Borman (2004, in press).

Summary of Results

Figure 7.2 summarizes the results from two years of analyses of the teacher evaluation score-student achievement relationships at the four sites, in the form of average correlations between evaluation scores and empirical Bayes intercept residuals that represent the average relative level of measured student achievement in the classroom, controlling for prior learning and student characteristics.

Figure 7.2. Average Correlations Between Teacher Evaluation Ratings and Estimates of Average Student Achievement Within Classrooms for Three Research Sites

Site	*Tested Subject*		
	Reading	Math	Other
Cincinnati			
01–02	0.48	0.41	0.26 (Science)
02–03	0.28	0.34	−0.02* (Science)
Coventry			
All Years Combined	0.24	0.03*	—
Vaughn			
00–01	—	—	0.36 (Reading, Math, & Language Arts Average)
01–02	0.58	0.42	0.42 (Language Arts)
Washoe			
01–02	0.21	0.19	—
02–03	0.25	0.24	—
* Confidence interval includes 0.			

These correlations show that ratings from standards-based teacher evaluation systems can have a substantial relationship with measures of the student achievement of the teachers' students. However, the size of the relationship varied across research sites, and across academic subjects. The correlations also vary substantially by grade (not shown). Some of this variation is likely attributable to differences in programs across sites and across evaluators for different grade levels or subjects (especially in Cincinnati, where evaluators from outside each school were assigned to evaluate specific teachers based on their grade level and subject experience). Measurement error in the tests of student achievement and the evaluation scores may also explain some of the variability, and a considerable portion could be because of sampling error, because the number of teachers included in each site, subject, and grade analysis was not that large. The largest samples were found in Washoe, where data for about 120 teachers-per-grade

Teacher Accountability Measures and Links to Learning   149

were available, but samples in Cincinnati and Vaughn were much smaller, at 20–40 per-grade and subject.[4]

To show the potential importance of having a more highly rated teacher, we also calculated the average estimated change in average classroom student achievement associated with a one-level change in teacher evaluation score. Specifically, we calculated the number of standard deviations in test scores that were associated with a change in teacher ratings of one overall level (i.e. from basic to proficient or proficient to distinguished on all domains). Figure 7.3 presents these results.

Figure 7.3. Effect of a One Level Change in Teacher Evaluation Score on Student Achievement, (in Standard Deviation Units) Averaged Across Grades

	Tested Subject		
Site	Reading	Math	Other
Cincinnati			
01–02	0.26	0.23	0.09 (Science)
02–03	0.14	0.18	–0.01 (Science)
Coventry			
All Years Combined	0.13	0.01	—
Vaughn*			
01–02	0.24	0.36	0.27 (Language Arts)
Washoe			
01–02	0.12	0.12	—
02–03	0.14	0.19	—
* Information for 00–01 school year not available.			

Again, there are substantial variations by site and subject. However, it would appear that an effect of about 0.10 to 0.15 standard deviations could be considered a reasonable expectation, notwithstanding the two near-zero effects in Cincinnati (for science in 2002–2003) and Coventry (for math). Although this

---

4 Note that use of the *EB* residuals to represent average classroom student achievement leads to a somewhat conservative estimate of the relationship between student achievement and teacher evaluation ratings, because these residuals are shrunk back toward the mean, quite substantially in cases where teachers have relatively few students. Correlations with OLS residuals are higher, but likely to be less reliable.

may not seem very impressive, the effects could be quite important to a district seeking to improve student achievement. If, over time, a critical mass of teachers could improve their performance by one level, and therefore give students the opportunity of being assigned to three top-rated teachers in consecutive years, the cumulative gain in achievement in comparison to a student assigned to three lower-rated teachers consecutively would be substantial. When we controlled for teacher experience (results not shown), the relationship between evaluation ratings and student achievement were similar, although slightly weaker at Vaughn and in Washoe, and stronger in Cincinnati. It would appear that the evaluation-score student-achievement relationships we found are not dependent on teacher experience.

We also explored the relationship between teacher experience, which is now almost universal as a basis for teacher compensation, and student achievement. We wanted to know if standards-based teacher evaluation scores were better predictors of classroom-average student achievement than teacher experience. To find out, we calculated the correlations between the *EB* intercept residuals and teachers' years of experience, as represented by their step position in Cincinnati and Washoe and the years of experience with the district for Coventry and Vaughn. We then combined the correlations across grades. Figure 7.4 shows these correlations.

Figure 7.4. Correlations Between Teacher Experience and Estimates of Average Student Achievement

	Tested Subject		
Site	Reading	Math	Other
Cincinnati			
01–02	0.15*	0.07*	0.09* (Science)
02–03	–0.19*	–0.20*	–0.02*(Science)
Coventry			
All Years Combined	0.18	–0.00*	
Vaughn			
01–02	0.20*	0.32*	0.23* (Language Arts)
Washoe			
00–01	0.16	0.14	—
01–02	0.15	0.16	—
* Confidence interval includes 0.			

In most cases, these correlations are lower than the evaluation-score student-achievement correlations reported in Figure 7.2 and in some cases are negative. This suggests that experience is not as good a predictor of student performance as the teacher evaluation scores. It also suggests that, although teacher evaluation scores are not as strongly related to student achievement as one might like, they are more strongly related than teacher experience. It may therefore be worthwhile to consider supplementing, if not replacing, the experience dimension of the current teacher salary schedule with some type of performance pay based on evaluation scores. A variety of designs for this are presented by Odden and Kelley (2002) and Milanowski (2002).

Other Aspects of Standards Based Evaluation for Teacher Accountability

To successfully use standards-based teacher evaluation as part of teacher accountability, and especially as part of a teacher pay for performance system, more is needed than a substantial relationship between evaluation ratings and student achievement. In order for teachers to accept the system, they must see the standards as appropriate, the goal of high performance achievable, and the evaluation process as fair. To help teachers work toward improving performance, and to build capacity to respond to test-based accountability pressures, evaluation systems need to emphasize teacher development as well as teacher accountability. Field research at three of the four sites was done to explore these issues, and results presented in papers by Heneman and Milanowski (in press); Milanowski and Heneman (2001); Kimball (2002); Kimball, Milanowski, and Heneman (2003); Kellor (2003); Kellor, Milanowski, Odden, and Gallagher (2001).

In general, we found that teachers accepted the standards as appropriate. Most felt that they were consistent with their conception of good teaching and were worth working toward. However, some teachers had concerns that the teaching described at the highest rubric level, although desirable, was not possible with their specific students. Problems with prior student preparation, family engagement, poverty, and similar factors were often cited as reasons why top level performance could not be achieved. Teacher perceptions of fairness were mixed. At Washoe, where performance ratings have low stakes for most teachers, the system was perceived as quite fair. In Cincinnati, where the system was originally designed for use in a performance pay system, many teachers expressed fairness concerns. These included concerns that the external evaluators would not understand their classroom context, that evaluators' decisions were subjective, and that they did not receive enough help to improve their performance. These concerns were heightened by implementation problems with portfolio guidelines and deadlines and miscommunications, such as the rumor that the district had imposed a quota on the number of teachers that could be rated at the highest level. At Vaughn, fairness concerns were also apparent in the first year. Teachers had concerns about vagueness in the initial versions of the rubrics and evaluator subjectivity. After modifications to the system, greater teacher participation in the design, and much discussion about the system at staff meetings, many fairness issues were addressed and perceptions of fairness improved markedly (Kellor, 2003; Kellor, Milanowski, Odden, & Gallagher, 2001).

In Cincinnati and at Vaughn, initial implementation glitches reduced teacher acceptance of the systems. In Cincinnati, initial ambiguity about portfolio requirements and deadlines, misunderstandings about what the evaluators were looking for, underestimation of the evaluator workload, and rumors of a quota on high ratings reduced the credibility of the system to many teachers. Many seem to have perceived these stumbles as reasons to doubt the validity of the system and excuses not to take its higher performance expectations seriously. Although the district did invest in communication, many teachers did not hear the message. Many building administrators and union building representatives appear to have provided little explanation and support for the system. Some problems with initial understanding of the system also arose at Vaughn, but the small size and cohesive culture of the school made them easier to address quickly. Even at Vaughn, some of the disputes over the initial design and implementation of the system caused some strains on staff collegiality.

There were fewer perceived implementation problems in Washoe County. This could be because of the lower stakes attached to the evaluation results and the longer phase-in of the system, with a two-year field test carried out before full implementation. Although there were anecdotal reports of difficulties with administrator subjectivity and use of the process as a punitive tool, most teachers understood and accepted the system's standards and requirements.

The degree to which these standards-based evaluation systems helped teachers improve their teaching was mixed. In Cincinnati, the emphasis on efficiently obtaining reliable, valid, and objective evaluations—a goal we believe the district has had considerable success achieving—has overshadowed the formative role of evaluation. Teachers generally did not feel that the evaluation system provided enough feedback and coaching to help them improve. Most teachers told us that they had made only relatively superficial changes in their teaching as a result of the evaluation, but some administrators told us that the system was a powerful force in getting teachers to pay attention to the district's *student* performance standards. The system was not initially designed to provide much assistance to the teachers who are evaluated, the assumption apparently being that existing resources were sufficient to help teachers improve. But many teachers on the comprehensive evaluation did not perceive that they had the resources to improve their performance. Over time, the district has added programs to support performance improvement, such as greater alignment of professional development offerings to the standards, and teacher study groups focusing on a specific set of standards each year. These changes were intended to support teachers in improving their practice.

At Vaughn, lack of feedback and coaching was also an issue in the initial years of system operation, but after the first two years of operation, efforts were made to provide teachers with more help. The peer evaluator, in particular, has been used as a source of feedback and assistance, reducing teachers' concerns in this area. In the third year of operation, evaluators tried to provide concrete suggestions for performance improvement along with performance level feedback. As a single school, Vaughn does not have the resources to build an extensive professional development program, but has been able to build capacity by carefully choosing external training programs addressing key competencies and by relying on peer assistance.

The evaluation system in Washoe County was designed to provide both formative recommendations and summative decisions on teacher performance. Teachers commonly referred to both purposes when characterizing the system, but they tended to emphasize the formative aspects. Although some teachers believed that the system helped them make substantial changes in their practice, particularly novice teachers, reports of deep changes to instructional practice or teacher professional development plans were uncommon. It could be that evaluators lacked the knowledge, time, or ability to provide helpful feedback. Evidence also suggests that some evaluators avoid being perceived by teachers as harsh and emphasize the positive in evaluation discussions and written narratives. These evaluators may overly temper their commentary on teacher performance, which limits the impact of feedback. To help improve the link between the evaluation process and teachers' professional growth, the district has attempted to align professional development offerings to the evaluation performance domains.

Implications for Using Standards-Based Teacher Evaluation as Accountability and Reward Measure

These results provide evidence that ratings from standards-based teacher evaluation systems can have a substantial relationship with measures of student achievement. There is evidence that these evaluation systems are holding teachers accountable for behaviors and competencies related to student achievement. These results also reassure us that holding teachers accountable for their performance is worthwhile in terms of the outcome policymakers and much of the public feel is most important. The stronger correlations found in Cincinnati and Vaughn support the use of these evaluation systems as a basis for teacher pay differentiation. These correlations are also comparable to the average correlations between objective measures of performance and performance appraisal scores found in meta-analyses of studies from private sector organizations by R. Heneman (1986) and Bommer et al. (1995).

We also believe that rigorous standards based evaluation can have an indirect effect on teacher accountability and instructional practice. We speculate that the strongest effect of the system on instruction at Vaughn may be to discourage teachers who are not willing to be accountable for teaching according to the Vaughn model from accepting a job or staying. Those that do stay are more likely to agree among themselves about what constitutes good instruction and what teachers and schools should be accountable for. This, in turn, should make it more acceptable to hold teachers accountable.

Our research also suggests that the design and implementation of the system matters. Although we have too few sites to make definitive attributions of differences in the size of correlations to design and implementation features, the sites with stronger correlations, Cincinnati and Vaughn, used multiple rater systems, whereas Coventry and Washoe used building administrators as the sole rater. Interviews in Cincinnati and Vaughn suggested that using multiple raters counteracted tendencies toward leniency that may have been stronger in Washoe and

Coventry. Cincinnati spent considerably more time and effort on rater training than the other three sites. Vaughn's small size and strong school culture probably reduced the need for extensive training, and facilitated consensus on the frame of reference to be applied to teacher performance. Both also designed their systems to be used as the basis for performance pay, rather than primarily for development.

The quality of initial implementation is also important, because it influences teacher acceptance. Teachers are unlikely to accept and work toward accountability measures that they believe are misunderstood or poorly implemented, or perceive as unfair. Here, the instrumentation is less important than how the system is introduced. It is important to develop and implement an intensive communication program to counteract rumors and misunderstandings, to fully develop and test all procedures, and to move quickly to address implementation glitches. If standards-based teacher evaluation systems are to be used for high stakes, such as pay differentiation, more attention also needs to be paid to preparing teachers for the higher expectations of a more rigorous evaluation. In Cincinnati, introducing a more rigorous system caused stress for many teachers. Most of the district's veteran teachers had limited experience with rigorous performance assessment, having had their last serious evaluation in their third year of teaching. Although the district developed ways to help prepare teachers, including orientation sessions, courses on the evaluation system, and a postobservation conference, these were not enough to immediately ameliorate teacher stress. To help improve teacher performance, and to help develop capacity to respond to outcome-based accountability, administrators of standards-based systems need to ensure that teachers receive useful feedback, including concrete suggestions for practice change, provide struggling teachers with someone to turn to for assistance, and offer professional development programs aimed at the specific competencies being evaluated. Cincinnati's study groups are one promising strategy. Another might be to get school administrators and peers more involved in providing developmental feedback and coaching performance. This, in turn, would require providing training in observation, providing feedback, and coaching.

Improving Teacher Evaluation Systems for Use as Accountability Systems

Our field research has suggested a number of changes that might be made to improve standards-based teacher evaluation systems for use as accountability systems. First, although the generic teaching behaviors emphasized in systems based on the Framework for Teaching are important, it may also be useful to explicitly evaluate teachers on their skill in implementing specific instructional programs important to the organization's strategy to improve student achievement. For example, if models like Success for All or Direct Instruction are part of the strategy to achieve school or district goals, teachers should be evaluated on how well they are implemented in the classroom.

Second, if more skill in content-specific pedagogy and higher levels of pedagogical content knowledge are needed to facilitate a major boost in student achievement, evaluation systems may need to place more emphasis on these competencies. Unfortunately, this would require more training of evaluators, or the use of subject-expert evaluators, because it takes more specialized expertise than most school administrator have been able to acquire to recognize these skills in use. Although the use of more highly trained evaluators would likely benefit teachers and improve the validity of the evaluation ratings, this may be too costly for many districts to afford.

Third, standards-based evaluation systems might also be streamlined to collect the most important information more efficiently. Although it is probably not wise to reduce the number of observations or extent of other evidence collected, it may be possible to reduce the number of standards or dimensions measured. However, because performance standards serve important communicative and developmental functions, organizations should be cautious about deleting dimensions from these systems, even though doing so would make them easier to administer.

Fourth, because classroom observations can be time consuming for evaluators and difficult to schedule, we would encourage districts and schools to experiment with technology to streamline the process. The use videos of teacher practice rather than direct observations for some of the evidence on classroom instruction would reduce administrative burden substantially, create a permanent record of instructional practice, and even allow the system to have a series of demonstration lessons for different subject areas and different performance levels. These demonstration lessons could be used to show teachers what good performance looks like, thereby providing more guidance on how to improve.

Finally, organizations using these systems for accountability purposes should measure and monitor the relationship between student achievement and teacher evaluation scores. To prevent behavior-based accountability from becoming an end unto itself, organizations need to make sure there is evidence that behaviors for which they are holding teachers accountable are contributing to student achievement. Over time, evaluation systems may lose some of their rigor as they become routinized and more reform strategies are overlaid on busy principals and teachers. This could result in teachers taking the process less seriously and evaluators not making as valid performance distinctions, if they make any at all. A decline in the relationship between evaluation scores and student achievement could be a warning that this is occurring.

Directions for Future Research

There are three directions we will pursue to provide additional evidence relevant to the validity and usefulness of standards-based evaluation systems. First, we will be replicating our analyses with another year of data from three of our sites. Because our samples are relatively small, an additional year of data could lead to more confident conclusions. Second, we are doing additional research on evaluator decision-making processes. Because evaluators are an important part of these relatively high-inference performance assessment systems, studying evaluator decision-making processes provides useful evidence on the construct validity of the evaluations as representations of teacher performance. Our study may also suggest ways to improve the assessment process. Third, we intend to do more intensive analysis of the data, including looking for possible bias in our results from excluding students with missing data, and whether teachers are differentially effective for students with different levels of prior achievement, from different ethnic backgrounds, or of different socioeconomic status. We have begun to explore the latter issue using data from Washoe (see Borman & Kimball, 2004). We hope this work will contribute to a better understanding of standards-based teacher evaluation as a strategy for both teacher accountability and developing capacity to respond to outcome-based accountability requirements such as those in the NCLB legislation.

References

Bommer, W. H., Johnson, J. L., Rich, G. A., Podsakoff, P. M., & MacKenzie, S. B. (1995). On the interchangeability of objective and subjective measures or employee performance: A meta-analysis. *Personnel Psychology* 48, 587–605.

Borman, G. D., & Kimball, S. M. (2004). Teacher quality and educational quality: Do teachers with higher standards-based evaluation ratings close student achievement gaps? Paper presented at the American Educational Research Association, San Diego, CA.

Danielson, C. (1996). Enhancing professional practice: A framework for teaching. Alexandria, VA: Association for Supervision and Curriculum Development.

Danielson, C., & McGreal, T. (2000). Teacher evaluation to enhance professional practice. Alexandria, VA: Association for Supervision and Curriculum Development.

Ellett, C. D. (1997). Classroom-based assessments of teaching and learning. In J. Stronge (Ed.) *Evaluating Teaching: A Guide to Current Thinking and Best Practice*, pp. 107–128. Newbury Park, CA: Sage.

Ellett, C. D., Annunziata, J., & Schiavone, S. (2002). Web-based support for teacher evaluation and professional growth: The professional assessment and comprehensive evaluation system (Paces). *Journal of Personnel Evaluation in Education* 16(1), 63–74.

Fritsche, L., Weerasinghe, D., & Babu, S. (2003). Making the connection: Linking the teacher evaluation results to the district accountability system. Paper presented at the American Educational Research Association, Chicago, IL.

Fuhrman, S. H. (2003). Redesigning accountability systems for education (CPRE Policy Brief RB-38). Philadelphia: Consortium for Policy Research in Education, University of Pennsylvania.

Gallagher, H. A. (in press, 2004). Vaughn Elementary's innovative teacher evaluation system: Are teacher evaluation scores related to growth in student achievement. *Peabody Journal of Education.*

Heneman, H. G. III, & Milanowski, A. T. (in press, 2004). Continuing assessment of teacher reactions to a Standards-Based Teacher Evaluation System. *Journal of Personnel Evaluation in Education.*

Heneman, H. G. III, & A. T. Milanowski. (in press, 2004). Alignment of human resource practices and teacher performance competency. *Peabody Journal of Education.*

Heneman, R. L. (1986). Relationship between supervisory ratings and results-oriented measures of performance: A meta-analysis. *Personnel Psychology* 39, 811–26.

Kelley, C., Heneman, H. G. III, & Milanowski, A. T. (2001). School-based performance awards: Research findings and future directions. *Educational Administration Quarterly.*

Kellor, E. M. (2003). Catching up with the Vaughn express: Four years of performance pay and standards-based teacher evaluation (CPRE-UW Working Paper TC-03–02). Madison, WI: University of Wisconsin-Madison, Wisconsin Center for Education Research, Consortium for Policy Research in Education.

Kellor, E. M., Milanowski, A. T., Odden, A. R., & Gallagher, H. A. (2001). How Vaughn Next Century Learning Center developed a knowledge-and skill-pay program. Madison, WI: University of Wisconsin, Wisconsin Center for Education Research, Consortium for Policy Research in Education.

Kimball, S. M. (2002). Analysis of feedback, enabling conditions and fairness perceptions of teachers in three school districts with new standards-based evaluation systems. *Journal of Personnel Evaluation in Education* 16(4), 241–268

Kimball, S., Milanowski, A. T., & Heneman, H. G. III (2003). Research results and formative recommendations from the study of the Washoe County teacher performance evaluation system. Paper presented at the American Evaluation Association, Sparks, Nevada.

Kimball, S., White, B., Milanowski, A. T., & Borman G. (in press, 2004). Examining the relationship between teacher evaluation and student assessment results in Washoe County. *Peabody Journal of Education.*

Koretz, D. M. (2002). Limitations in the use of achievement tests as measures of educators' productivity. *Journal of Human Resources,* 37(4), 752–777.

Medley, D. M., & Coker, H. (1987). Accuracy of principals' judgments of teacher performance. *Journal of Educational Research* 80(4), 242–247.

Milanowski, A. T. (in press, 2004). Relationship between teacher performance evaluation scores and student achievement: Evidence from Cincinnati. *Peabody Journal of Education.*

Milanowski, A. T. (2004). Relationships among dimension scores of standards-based teacher evaluation systems, and the stability of evaluation score-student achievement relationships over time. Paper presented at the American Educational Research Association, San Diego, CA.

Milanowski, A. T. (2002). Varieties of knowledge and skill-based pay design: A comparison of seven new pay systems for K-12 teachers. *Education Policy Analysis Archives* 11(4). Retrieved June, 2004. from http://epaa.asu.edu/epaa/v11n4/.

Milanowski, A. T., & Heneman, H. G. III. (2001). Assessment of teacher reactions to a standards-based teacher evaluation system: A pilot study. *Journal of Personnel Evaluation in Education* 15(3). 193–212.

Milanowski, A. T., Kimball, S., & White, B. (2004). The relationship between standards-based teacher evaluation scores and student achievement: Replication and extensions at three sites. Paper presented at the American Educational Research Association, San Diego, CA.

Odden, A., & Kelley, C. (2002). Paying teachers for what they know and do: New and smarter compensation strategies to improve schools. (2nd ed.) Thousand Oaks, CA: Corwin Press.

Peterson, K. D. (2000). Teacher evaluation: A comprehensive guide to new directions and practice. (2nd ed.) Thousand Oaks, CA: Corwin Press.

Porter, A., Youngs, P., & Odden, A. (2001). Advances in teacher assessment and their uses. In V. Richardson (Ed.) *Handbook of Research on Teaching,* (pp. 259–297). New York: Macmillan.

Rowan, B., Correnti, R., & Miller, R. J. (2002). What large-scale, survey research tells us about teacher effects on student achievement: Insights from the *Prospects* study of elementary schools. *Teachers College Record,* 104(8), 1525–1567.

Shadish, W. R., & Haddock, C. K. (1994). Combining estimates of effect size. In H. Cooper and L. V. Hedges (Eds.) *Handbook of Research Synthesis.* New York: Russell Sage Foundation.

Snijders, T., & Bosker, R. (1999). Multilevel analysis: An introduction to basic and advanced multilevel modeling. London: Sage Publications.

Stronge, J. (1997). Improving schools through teacher evaluation. In J. Stronge (Ed.) *Evaluating teaching: A guide to current thinking and best practice,* (pp. 1–23). Newbury Park, CA.

White, B. (2004). Relationship between teacher evaluation scores and student achievement: evidence from Coventry, RI. Paper presented at the American Educational Research Association, San Diego, CA.

Appendix

Measures of Student Achievement

At Vaughn, the Stanford 9 test was the measure of student achievement used for all grades in both years. Because of this uniformity, and because this test is supposed to be scaled so that one year's test scores are comparable with those from other years, we combined grades in the Vaughn models and included grade-level dummy variables, rather than estimating separate models by grades.

For the other sites, the measures of student achievement used are shown in the tables below.

Figure 7.5. Student Achievement Measures by Grade–Cincinnati

Grade	Year	Current Year Achievement Measure	Prior Year Achievement Measure
3	2001–2002	District Test	District Test
3	2002–2003	District Test	District Test (reading and math for science*)
4	2001–2002	State Proficiency Test	District Test
4	2002–2003	State Proficiency Test	District Test
5	2001–2002	TerraNova	State Proficiency Test
5	2002–2003	TerraNova	State Proficiency Test
6	2001–2002	State Proficiency Test	District Test
6	2002–2003	State Proficiency Test	District Test
7	2001–2002	District Test	State Proficiency Test
7	2002–2003	District Test	State Proficiency Test
8	2001–2002	State Proficiency Test	District Test
8	2002–2003	TerraNova	District Test

*Because no science test was given in third grade for 2001–2002, the both prior year reading and mathematics tests given in grade three were used as a control for prior student achievement for the science fourth grade analysis.

Figure 7.6. Student Achievement Measures by Grade—Coventry

Grade	Year	Current Year Achievement Measure	Prior Year Achievement Measure
2	1999–2000	Stanford 9, Reading & Math	Grade 1 Stanford 9, Reading & Math
2	2000–2001	Stanford 9, Reading & Math	Grade 1 Stanford 9, Reading & Math
3	1999–2000	Stanford 9, Reading & Math	Grade 2 Stanford 9, Reading & Math
3	2000–2001	Stanford 9, Reading & Math	Grade 2 Stanford 9, Reading & Math
4	2000–2001	New Standards Reading & Math	Grade 3 Stanford 9, Reading & Math
4	2001–2002	New Standards Reading & Math	Grade 3 Stanford 9, Reading & Math
6	1999–2000	Stanford 9, Reading & Math	Grade 5 Stanford 9, Reading & Math

Figure 7.7. Student Achievement Measures
by Grade and Year—Washoe

Grade	Year	Current Year Achievement Measure	Prior Year Achievement Measure
3	2001–2002	State Proficiency Test (Spring 2002)	District Criterion Referenced Test (Spring 2001)
4	2001–2002	TerraNova (Spring 2002)	TerraNova (Fall 2001)
4	2002–2003	District Criterion Referenced Test (Spring 2003)	State Proficiency Test (Spring 2002)
5	2001–2002	State Proficiency Test (Spring 2002)	TerraNova (Spring 2001)
5	2002–2003	State Proficiency Test (Spring 2003)	TerraNova (Spring 2002)
6	2002–2003	District Criterion Referenced Test (Spring 2003)	State Proficiency Test (Spring 2002)

8

Revealed-Preference Measures of School Quality

Lori L. Taylor

Introduction

The No Child Left Behind (NCLB) Act of 2001 makes standardized testing a cornerstone of educational accountability. Under NCLB, states are obliged to develop curriculum-based exams in mathematics, reading, and science and to evaluate their schools and districts on the basis of such instruments. States must define "adequate yearly progress"; so all students are expected to improve, and in 12 years all students will meet the state's standard for proficiency. Schools that do not show adequate progress for two consecutive years will be flagged as failing.

Studies of educational productivity and adequacy also rely heavily on test scores to measure school quality. Test scores are the primary measure of school quality in cost function analyses of school districts.[1] They are also major determinants of those districts deemed successful in the Successful Schools analyses of educational adequacy (Baker, Taylor, & Vedlitz 2004).

Arguably, there are many other potential measures of educational outcomes and quality that are not included in such analyses. Of particular appeal are measures that are based on the revealed-preferences of the primary educational consumers—students and their parents. Schools that are perceived as high quality attract students, resulting in increases in enrollment and/or increases in the price parents are willing to pay to live within the school's attendance zone. Therefore, the capitalization of school attendance zones into home prices, and the migration/enrollment patterns of students could be useful tools for measuring school quality.

---

1 For example, see Gronberg, Jansen, Taylor, & Booker (2004), Duncombe, Lukemeyer, & Yinger (2003) or Reschovsky & Imazeki (2001, 2003).

This chapter surveys the literature on revealed-preference measures of school quality and highlights the advantages and disadvantages of using such measures for accountability and adequacy purposes.

Revealed-Preference Models of School Quality

In a seminal article, Charles Tiebout (1956) hypothesized that the free movement of individuals across jurisdictions creates market-like incentives for governments and induces residents to reveal their preferences for governmental amenities. The Tiebout Hypothesis gives rise to two related lines of research, both of which have been used to measure school quality. The most prominent of these approaches is the hedonic housing model. However, interest has also turned recently to discrete choice models that directly examine migration and location.

The Hedonic Housing Model

A house is a collection of desirable characteristics such as shelter, comfort, and location. Therefore, the price buyers are willing to pay for a house should be related to the prices they are willing to pay for its component characteristics. By treating a house as the sum of its parts, a hedonic housing model generates estimates of the consumer's willingness to pay for each component characteristic.

Most hedonic housing models trace their roots, either explicitly or implicitly, to a model developed by Rosen (1974). In these models, consumers attempt to maximize their own happiness, taking the housing stock as given. Consumers derive utility from consuming all sorts of housing characteristics ($Z = z_1, z_2, \ldots z_n$) and a composite good (x). They earn an income (y) regardless of their chosen residence and can only consume combinations of Z and x that are affordable given that income. There are many types of consumers, and tastes for Z and x differ among those consumers according to socioeconomic characteristics (α) such as the person's age or educational attainment. In equilibrium, all consumers with identical preferences and income are able to achieve the same level of utility.

After some manipulation, the individual consumer's decision making can be described with a willingness-to-pay relationship or, more formally, a bid-rent function:

$$R = R(z_1, z_2 \ldots z_n; y, \alpha) \tag{1}$$

The value of the bid-rent function represents the amount the consumer is willing to pay to rent a home with certain characteristics (Z), given the consumer's income level and socioeconomic type. Partial derivatives of the bid-rent function with respect to housing characteristics represent the consumer's willingness to pay for those characteristics.

The price a potential buyer would be willing to pay for a house represents the present discounted value of the after-tax stream of bid rents.[2] If τ_R is the tax rate

---

2 This discussion ignores the differential tax treatment of renters and owners.

chosen by the jurisdiction for real estate, θ represents the discounting factor, and housing is an infinitely lived asset, then the bid price of a house (P) would be

$$P = \frac{R - \tau_R P}{\theta} \qquad (2)$$

or equivalently,

$$P = \frac{R(z_1, z_2 \ldots z_n; y, \alpha)}{\theta + \tau_R} \qquad (3)$$

If the supply of housing characteristics is fixed, then equation (3) indicates the market price for a house with Z characteristics. However, if the supply of Z is not fixed—either because there is undeveloped land in a market or because relevant locational characteristics are changeable—then the observed hedonic price function need not be the same as the bid-rent function (Bartik & Smith 1987). To interpret the hedonic price function as measuring the consumer's willingness to pay for housing characteristics, one must control for factors that can shift the supply curve of such characteristics. Few researchers incorporate such controls, relying instead on a presumption that housing supply is fixed or on techniques that incorporate house-specific fixed effects (e.g. Figlio & Lucas 2004). However, Downes and Zabel (2002) find evidence that school characteristics are endogenous even in a specification that controls for house-specific fixed effects. Although their finding of endogeneity may reflect nothing more than the data limitations that prevent them from precisely matching houses with school attendance zones, it reinforces the need for caution when interpreting hedonic housing models.

When using the hedonic housing model in equation (3) to evaluate schools, researchers concentrate specifically on the locational characteristics of houses. The underlying premise is that competition among potential residents will bid up the price of housing in the attractive location (all other things being equal). Therefore, the premium paid for houses in a specific location will reflect the price that residents and potential residents are willing to pay for the unique characteristics of that location. Because one potentially important locational characteristic is the right to attend a particular school, systematic variations in housing values can reveal not only the value that residents place on their neighborhood school, but also the specific characteristics of the school that are most valued by residents.

A major sticking point when using hedonic housing models to examine schools is disentangling the house price impact of the neighborhood school from the house price impact of all the other characteristics of the neighborhood. The virtues of even the highest-quality school can be completely overshadowed by a smokestack next door or by other characteristics of urban blight. Neighborhood demographics and school demographics can be highly correlated. If the nonschool neighborhood characteristics are not adequately addressed, then the hedonic housing model can give a misleading impression of school quality.

Recently, researchers have used a number of analytic approaches to control for nonschool neighborhood characteristics. Black (1999) triggered renewed interest in school capitalization analysis by developing a new way of measuring neighborhoods. She limits her attention to houses that were less than seven-tenths of a mile from the internal boundary lines that divide school attendance zones within school districts and uses those boundaries to define neighborhoods. Houses within a short distance on either side of the line are in the same neighborhood—regardless of how long the boundary line itself may be. Black then uses fixed effects for each boundary line to control for the common characteristics of the neighborhood. Other researchers adopting Black's technique include Brasington (2003a, 2003b); Kane, Staiger, and Samms (2003); and Kane, Staiger, and Riegg (2004).

Figlio and Lucas (2004) also use fixed effects to control for neighborhood characteristics. They define neighborhoods as platted subdivisions and include in their model annual fixed effects for each subdivision. They use multiple years of data on sales and incorporate house-specific fixed effects, so any time-invariant effects of neighborhood characteristics within subdivisions are also taken into account.

Kane, Staiger, and Samms (2003) and Kane, Staiger, and Riegg (2004) construct pseudo-neighborhoods by overlaying a grid pattern on their data. All houses are assigned to one of the grid's blocks. Each block is 2,500-feet square. Houses within the same block are presumed part of the same neighborhood. Fixed effects for the pseudo-neighborhoods control for actual neighborhood effects.

Most other researchers have used census tracts as a proxy for neighborhoods.[3] Among such studies, two stand out as devoting particular interest to the question of nonschool neighborhood effects. Weimer and Wolkoff (2001) assume that the values of nearby houses provide a summary statistic on neighborhood quality, and use the median home value in each census tract as their measure of neighborhood quality. They address the potential endogeneity of median home values using tract characteristics as instruments.[4] Downes and Zabel (2002) rely on a particularly rich set of census characteristics to control for neighborhood effects. In particular, Downes and Zabel control for the income, age, ethnicity, educational attainment, and occupation of census tract residents. They also control for general characteristics of the neighborhood housing stock, distance from the central business district, and a measure of air quality.

None of the various strategies is the definitive answer to the problem of neighborhood effects. Black's boundary effects model presumes that attendance zone boundaries bisect neighborhoods. If instead, the boundaries *define* neighborhoods, then boundary effects will have little power to isolate school effects. For example, if school boards are reluctant to split established neighborhoods

---

3 For example, see Brunner, Murdoch, & Thayer (2002); Brunner, Sonstelie, & Thayer (2001); Haurin & Brasington (1996); and Bogart & Cromwell (2000).

4 They also include fixed effects for nonschool political jurisdictions. The jurisdictional fixed effects captured variations in the bundle of nonschool taxes and services.

when drawing attendance zones, then houses on opposite sides of an attendance boundary are not part of the same perceived neighborhood and the underlying assumption of the boundary effects model is violated. Furthermore, both Kane, Staiger, and Samms (2003) and Kane, Staiger, and Riegg (2004) point out that once boundary lines are drawn, Tiebout sorting can lead to shifts in the capital stock or in the demographic profile on either side of the line. Capitalization may lead owners on the more desirable side of the line to invest more in maintaining their property. Highly desirable neighbors may flock to the academically sunny side of the street. Even if the line originally bisected a neighborhood, after a while it no longer may intersect the vicinity.[5]

Relying on fixed effects for platted subdivisions and house-specific fixed effects, as in Figlio and Lucas (2004), largely addresses neighborhood concerns, but only if school attendance zones are sufficiently distinct from subdivision boundaries. Furthermore, the use of house-specific fixed effects transforms the model into a repeat sales analysis, and repeat sales analyses can be biased because they are based on a nonrandom sample of houses (Kiel & Zabel 1997). Constructing pseudo-neighborhoods may fail to capture neighborhood characteristics because the actual neighborhoods may not correspond to those used in the estimation. Strategies that rely on census characteristics to control for neighborhood effects are vulnerable to omitted variables bias and raise the question of whether census tracts are reasonable proxies for neighborhoods.

Regardless of methodology, the recent emphasis on controlling for neighborhood effects has strengthened the evidence concerning capitalization of school characteristics. In at least 11 studies over the past 5 years, researchers have found evidence of significant capitalization.

The primary focus of the recent literature has been the capitalization of standardized tests. Except work by Bogart and Cromwell (which incorporated test scores only as robustness check on the capitalized value of changes in attendance boundaries).[6] all the researchers have found a significant, positive relationship between tests scores and property values. A one standard-deviation difference in test scores can lead to as much as a 25 percentage point difference in property values (Kane, Staiger, & Samms, 2004).

Interest in expenditures as a potentially capitalized school characteristic has waned. Among recent studies, only Downes and Zabel (2002); Brunner, Murdoch, and Thayer (2002); and Brasington (1999) report on the relationship between school expenditures and property values. All three find that property values are significantly higher where school-district spending is higher, although Brasington finds capitalization only in some cases.

---

5 One implication of this critique is that fresh boundary lines are more likely to lie on the interior of neighborhoods than are well-established boundary lines. Therefore, the boundary effects model may be particularly well suited to analyses of redistricting as in Kane, Staiger, & Riegg (2004).

6 Bogart & Cromwell, 2000.

Two of the recent studies specifically examine the information value associated with school report cards of the type required under the NCLB Act of 2001. Figlio and Lucas (2004) explore the announcement value of the school grading system in Florida, whereas Kane, Staiger, and Samms (2003) explore the impact of a similar system in North Carolina. In Florida, Figlio and Lucas find that "the market responds to the assignment of school letter grades." A house in the attendance zone of an A-rated school commands an 8% premium over a house in the attendance zone of a B-rated school, which in turn commands an even greater premium (in percentage terms) over a house in the attendance zone of a C-rated school. In contrast, Kane, Staiger, and Samms find no relationship between North Carolina's rating system and property values. Kane, Staiger, and Samms attribute the difference in findings to the likelihood that in North Carolina the identities of low performing schools "were known to buyers even without the state labels." However, significant differences in the grading systems of the two states and in state policy regarding high- and low-performing schools may also play a role. For example, the Florida grading system provides homebuyers with information about test scores and the distribution of test scores, whereas the North Carolina system provides information on test scores and a measure of value added.[7] One interpretation of the difference between the Florida and North Carolina studies is that homebuyers value consistently high performance across student groups but not value added, per se.

Such an interpretation would reinforce a more general conclusion that the capitalization of student test scores probably reflects peer effects rather than value-added school effects. Researchers have long understood that test scores can be decomposed into that which is attributable to the school (school effects) and that which would be expected given the student demographics (peer effects). Hayes and Taylor (1997) were the first to incorporate this decomposition into a model of housing values. Their analysis of 1987 data suggested that homebuyers in North Dallas paid a premium for the value added by schools. However, their measure of value added was based on school-level rather than student-level data, and their analysis had limited controls for neighborhood effects. Subsequent analyses have not found evidence of capitalization of value added. Brasington (1999) found essentially no evidence that district-level changes in student performance were capitalized into housing values. Downes and Zabel (2002) argue that capitalization of value added implies that prior test scores for a given student cohort should be negatively capitalized when current

---

7　The Florida system requires schools to achieve high-performance levels with all student groups to receive the highest grade, whereas the North Carolina system requires high average scores and that schools meet or exceed expectations regarding improvements in test scores.

test scores are positively capitalized.[8] Because they find positive capitalization of the prior score, they conclude that value added is not capitalized. Kane, Staiger, and Samms (2003) and Kane, Staiger, and Riegg (2004) use student-level micro data to generate estimates of the value added by schools and include such estimates in their hedonic housing models. Regardless of the strategy used to control for neighborhood effects, they also find no evidence that value added is capitalized into housing values.

Figure 9.1 presents an update of the Hayes and Taylor (1997) analysis, using 1997 data generously provided by Linda Loubert (in press) on sales of single-family homes in Dallas County, Texas.[9] Unlike the Hayes and Taylor analysis, which focused exclusively on the Dallas Independent School District (ISD), this estimation includes most school districts in Dallas County.[10] Nonschool neighborhood effects are controlled for using a grid pattern to construct pseudo-neighborhood fixed effects. Only blocks that contain observations from two or more schools are included in the analysis. The measures of school effects and peer effects are the average of the sixth-grade math and reading effects used in Grosskopf, Hayes, and Taylor (2004) and were estimated from student-level microdata. The school effect is the predicted performance of a student with average characteristics who attends school j; the peer effect is the predicted performance of the actual students attending school j, assuming that they had attended the average Texas school. Given the volatility found by Kane and Staiger (2002), the housing hedonic uses three-year moving averages of all test scores, school effects, and peer effects. Figure 9.2 presents demographic statistics for the data used in this analysis.

---

8 This presumption requires that prior test scores would not be positively capitalized in their own right.

9 Houses that sold for more than $1 million are excluded from the estimation, as are houses that sold for less than $10 per square foot or for more than $250 per square foot. On average, houses in Dallas County sold for $65 per square foot in 1997.

10 Garland ISD is excluded because it is an open enrollment district wherein residence does not determine the school attended. A few smaller districts were also lost because there were not enough sales in eligible grid blocks. The

Figure 8.1: Hedonic Housing Models for Dallas County

Parameter	Model I		Model II		Model III		Model IV	
	Estimate	Robust Standard Error	Estimate	Robust Standard Error	Estimate	Robust Standard Error	Estimate	Robust Standard Error
Square Feet of Living Area (log)	0.0551[a]	0.0024	0.0548[a]	0.0024	0.0541[a]	0.0024	0.0484[a]	0.0022
Log Living Area, Squared	−0.0004[a]	0.0000	−0.0004[a]	0.0000	−0.0004[a]	0.0000	−0.0003[a]	0.0000
Age	−0.0086[a]	0.0015	−0.0087[a]	0.0015	−0.0089[a]	0.0015	−0.0101[a]	0.0015
Age, Squared	0.0001[a]	0.0000	0.0001[a]	0.0000	0.0001[a]	0.0000	0.0001[a]	0.0000
Number bathrooms	0.0924[a]	0.0094	0.0928[a]	0.0093	0.0910[a]	0.0092	0.0865[a]	0.0088
Pool	0.0991[a]	0.0088	0.0994[a]	0.0088	0.0987[a]	0.0088	0.0970[a]	0.0088
Average test score	0.0058[a]	0.0018			−0.0062[c]	0.0032		
Peer Effect			0.0089[a]	0.0021				
School Effect			−0.0101[b]	0.0046				
Percent of Students								
Low SES					−0.0021[c]	0.0012		
Limited English					−0.0016	0.0013		
Hispanic					−0.0012	0.0013		
Black					0.0000	0.0009		
Number of Observations		5,468		5,468		5,468		5,495
R-square		0.9028		0.9031		0.9046		0.9172

Note: The dependent variable in all five models is the natural log of the sales price. Models I, II, and III include fixed effects for 6 cities, 6 school districts, and 334 neighborhoods. Model IV includes fixed effects for 6 cities, 177 schools, and 334 neighborhoods.

a = significant at the 1% level; b = 5% level; c =10% level.

qualitative conclusions of the analysis are unchanged if the estimation is restricted to only those homes in the Dallas ISD and the city of Dallas.

Figure 8.2: Descriptive Statistics for Dallas County Hedonics

Parameter	Mean	Standard Deviation	Minimum	Maximum
Sales Price	$132,088.4	110,058.4	$10,000	$995,000
Square Feet of Living Area	1,882.18	811.57	552.00	8,232.00
Age	35.28	17.13	0.00	88.00
Number of bathrooms	2.07	0.79	1.00	4.50
Pool	0.15	0.36	0.00	1.00
Average test score	81.13	5.27	67.27	89.12
Peer Effect	80.03	4.69	67.51	88.73
School Effect	81.13	5.27	67.27	89.12
Dallas ISD	0.51	0.50	0.00	1.00
Percent of Students				
Low SES	48.22	29.85	0.00	96.20
Limited English Proficient	22.24	19.37	0.00	76.90
Hispanic	31.36	25.87	0.40	96.10
Black	20.53	19.76	0.20	99.30

The estimation indicates that test scores are positively capitalized into property values. A one standard-deviation increase in the average test score is associated with a 3.2% increase in property values, all other things being equal. However, as Models II and III illustrate, the positive relationship between property values and test scores is driven by the capitalization of peer effects. There is no evidence that school effects are capitalized into property values. If anything, the models suggest that property values are lower where school effects are higher. Given the similar findings by Kane, Staiger, and Samms (2003) and Kane, Staiger, and Riegg (2004), the weight of the empirical evidence suggests that whereas test scores are capitalized into housing values, the school effects aspects of test scores are not.

Discrete Choice Models of Household Location and Migration

Although the hedonic housing model is well established as a strategy for examining school quality, the other line of Tiebout-inspired literature is relatively embryonic. This line of research focuses directly on the migration patterns and residential location decisions underpinning the hedonic housing model. Its empirical foundation is a random utility model developed by McFadden (1978).

In the random utility model, households choose to locate in the house that maximizes their utility, and utility is a function of household and location characteristics. Because some of the determinants of utility are unobservable,

$$U_{hj} = V_{hj} + \varepsilon_{hj} \tag{4}$$

where V_{hj} is the part of utility explained by observable characteristics and ε_{hj} is the part of utility explained by unobservables. If there are K possible housing types to choose from, then the probability that household h chooses housing type j is[11]

$$P_{hj} = \frac{e^{V_{hj}}}{\sum_{k} e^{V_{hk}}} \tag{5}$$

Equation (5) can be estimated using a maximum likelihood approach.

In her analysis using the random utility model, Lisa Barrow (2002) compares the location decisions of households with children to those of households without children. Barrow uses the 5% Individual Public Use Microdata Series (IPUMS) from the 1990 Census to evaluate location patterns in the Washington, D.C. metropolitan area, restricting attention to individuals who were living in the area from 1985 thorough 1990. Such a restriction allows her to argue that the residents were well informed about relative school quality in the D.C. area. She uses average SAT scores as the measure of school quality and controls for neighborhood effects with census data and a variety of other area characteristics such as the number of D.C. metro stations and the crime rate.

Barrow finds that households with children are disproportionately drawn to areas with relatively high SAT scores. A 100 point increase in the average SAT score increases the probability that households with and without children will locate in a particular area. However, the impact of SAT score differences is greater for households with children than for households without children. Using data on the rents paid in various locations, Barrow concludes that white households with children would be willing to pay more than $1,800 per year more than white households without children to live where average SAT scores are 100 points higher. She finds no evidence that African-American households are willing to pay such premiums, a pattern that Barrow attributes to a more restricted set of residential choices for African-American households.

Although innovative, Barrow's analysis is severely limited by her reliance on IPUMS data. The smallest unit of geography in the IPUMS is the Public Use Microdata Area (PUMA). Each PUMA has a population of 100,000 individuals, and the boundaries were not drawn to facilitate the analysis of school districts. Washington, D.C. is a market where the geographic detail available in the IPUMS corresponds reasonably well with school districts. In many other parts of the country, PUMAs straddle multiple school districts, subsume multiple districts, or both. It is not possible to use PUMA data to examine differences in school quality across schools within districts.

---

11 This specification also assumes that the, ε_{hj} are independently and identically extreme value distributed.

Furthermore, the lack of geographic detail in the IPUMS prevents Barrow from using boundary fixed effects or other similar techniques to control for neighborhood characteristics. Instead, Barrow argues that neighborhood characteristics have the same effect on households with and without children, households with children value public education more highly than households without children, and comparisons across the two groups can therefore isolate the marginal impact of school characteristics. Although such an argument is plausible, it would be better to control for neighborhood effects directly.

Bayer, Ferreira, and McMillan (2003, 2004) and Bayer, McMillan, and Rueben (2004) are able to incorporate such direct controls because they have access to the confidential census data underlying the 1990 IPUMS. The restricted-use microdata specify not only the PUMAs in which the householder lives and works, but also the census blocks (geographic areas designed to have a population of 100 individuals). Analysis using the restricted use microdata can be conducted at a level of geographic detail comparable to that used in the hedonic housing price literature.

Bayer, Ferreira, and McMillan (2003, 2004) and Bayer, McMillan, and Rueben (2004) analyze the residential location patterns in the San Francisco Bay Area and conclude that test scores are capitalized into housing values. As one might expect, they also find that households with more education and income are willing to pay more for test scores than households with less education and income. More important, they also find that schools with high test scores raise housing prices by attracting educated, high-income households, and thereby enhancing the demographic mix of the school's attendance zone. According to Bayer, Ferreira, and McMillan (2003), this indirect effect on housing values is typically between 70% and 75% as large as the direct effect of the test scores themselves. Together, the direct and indirect effects indicate that a one standard-deviation increase in test scores leads to a 4% increase in housing values (Bayer, Ferreira, & McMillan 2003).

Bayer, Ferreira, and McMillan (2003, 2004) and Bayer, McMillan, and Rueben (2004) incorporate boundary fixed effects as in Black (1999) to control for the correlation between school quality and neighborhood characteristics. However, where Kane, Staiger, and Samms (2003) and Kane, Staiger, and Riegg (2004) argue that Tiebout sorting undermines the extent to which boundary fixed effects can control for the correlation between unobservable neighborhood characteristics and school quality, Bayer, Ferreira, and McMillan (2003, 2004) and Bayer, McMillan, and Rueben (2004) exploit the Tiebout sorting to examine the extent to which school characteristics influence neighborhood sociodemographics.

Using Reveled-Preference Measures for Accountability and Adequacy

The appeal of revealed-preference measures is obvious. There is little disagreement that test scores and other similar measures of school outcomes offer an incomplete picture of school quality. Revealed-preference techniques offer a way of getting at differences among schools that are not observed by researchers but are well known to residents. Unfortunately, there are also significant drawbacks to using revealed-preference measures of school quality in accountability systems or adequacy analyses.

Perhaps the most problematic drawback comes from the nature of revealed-preference models themselves. The Tiebout model rests on the presumption that the income of residents is independent of their chosen residence. As such, Tiebout-based methodologies measure the relative attractiveness of schools and districts within a single labor market. The best schools and districts in each market will attract a disproportionate share of households with children and command a housing premium from potential residents. However, the Tiebout model does not lend itself to comparisons of school quality across labor markets. Residents in one labor market may pay a substantial premium to live in the attendance zone of a school that would be considered mediocre in another setting, simply because it is the best of a bad lot. Without some method for calibrating the premium paid in one market with the premium paid in another, it would be very problematic to incorporate a revealed-preference measure of school quality into an accountability system.

A related drawback arises because capitalization is the result of scarcity. People are willing to pay a premium to live in an attendance zone because it is the only way to acquire the desirable educational services. In markets with many charter, magnet, or private schools, there is less need to pay such a premium. There is also less need to pay a premium when the attractive school is located in an undeveloped area than when it is located in a fully developed area. In a developed area, the supply of houses associated with the attractive school is fixed; in a developing area, the supply can expand to meet demand. Even after controlling for boundary fixed effects, Brasington (2003) finds that the premium paid for test scores is almost 30% weaker toward the edge of an urban area where developer activity is greater. Because the hedonic price function can reflect the supply as well as the demand for housing characteristics, extracting information on perceived quality from housing premiums can be tricky.

It is also important to adequately control for differences in effective tax rates across school districts. Because taxes have a negative impact on values, inadequate controls can lead to an overestimate of the school premium in low tax districts and an underestimate of the premium in high tax districts. Imperfect controls for tax capitalization would be particularly problematic in the context of school accountability systems because they could lead to the false conclusion that schools are low quality when in fact they have low tax bases and correspondingly high tax rates.

Finally, the empirical literature suggests that peer effects are an important determinant of revealed-preference measures of school quality. Peer effects are an important aspect of the educational environment, and it is not surprising to find that parents are willing to pay a premium to acquire a desirable peer group for their children. However, peer effects are also largely outside of school-district control. Although districts can and do drawn attendance boundaries to achieve a particular mix of students in specific schools (e.g. Bogart & Cromwell, 2000), and Tiebout sorting implies that over time districts can influence their demographics through their policy choices, the primary determinants of peer characteristics in a school are likely to be the local housing stock, commuting distances, and neighborhood effects. As factors largely outside of school-district control, peer effects do not belong in either an accountability system or as an outcome measure in an adequacy study. To the extent that revealed-preference measures of school quality reflect peer effects, they also do not belong in such contexts. (Of course, to the extent that average test scores and other common measures of school quality reflect peer effects, they also do not belong in such contexts.)

Despite all the drawbacks, a revealed-preference approach remains appealing because it has the potential to measure aspects of education that are within school-district control but not reflected in test scores. Clearly, the evidence suggests that peer effects are capitalized. However, the evidence does not reject the possibility that nontest, nonpeer aspects of school quality are also capitalized. Revealed-preference measures may be the only way to get at those aspects of school quality.

To explore that possibility, I use the hedonic approach to estimate school-level fixed effects for 175 elementary/middle schools in Dallas County, Texas. As before, pseudo-neighborhood fixed effects control for nonschool characteristics of the neighborhood, and only those pseudo-neighborhoods that straddle school or district boundaries are included in the analysis. Figure 9.1 presents the estimation as Model IV.

The school-level fixed effects estimated in Model IV represent a noisy estimate of school quality. Differences in peer characteristics and tax rates may explain much of the variation. Because the estimates are drawn from the core county of a single major metropolitan area, differences in charter or private school options and developer activity should be negligible (less than 0.5 percent of the houses in the sample are new construction), but there may still be other supply-side factors that are captured in the hedonic. Therefore, I use a second-stage estimation to examine the extent to which the revealed-preference measures reflect peer effects, tax rates, and potential supply factors. The dependent variable in the second stage is the school-level fixed effect from Model IV. The independent variables are characteristics of the neighborhood school taken from the Academic Excellence Indicator System of the Texas Education Agency (which was available on-line to any interested home buyer). Potential peer characteristics are the shares of the student body who are economically disadvantaged, limited English proficient, black, and Hispanic. The district tax rate is the standardized total tax rate effective for the 1997 calendar year. Given the strong economies of scale in education, the log of school enrollment is included as a cost factor that could influence the supply of school quality. However, because enrollment itself can be an endogenous reflection of *voting with your feet*, I instrument for enrollment using lagged enrollment from the previous three years. Schools that did not exist in 1994 are assigned a prior enrollment of zero and flagged with an indicator variable. To reflect the varying degrees of precision with which the dependent variable is estimated, I use weighted 2SLS where the weights are the inverse of the standard error for the school fixed effects (from Model IV).[12]

---

12 For prior work using a similar weighting scheme, see Hanushek, Rivkin, & Taylor (1996).

As Figure 9.3 illustrates, student demographics, tax rates, and school economics of scale can explain almost 19% of the variation in housing premiums. Residents pay a significant premium to locate in the attendance zone of a school with fewer economically disadvantaged students. Controlling for English proficiency, there is a positive relationship between the share of Hispanic students and the school housing premiums. Tax rates appear to have been positively capitalized into values, but the relationship is not statistically significant. The 13 new schools command a substantial premium, but differences in school enrollment are not capitalized.

Figure 8.3: Second Stage Regressions: Explaining the Housing Premiums

	Model V		Model VI		Model VII	
	Estimate	Robust Standard Error	Estimate	Robust Standard Error	Estimate	Robust Standard Error
Intercept	−4.0839 [c]	1.8287	−5.3124 [a]	1.0775	−1.3396	1.7150
Percent of Students						
Low SES	−0.0099 [a]	0.0039	−0.0098 [b]	0.0037	−0.0105 [b]	0.0036
Limited English Proficient	−0.0051	0.0058	−0.0046	0.0061	0.0001	0.0060
Hispanic	0.0112 [a]	0.0043	0.0105 [c]	0.0045	0.0068	0.0052
Black	0.0043	0.0046	0.0044	0.0042	0.0041	0.0041
New School Indicator	0.1541 [c]	0.0697	0.1738 [b]	0.0613	0.1526	0.0978
School Enrollment (log)	0.2895	0.1727	0.4454 [b]	0.1436	0.4984 [a]	0.1298
Tax Rate	1.3795	1.2004	0.9003	0.8504	0.3833	1.0048
Budgeted Per-Pupil Expenditures			0.0003 [a]	0.0001		
Instructional Share					−0.0149	0.0098
Pupil-Teacher Ratio					−0.0732 [a]	0.0147
Average Teacher Experience					−0.0184	0.0153
Number of Observations	175		175			175
R-square	0.1866		0.2505			0.2792

Note: The dependent variables in all models are the school fixed effects from the housing hedonic. All three models are estimated using weighted 2SLS with clustered errors where the weights are the inverse of the standard errors from the first stage regressions and the errors are clustered by school district. The instrument for school enrollment is school enrollment three years previously.

a = significant at the 1% level; b = 5% level; c = 10% level.

The substantial premium associated with a new school suggests that school resources may be an important determinant of perceived school quality. Models VI and VII explore the relationship between the school housing premiums and school resources. As the models illustrate, school resources are capitalized into housing values. In particular, housing premiums are higher where the pupil-teacher ratio is lower. Furthermore, after controlling for school resources, there is a premium associated with larger schools, a pattern that is inconsistent with commonly expressed belief that small schools are better but is consistent with a supply interpretation—economies of scale allow larger schools to produce more educational outputs from the same resources.

Because the school housing premiums are sensitive to demographic and scale differentials, they are at best noisy measures of the aspects of school quality within school-district control. For that reason alone it would be problematic to include them in an accountability system. However, it would not be unreasonable to explore their use in analyses of school productivity or educational adequacy.

In the adequacy context, test scores are frequently used to identify successful schools worthy of further analysis. Arguably, the school housing premiums could be put to similar use. If the revealed-preference measures were used to identify the top-performing quartile of schools in Dallas county, only 12 of the top 44 schools would be in Dallas ISD, a very low share given that the district comprises nearly half of the sample. The top schools would be disproportionately affluent and Anglo (Figure 9.4). Top schools would have less student turnover than other schools, but potentially more teacher turnover.[13] (Teacher experience and tenure are both significantly lower at high-performing schools.) Interestingly, although top schools have a more advantaged student body and spend more per pupil than other schools, there is no difference in average test scores.

---

[13] Student turnover is measured as the percentage of students who attend a school for part of the school year, but for less than 83% of the school year. This measure is part of the AEIS system.

Figure 8.4: The Characteristics of High-Performing Districts

		Housing Premium	
		Mean	Standard Error
Average Test Score	high	80.36	0.76
	other	79.19	0.47
School Enrollment	high	656.55	27.94
	other	648.15	17.55
Share Instructional Spending	high	71.48	0.69
	other	71.53	0.35
Expenditures per Student	high	3,650.91 [a]	73.42
	other	3,451.23 [a]	38.70
Pupil-Teacher Ratio	high	16.58 [c]	0.32
	other	17.25 [c]	0.18
Average Teacher Experience	high	10.87 [a]	0.35
	other	12.22 [a]	0.25
Average Teacher Tenure	high	7.35 [a]	0.39
	other	9.25 [a]	0.24
DISD	high	0.27 [a]	0.07
	other	0.55 [a]	0.04
% Low SES	high	46.21 [b]	5.05
	other	57.89 [b]	2.63
% Limited English Proficient	high	20.41	3.00
	other	24.01	1.94
% Hispanic	high	31.47	4.27
	other	33.10	2.49
% Black	high	17.07 [b]	3.59
	other	27.00 [b]	2.34
% White	high	44.29 [c]	4.53
	other	35.46 [c]	2.65
% Special Education	high	9.48	0.64
	other	8.60	0.37
% Student Turnover	high	20.05 [a]	1.17
	other	24.18 [a]	0.80

Note: a = significant at the 1% level; b = 5% level; c =10% level.

Revealed-Preference Measures of School Quality

Average Test Score		Value-Added Test Score		Adjusted Premium	
Mean	Standard Error	Mean	Standard Error	Mean	Standard Error
86.35 [a]	0.22	79.39	0.81	78.66	0.78
77.18 [a]	0.35	79.52	0.47	79.76	0.47
512.05 [a]	21.27	688.95	29.39	649.55	27.18
696.69 [a]	16.69	637.27	17.14	650.50	17.68
74.41 [a]	0.67	71.96	0.39	70.19 [b]	0.62
70.54 [a]	0.31	71.36	0.40	71.96 [b]	0.36
3,671.98 [a]	73.80	3,435.95	72.57	3,598.50 [c]	63.51
3,444.15 [a]	38.31	3,523.43	39.67	3,468.83 [c]	41.14
16.09 [a]	0.27	17.53	0.29	16.95	0.32
17.42 [a]	0.19	16.93	0.19	17.13	0.19
11.86	0.42	12.08	0.45	11.41	0.39
11.89	0.24	11.82	0.24	12.04	0.25
8.20	0.48	9.15	0.45	8.11 [c]	0.40
8.97	0.23	8.65	0.24	9.00 [c]	0.25
0.14 [a]	0.05	0.77 [a]	0.06	0.41	0.07
0.60 [a]	0.04	0.38 [a]	0.04	0.50	0.04
17.05 [a]	2.42	68.53 [a]	4.04	57.96	4.82
67.69 [a]	2.10	50.39 [a]	2.75	53.94	2.73
7.77 [a]	1.17	29.52 [b]	3.35	23.17	3.15
28.26 [a]	1.96	20.95 [b]	1.84	23.09	1.92
10.73 [a]	1.54	40.67 [b]	4.58	33.83	4.15
40.07 [a]	2.51	30.01 [b]	2.38	32.31	2.51
9.72 [a]	1.47	31.75 [b]	4.33	26.15	4.81
29.47 [a]	2.47	22.07 [b]	2.19	23.95	2.12
70.92 [a]	2.60	23.33 [a]	3.58	33.91	4.51
26.52 [a]	2.21	42.50 [a]	2.70	38.95	2.67
9.96 [a]	0.54	6.52 [a]	0.47	8.88	0.57
8.44 [a]	0.39	9.60 [a]	0.38	8.81	0.39
14.08 [a]	1.12	25.89 [b]	1.38	22.63	1.18
26.28 [a]	0.62	22.33 [b]	0.77	23.32	0.82
Note: a = significant at the 1% level; b = 5% level; c =10% level.					

In contrast, if average test scores were used to identify high-performing schools, they would identify only six Dallas ISD schools as top schools.[14] On the basis of average test scores, top schools are smaller than other schools and have lower pupil-teacher ratios. As with the housing premiums, the schools identified as top schools according to average test scores serve a student body that is disproportionately Anglo with relatively few students who are economically disadvantaged.

Interestingly, there is only a modest overlap between the top schools according to the housing premiums and the top schools according to average test scores. Only 15 schools make both lists. Schools that are in the top quartile according to the housing premium, but not according to test scores are much larger and serve substantially less advantaged student bodies than the schools that would be identified as successful using test scores alone.

If one identified top schools as those schools that were outperforming expectations (i.e. producing high value added) then Dallas ISD would have 34 top schools. Only 11 of the 34 would have been identified as high performing by either average scores or housing premiums, and none would have been top performing by both criteria. Schools that were outperforming expectations would be disproportionately nonwhite and economically disadvantaged.

Finally, Model V could be used to strip uncontrollable factors from the housing premium. The relationship between the resulting adjusted premium (the residual from Model V) and the original school fixed effect would be roughly analogous to the relationship between the average test score and the value-added test score. Such adjustments would break the link between student demographics and housing premiums (Figure 9.4), and eliminate the correlation between the housing premium and average test scores (Figure 9.5). Schools that are top performing according to the adjusted housing premium spend more than other schools, but spend a smaller share of their budgets on instruction or instructional leadership. Ten of the 44 top schools according to the housing premium would no longer be in the top quartile after the adjustments. Of the 10 schools identified as top schools according to the adjusted premium but not identified according to the unadjusted premium, none would have been in the top quartile according to test scores, but five would have been in the top quartile according to value-added tests scores.

---

14 For this part of the analysis, average sixth-grade scores and value-added scores are assigned to each of the 175 campuses for which a fixed effect can be calculated. Elementary schools that do not serve the sixth grade are assigned the average scores for the middle school their students will attend for the sixth grade.

Figure 8.5: The Correlations Across Quality Measures

	Housing Premium	Average Test Score	Value-Added Test Score	Adjusted Premium
Housing Premium	1.0000	0.1908	-0.0681	0.8963
Average Test Score		1.0000	0.1384	-0.0460
Value-Added Test Score			1.0000	0.0090
Adjusted Premium				1.0000

Conclusions

Studies of educational efficiency and adequacy rely heavily on test scores to measure school quality. No one believes that test scores capture all the important aspects of school quality, but there are few quantitative alternatives. One such alternative is suggested by the burgeoning literatures on hedonic housing models and household location choices. The recent evidence strongly suggests that parents are willing to pay a premium to live within the attendance zone of particular schools. These premiums have the potential to be used to measure aspects of school quality that are not reflected in test scores.

Caution must be used when relying on revealed-preference measures of quality, however. The Tiebout foundations of the methodology make it difficult to make comparisons across labor markets, and the need to isolate demand from supply can make it tricky to make comparisons within labor markets. Furthermore, the empirical evidence strongly suggests that capitalized values reflect the characteristics of the children attending the school rather than purely characteristics within school-district control.

Given the inherent imprecision of the methodology and the strong possibility that housing premiums reveal a preference for student characteristics outside of school-district control, it would be problematic to incorporate revealed-preference measures into school accountability systems. However, analyses of school productivity and adequacy could potentially benefit from incorporating the information about nontest educational outcomes that may be embedded in revealed-preference measures of school quality.

Revealed-preference measures also have the potential to greatly change perceptions of school quality. In the example presented here, the correlation between housing premiums and test scores is relatively modest whereas the correlation between housing premiums and value-added test scores is statistically insignificant. Among the 175 elementary and middle schools within Dallas County, Texas, for which a school premium could be estimated, 107 are in the top quartile on at least one of the four measures of school quality (school premiums, test scores, value-added test scores, and adjusted housing premiums). No schools are in the top quartile with respect to all four measures. Thus, the evidence suggests that revealed-preference measures may be the only way to get at important aspects of school quality that are not reflected in test scores and cannot be quantified in other obvious ways. If so, then revealed-preference measures have the potential to greatly alter perceptions of educational adequacy, productivity and efficiency.

References

Baker, B. D., Taylor, L. D., & Vedlitz, A. (2004). Measuring educational adequacy in public schools. Manuscript.

Bartik, T. J., & Smith, V. K. (1987). Urban amenities and public policy. In E. S. Mills, (Ed.), *Handbook of regional and urban economics* (pp.1207–54). Amsterdam: North Holland.

Bayer, P., Ferreira, F. V., & McMillan, R. (2003). Unified framework for measuring preferences for schools and neighborhoods. (Discussion Paper No. 892.) Yale University Economic Growth Center, New Haven: CT.

Bayer, P., Ferreira, F. V., & McMillan, R. (2004). Tiebout sorting, social multipliers and the demand for school quality. Manuscript.

Bayer, P., McMillan, R., & Rueben, H. (2004). An equilibrium model of sorting in an urban housing market. Manuscript.

Barrow, L. (2002). School choice through relocation: Evidence from the Washington, D.C. area. *Journal of Public Economics, 86*(2), 155–189.

Black, Sandra E. (1999) Do Better Schools Matter? Parental Valuation of Elementary Education. *Quarterly Journal of Economics* 114(2): 577–99.

Bogart, W. T., & Cromwell, B. J. (2000). How much is a neighborhood school worth? *Journal of Urban Economics, 47*(2), 280–305.

Brasington, D. M. (1999). Which measures of school quality does the housing market value? *Journal of Real Estate Research, 18*(3), 395–413.

Brasington, D. M. (2003a). Can new insights on location and Black's (1999) test help resolve the 5-decades-old debate over capitalization. Manuscript.

Brasington, D. M. (2003b). Supply of public school quality. *Economics of Education Review, 22*(4), 367–77.

Brunner, E. J., Murdoch, J., & Thayer, M. (2002). School finance reform and housing values. *Public Finance and Management. 2*(4), 535-65.

Brunner, E. J., Sonstelie, J., & Thayer, M. (2001). Capitalization and the voucher: An analysis of precinct returns from California's proposition 174. *Journal of Urban Economics, 50*(3), 517–36.

Downes, T. A., & Zabel, J. E. (2002). The impact of school characteristics on housing prices: Chicago 1987–1991. *Journal of Urban Economics, 52*(1), 1–25.

Duncombe, W., Lukemeyer, A., & Yinger, J. (2003) Financing an adequate education: A case study of New York. In William J. Fowler (Ed.) *Developments in School Finance: 2001–02 (pp. 127–153)*. Washington, DC: National Center for Education Statistics.

Figlio, D. N., & Lucas, M. E. (2004). What's in a grade? School report cards and house prices (pp. 127–53). *American Economic Review, 94*(3), 591–604.

Gronberg, T. J., Jansen, D. W., Taylor, L. L., & Booker, K. (2004). School outcomes and school costs: The cost function approach. Manuscript.

Grosskopf, S., Hayes, K. J., & Taylor, L. L. (2004). Competition and efficiency: The impact of charter schools on public school performance. Manuscript.

Hanushek, E. A., Rivkin, S. G., & Taylor, L. L. (1996). Aggregation and the estimated effects of school resources. *Review of Economics and Statistics*, 78(4), 611–627.

Haurin, D. R., & Brasington, D. (1996). School quality and real house prices: Inter-and intrametropolitan effects. *Journal of Housing Economics*, 5, 351–368.

Hayes, K. J., & Taylor, L. L. (1996). Neighborhood school characteristics: What signals quality to homebuyers? *Federal Reserve Bank of Dallas Economic Review*, Fourth Quarter, 2–9.

Kane, T. J., & Staiger, D. O. (2002). The promise and pitfalls of using imprecise school accountability measures. *Journal of Economic Perspectives*, 16(4), 91–114.

Kane, T. J., & Staiger, D. O., & Riegg, S. K. (2004). Do good schools or good neighbors raise property values? Manuscript.

Kane, T. J., & Staiger, D. O., & Samms, G. (2003). School accountability ratings and housing values. *Brookings-Wharton Papers on Urban Affairs.* 83–127.

Kiel, K. A., & Zabel, J. E. (1997). Evaluating the usefulness of the American Housing Survey for creating house price indices, *Journal of Real Estate Finance and Economics*, 14, 189–202.

Loubert, Linda (in press). Housing markets and school financing. *Journal of Education Finance.*

McFadden, D. (1978). Modeling the choice of residential location. In A. Karlquist et al. (Eds.) *Spatial interaction theory and planning models* (pp. 75–96). New York: Elsevier North Holland.

Reschovsky, A., & Imazeki, J. (2001) Achieving educational adequacy through school finance reform. *Journal of Education Finance*, 26(Spring), 373–396.

Reschovsky, A., & Imazeki, J. (2003). Let no child be left behind: Determining the cost of improving student performance. *Public Finance Review* 31(May), 263–290.

Rosen, S. (1974). Hedonic prices and implicit markets: Product differentiation in pure competition. *Journal of Political Economy* 82 (January/February), 34–55.

Tiebout, C. M., (1956). Pure theory of local expenditures. *Journal of Political Economy* 64, 416-424.

Weimer, D. L., & Wolkoff, M. (2003). School performance and housing values: using non-contiguous district and incorporation boundaries to identify school effects, *National Tax Journal*, 54(2), 231–253.

9

Rethinking Educational Productivity and its Measurement: A Discussion of Stochastic Frontier Analysis Within a Budget-Maximizing Framework

Anthony Rolle

Introduction

Education finance and economics researchers tend to investigate three types of efficiency when examining the efficacy of the schooling process (Mayston, 1996):

- *Technical efficiency:* Attempts to maximize student learning and organizational policy outcomes while utilizing given sets of financial and human resource inputs.

- *Allocative efficiency:* Attempts to maximize student learning and organizational policy outcomes, given prices for inputs and the effectiveness of management strategies, while utilizing financial and human resources in optimal proportions.

- *Total economic efficiency:* Attempts to maximize student learning and organizational policy outcomes while pursuing allocative and technical efficiency simultaneously.

When conducting efficiency analyses, education researchers typically employ the use of statistical relationships called production functions—or cost functions in the dual sense (Levin, 1974; see also Schwartz, Stiefel, & Bel Hadj Amor, Chapter 4 in this volume). Based on economic theories of the firm, these statistical formulations assume that public organizations act similarly to private businesses, and accordingly, administrators of public organizations pursue cost-minimizing management strategies.

A generalized expression for a basic educational algorithm that is designed to predict levels of student learning costs looks like:

$$\text{Student Learning Costs} = \text{A Combination of } (C, H, I, P, S)$$

where C represents community characteristics, H represents household characteristics, I represents individual student characteristics, P represents peer influence characteristics, and S represents school resource characteristics. Mathematically, the algorithm described above can be represented as:

$$C_i = \alpha + \sum_{\rho=1}^{P} B_\rho Y_{\rho i} + u_i \qquad (1)$$

where C_i represents student learning costs, α represents a computational constant, B_ρ represents the direction and degree to which $Y_{\rho i}$ influences student learning outcomes, $Y_{\rho i}$ represents many characteristics that influence student learning costs, and u_i represents measurement error. As a consequence of using cost and production functions for economic efficiency analyses of educational organizations, several generalizations about what resources consistently improve educational outcomes have been substantiated (Hoenack, 1994; King & MacPhail-Wilcox, 1994; Monk, 1990, 1992): a) positive teacher attributes such as high verbal abilities and quality training, b) progressive administrative policies such as high levels of collaborative management and small class sizes, and c) proper fiscal and physical assets such as stable student expenditure levels and contemporary facilities.

More recently, education finance researchers are attempting to improve these conventional education-cost and production-function approaches by focusing primarily on several areas of interest (Levin, 1997; Rice, 2001; Schwartz & Stiefel, 2001; Verstegen & King, 1998):

- ◆ Improving statistical relationships between purchased school inputs, nonpurchased school inputs, student learning, and organizational policy outcomes
- ◆ Understanding relationships between human resources allocation, organizational incentives, and the individual preferences of administrators, faculty, and students
- ◆ Creating incentives that transform individual and institutional productivity efforts into pursuits of increased student learning and organizational policy outcomes
- ◆ Developing systematic district-, school-, and classroom-level data collection, management, reporting, and dissemination mechanisms that accurately reflect the aforementioned relationships

Still, despite the promise of these investigative efforts, major challenges continue to complicate the employment of educational cost and production functions (Rolle, 2004a):

- There is a need to expand the traditional two-stage statistical relationship (i.e., dollars purchase educational services, and these services generate outcomes) into multistage models (e.g., dollars purchase personnel, personnel provide services, services are used by students, and students generate outcomes) that accurately portray the educational process.

- There is a need to analyze distinct subgroups (e.g., by levels of language ability, poverty, or urbanicity)—using the expanded models mentioned above—to improve statistical relationships that accurately represent the educational process for various types of students being educated in multiple contexts.

- There is a need to investigate the effects of time—and time-lagged effects—on levels of educational productivity and its measurement that accurately represent the educational process for various types of students being educated in multiple contexts.

In opposition to these efforts to improve conventional measures of efficiency, researchers from Mises (1944) to Levin (1976) to Barnett (1994) assert that educational organizations are structured for bureaucratic management—not for efficient management—strategies which are supported by centralized authorities, hierarchical rule orientations, and external (i.e., economic, political, and social) influences. In addition, seminal research developing economic theories for bureaucratic organizations—and research regarding the behavior of public-sector administrators—indicates that it is highly implausible that district and school administrators act to minimize costs (Boyd & Hartman, 1988; Buchanon & Tollison, 1984; Downs, 1967, 1998; Hentschke, 1988; Peacock, 1992; Tullock, 1965). As a matter of fact, because educational quality is measured primarily by levels of—but not optimal use of—financial and human resource inputs, educational agencies seem much more likely to be budget maximizers (Barnett, 1994; Niskanen, 1968, 1971; Grosskopf & Hayes, 1993).

As a result of these findings, education-cost and production-function analyses used to measure levels of efficiency in educational organizations may be predisposed to show weak statistical relationships in at least three ways because (Deller & Rudnicki, 1993):

- There is an assumption that all students, teachers, and administrators are performing optimally; but no universally accepted determination of this optimality—or its measurement—exists for student effort, teacher effectiveness, or education management.

- There is a casualness that surrounds the construction of statistical models used to estimate student learning costs; but no universally accepted pedagogical or curricular—and therefore no statistical—structure exists for the educational production process.

- There is education policy research that refers to the significant influences of community, household, and peer characteristics; but no universally accepted definitions for these characteristics—or their measurement.

Moreover, given that these findings challenge the applicability of cost-minimizing analytical frameworks to public educational institutions, it is unfortunate that education-finance researchers devote little attention to measuring levels of efficiency outside of conventional analytical paradigms. As such, the purpose of this monograph is to contribute to our knowledge about the measurement of educational efficiency using a relative measure of technical efficiency—stochastic frontier analysis—within a budget-maximizing framework. Specifically, this chapter will provide a brief literature review that outlines budget-maximization theory, describes and critiques the stochastic frontier analysis methodology, and suggests recommendations to improve its application to public educational organizations.

A Budget-Maximizing Framework
for Examining Educational Productivity

Economic efficiency research on how public schools behave consists mainly of cost and production function studies that assume implicitly that schools are cost-minimizing or outcome-maximizing organizations. However, patterns among education organizations seem to be characterized by annual increases in size, fiscal resources, and constancy—or decreases—in educational outcomes (Sowell, 1993; Walberg & Fowler, 1987; and Walberg & Walberg, 1994). As a result, applying economic efficiency measures designed to incorporate the behavior of private industries seem to be inappropriate for public schools. On the other hand, investigating concepts of economic efficiency in public schools within the context of the theory of budget-maximizing bureaucratic behavior does seem appropriate (Niskanen, 1968, 1971, 1973). This alternative economic framework describes public schools as *budget-maximizing* agencies—as opposed to cost-minimizing or output-maximizing organizations—whose costs are determined by a sociopolitical process that acquires and distributes revenue (Duncombe, Miner, & Ruggiero, 1997; Romer & Rosenthal, 1984; Rolle, 2003; Stevens, 1993).

The Budget-Output Function:
A Mathematical Representation of Sponsor Preferences

From the vantage point of public education agencies, budget-maximization theory asserts that the preferences of the sponsor (i.e., the collective organization that ultimately determines expenditure levels and designations) can be summarized mathematically by a cost function called the budget-output function (Niskanen, 1971). Any point represented by this function represents the maximum total budget a sponsor is willing to grant to the bureau for a specific expected level of output. The function has the following properties:

- ♦ The first derivative of the budget-output function is positive and monotonic over a defined range.

- ♦ The second derivative of the budget-output function is negative and monotonic over a defined range.

In practical applications, these criteria model-spending patterns initially increase marginally, but ultimately reflect decreasing marginal investments. That is, over time, sponsors are reluctant to grant large budget increases to longstanding programs.

Several types of equations share these two properties, but Niskanen chose to use a quadratic function of the following form to represent the concave down budget-output function:

$$B_t = aQ_{t-1} - bQ^2_{t-1} \quad \text{subject to} \quad Q_{t-1}:Q_{t-1} \in [0, a/2b] \tag{2}$$

where: $B_t \equiv$ maximum total budget sponsor is willing to grant to bureau during a specific time period; $Q_{t-1} \equiv$ expected level of output by bureau during a specific time period; $t \equiv$ time in academic years; a and $b \equiv$ the coefficients for Q_{t-1} and Q^2_{t-1} respectively.

He claims a total budget-output function is a necessary building block for a theory of supply by bureaus because the exchange of promised activities, and expected output for a budget, is conducted "entirely in total" rather than in "unit" terms. The budget-output function, therefore, should be considered to be the product of two relationships (Niskanen, 1971):

1. The relationship between budget and level of service (e.g., the relationship between teacher salary and teacher quality)

2. The relationship between level of service and output (e.g., the relationship between teacher quality and student learning outcomes)

Furthermore, Niskanen states that a bureaucrat—in our case a superintendent or principal—usually can estimate the sponsor's (e.g., a state legislature's) budget-output function fairly accurately from previous budget reviews, recent changes in the composition of the collective organization, and by the levels of influence different constituencies exert on the sponsor (Niskanen, 1971). In addition, he believes a bureaucrat also possesses greater knowledge about the cost and production factors for the services provided than members of the sponsor organization. In contrast, budgets offered by the bureau reveal little about the minimum budget amount that would be sufficient to supply a given output. Therefore, Niskanen claims, a bureaucrat needs relatively little information—most of which can be estimated by the revealed preferences of the sponsor—to exploit the position as a monopoly supplier of a given service. The members of the sponsor organization, on the other hand, need a great deal of information—little of which can be estimated from revealed behavior—to exploit their position as a monopsony buyer of services (Niskanen, 1971). Therefore, the theory Niskanen developed originally assumed that the sponsor is passive and knows the largest budget it is prepared to grant for an expected level of services. These characteristics are assumed because there is no incentive or opportunity for the sponsor to obtain information on the minimum budget necessary to supply this service.

A Budget-Maximizing Single-Service Bureau

The single-service agency hypothesized above is monitored only by one sponsor, and it supplies only one service (i.e., education) in exchange for a total budget. For this general case, a school district purchases all of its production factors at a competitive price. Accordingly, Niskanen claims all expenditures necessary to supply this service are made during a single budget period. Thus, the basic model is a one-period model of a pure educational service bureau that purchases production factors competitively (Niskanen, 1971). Also, the school district is considered to be a monopoly supplier of the service. But, for either lack of incentive or opportunity, the sponsor is assumed not to exercise its monopsony power.

During any budget period, the total potential budget available to this school district is represented by the budget-output function mentioned previously:

$$B_t = aQ_{t-1} - bQ^2_{t-1} \quad \text{subject to} \quad Q_{t-1} : Q_{t-1} \in [0, \tfrac{a}{2b}] \tag{3}$$

Given the competitive purchase of factors, the minimum total cost (TC) during the budget period is represented by the following cost-output function (Niskanen, 1971):

$$TC_t = cQ_{t-1} + dQ^2_{t-1} \quad \text{subject to} \quad Q_{t-1} : Q_{t-1} \le 0; \tag{4}$$

where a and b are the coefficients for Q_{t-1} and Q^2_{t-1}, respectively. The constraint that the budget must be greater than or equal to the minimum total cost is represented as follows:

$$B_t \ge TC_t \tag{5}$$

These two functions and the budget constraint comprise the complete model for the costs of the school district.

A Budget-Maximizing Multiservice Bureau

Most school districts, however, supply two or more of instructional—and noninstructional—services. Consequently, Niskanen also evaluates the behavior of a multiservice organization to determine if its behavior differs from the summation of individual bureau behavior (Niskanen, 1971). In this scenario, a school district is assumed to be a monopoly supplier of several different educational services. This district also is assumed to face multiple sponsors (i.e., from the state, local, and federal levels) that provide its total financing and pay competitive prices for factors of production. The model Niskanen develops is specific to organizations that supply only two services, but he claims the results easily are generalizable to public agencies that supply three or more services.

School districts that supply two or more educational services face two or more different budget-output functions and also have different minimum cost functions. The budget-output function for one service is described by (Niskanen, 1971):

$$B_{1t} = a_1 Q_{1t-1} - b_1 Q^2_{1t-1} \text{ subject to } Q_{1t-1} : Q_{1t-1} \in [0, \tfrac{a_1}{2b_1}] \tag{6}$$

The budget-output function for the second service, either from the same or a different sponsor, is described by:

$$B_{2t} = a_2 Q_{2t-1} - b_2 Q^2_{2t-1} \quad \text{subject to} \quad Q_{2t-1} : Q_{2t-1} \in [0, \tfrac{a_2}{2b_2}] \tag{7}$$

In this case, the demands for the two educational services are completely independent. The minimum total cost function for the first service is described by:

$$TC_{1t} = c_1 Q_{1t-1} + d_1 Q^2{}_{1t-1} \text{ subject to } Q_{1t-1} : Q_{1t-1} \geq 0 \tag{8}$$

and the minimum total cost function for the second service is described by:

$$TC_{2t} = c_2 Q_{2t-1} + d_2 Q^2{}_{2t-1} \text{ subject to } Q_{2t-1} : Q_{2t-1} \geq 0 \tag{9}$$

The minimum total costs of the two educational services also are completely independent. This two-service bureau faces a budget constraint represented by:

$$B_{1t} + B_{2t} \geq TC_{1t} + TC_{2t} \tag{10}$$

Therefore, the output problem Niskanen presents here is to find the level of the output of the two services that maximizes $[B_{1t} + B_{2t}]$ subject to the budget constraint represented by $[TC_{1t} + TC_{2t}]$.

Niskanen's analysis shows that a bureau supplying two or more services with different demand and cost conditions have equilibrium budgets greater than the sum of individual bureaus supplying separate services (Niskanen, 1971). He claims the primary reason for this outcome is that bureaucrats—district superintendents or school principals—have the freedom to allocate expenditures for multiple services from a single budget. This free spending, coupled with the inability of a sponsor to know actual costs or control the level of services, contributes to higher equilibrium levels. As a result, the multiservice district will supply a combination of smaller outputs of superior services and larger outputs of inferior services (Niskanen, 1971). These properties suggest that school districts should be expected to add educational services—independent of productivity relationships—to those supplied presently.

Summary

Budget-maximization theory states that public sector managers—lacking the lure of performance-based salaries and benefits as rewards for increasing organizational efficiency—attempt to maximize their nonpecuniary benefits (e.g., prestige, scope of activities, or perquisites) through the pursuit of larger agency budgets (Niskanen, 1971). As a result of this budget-maximizing behavior, public bureaus generate organizational output in a manner that is economically inefficient. In other words, administrators of public districts and schools may place considerable value on preventing employees from understanding the administration fully and keeping employees responsive, cooperative, and effective to maintain agency reputation. Migue and Belanger (1974) and Niskanen (1975, 1991, 1994) amended Niskanen (1971) to state that sponsors are not passive, and discretionary funds—differences between total revenue received and overall costs—are spent on utility maximization for the bureaucrat. Rolle (2004b) provides additional support that public school districts act as budget-maximizing agencies; concomitantly, he also provides an addendum to Niskanen's amended theory: It is necessary to examine the sociopolitical history of a particular sponsor's expenditure preferences—to model concavity conditions properly—before attempting to determine if resources are being used efficiently.

A large body of research supports the notion that managers of public bureaus systematically request budget increases regardless of the level of organizational output generated. These ideas have been relatively unchallenged because Wildavsky (1964) claimed bureaucrats request moderate annual budget increases to maximize long-term budget goals. For example, Fiorina and Noll (1978), Lynn (1991), and Hayes, Razzolini, and Ross (1998) all have provided empirical evidence that public managers desire and request increased budgets. In particular, these researchers suggest that the welfare of educational constituents (e.g., students, families, and communities served by educational agencies) may not have any consistent relationship to the student learning or organizational policy goals pursued by administrators or teachers. They reason: Educational institutions tend to create opposing incentives that lead rational, self-interested individuals to behave in manners that involve attempts to satisfy as many constituents as possible. Therefore, public sector agencies do not spend efficiently—or inefficiently—in the traditional sense. Similarly, other research (e.g., Aucoin, 1991; Blais & Dion, 1991; Kiewiet, 1991; Young, 1991) has shown that:

- Budget controls exist because sponsors believe that managers of public agencies always will attempt to increase their budgets.
- Little or no relationship exists between the size (or rate of growth) of public agencies, staff salaries, and organizational performance.
- Managers of public agencies tend to favor political parties that support high levels of state intervention.
- School superintendents hold tax rates as high as possible without having to obtain voter approval.

It is within this historical and contemporary type of literature that evidence supports assertions that public managers tend to pursue increased budgets. More specifically, these research findings establish the necessity for exploring concepts of educational efficiency outside of conventional analytical paradigms. Employing budget-maximizing analytical assumptions—or other public choice economics frameworks that examine the efficacy of sociopolitical contexts on productivity—questions the veracity of utilizing cost-minimizing assumptions in determining absolute levels of educational productivity. Relative measures of economic efficiency—comparisons of the best economic performers to the worst—deserve considerations given the influence of exogenous factors on levels of productivity in the public policy arena.

Using Stochastic Frontier Analysis to Determine Levels of Relative Efficiency

This Niskanenian perspective is inconsistent with the conventional assumption that financial resources are chosen optimally by sponsors—and used optimally by administrators—to maximize educational outcomes across multiple program and policy goals. Furthermore, findings by Pritchett and Filmer (1999) assert that because school administrators have little discretion over determining optimal levels and proportions of input resources, research measuring levels of allocative efficiency in public schools may never be fruitful. An examination of average total costs and marginal costs are warranted in the private sector because most production functions are known—this phenomenon does not exist in the public sector. By contrast, public school spending is conducted such that no student's educational situation is made worse to improve the situation of another student. As a result, efficiency in public schools is concerned with the quantity and quality of educational services delivered to—and acquired by—students and at what cost. As such, it seems improper for a public school's level of allocative efficiency to be measured as a pursuit of what could be the unattainable: an absolute mathematical representation of a legislative process that determines and distributes resources to administrators who may or may not direct resources toward desired organizational goals.

Given this context, educational productivity can be defined as the amount of technical efficiency generated by combinations of financial and human resources, instructional and management strategies, and levels of student effort that maximize educational outcomes. Therefore, a different measure of production efficiency is warranted. Ordinary least squares (OLS) regression methods are designed to predict best *average* performances, not what the highest performers will achieve. If education finance researchers truly are interested in what high-performing educational institutions produce, the methods used should focus on comparisons of the best-observed performers to the worst—not on the average performers. The difficulty in developing mathematical relationships based on average performances used by conventional OLS measures may be the primary reason that an educational cost function—or production function—is yet to be found.

Stochastic Frontier Analyses

When acknowledging the influences of sociopolitical characteristics on the generation of educational outcomes, the efficiency measurement question to address becomes (Debreu, 1951; Farrell, 1957): When an organizational environment is determined to be nonoptimal economically, is it possible to develop a methodology that consistently measures the difference between relatively efficient and inefficient performers?

Stochastic frontier measures of economic efficiency are used commonly by economic- and public-finance policy researchers to evaluate levels of technical efficiency present in an organization relative to the best-performing organization(s) in the sample investigated (Murillia-Zamarano, 2004; Worthington, 2001). Accordingly, the focal point of the analysis lies in determining statistically the best-performing organization. If the statistically determined best-performing organization has higher levels of economic productivity than the remaining organizations, the residual organizations are labeled as inefficient producers in relative comparison to the best-performing organization(s) in its comparison group (Coelli, Rao, & Battese, 1998; Cubbin & Zamani, 1996).

Before a mathematical example, consider a given cost curve (i.e., this cost curve—also called an isoquant—represents combinations of outputs produced at lowest cost when inputs are used in a technically efficient manner), Schools A and C lie on the cost frontier and can be labeled efficient (see Figure 9.1 below). On the other hand, School B lies above the cost curve and is labeled inefficient. In this case, the estimated level of inefficiency for School B can be represented by the efficiency ratio (OB/OB*-1). The ratio gives the extent to which costs are above the estimated level of efficiency denoted by B (Barrow, 1991; Fare, Grosskopf, & Lovell, 1994; Kumbhakar & Lovell, 2000)

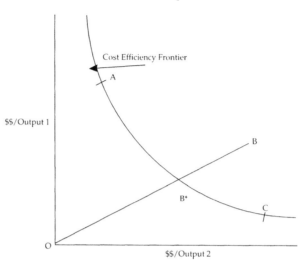

Figure 9.1. Graphic Example of Stochastic Frontier Analysis for School B

Besides measuring overall levels of efficiency, stochastic frontier analysis (SFA) also can allow for the distinct measurements of technical efficiency depending on its functional form and availability of data.

Mathematically, Aigner, Lovell, and Schmidt (1977) are credited with developing stochastic frontier analysis techniques. This method improved the deterministic frontier method by incorporating a technical efficiency term into the regression equation; and by isolating the effects of random error from the effects within the control of organizational managers. For the simplest case, where homogeneity is assumed, the single-output organization can be represented by the stochastic frontier model:

$$C_i = \alpha + \sum_{\rho=1}^{P} A_\rho Y_{\rho i} + \sum_{\rho=1}^{P} B_\rho Z_{\rho i} + (u_i + n_i) \quad \text{see footnote}[1] \tag{11}$$

where, C_i represents student learning costs, α represents a computational constant, A_ρ represents the direction and degree to which $Y_{\rho i}$ influences student

---

[1] At this point, regardless of the estimation method used, the composite error term needs to be separated for technical efficiency analyses. Jondrow, Lovell, Materov, & Schmidt (1982) were the first to show the expected value of n_i for the half-normal and exponential cases. Readers wanting more detailed statistical presentations are referred to Jondrow et al.; Coellli, Rao, and Battese (1998); and Kumbhakar, and Lovell (2000).

learning outcomes, Y_{pi} represents many purchased characteristics that influence student learning costs, B_p represents the direction and degree to which Z_{pi} influences student learning outcomes, and Z_{pi} represents many nonpurchased characteristics that influence student learning costs (Cooper & Cohn, 1997). The term $u_i + n_i$ is a composite error term, where u_i represents randomness and n_i represents technical inefficiency. The portion of the error term representing statistical noise, u_i, is assumed to be identical independent and identically distributed. With respect to u_i, it is assumed to be a nonnegative, one-sided error term that most frequently assumes a half-normal or exponential distribution. If the two error terms are assumed independent of each other, independent of the input variables, and independent of the distributions mentioned above, then either Maximum Likelihood (ML) or Corrected Ordinary Least Squares (COLS) estimates can be used to determine the appropriate estimates. The cost inefficiency ratio (CIR) then is calculated as:

$$CIR : (C_{actual} / C_{estimated}) - 1 \tag{12}$$

An Illustrative Example of Efficiency Measurement Using OLS and SFA

Discussions of efficiency have been central to systems of public school funding—and later at the heart of school finance litigation during the 1970s and beyond—since the seminal works of Cubberley (1906), Strayer and Haig (1922), and Mort (1924). Another of these discussions occurred when the Supreme Court of Tennessee ruled that the state school finance system violated the equal protection clause of the state constitution in *Tennessee Small School Systems v McWherter I, II, and III.* Following court mandates, the state of Tennessee enacted the Education Improvement Act (EIA) of 1993 which requires the implementation of changes to the state funding formula to support the Basic Education Program (BEP). The primary purpose of the BEP formula is to increase levels of education finance resources present in all Tennessee public school districts that create equal opportunities for students to learn. But, beyond the reporting requirements mandated by the No Child Left Behind (NCLB) Act of 2001, there has been little policy discussion surrounding the BEP with respect to how levels of educational productivity should be measured.

The construction of a Niskanenian budget-output function for education—which really is used as a mathematical proxy for the hypothesized indifference curve of a state legislature—is based on the model of a budget-maximizing agency. Specifically, this cost function that predicts total expenditures-per-pupil based on the ACT assessment is:

$$totpup02 = B_0 - B_1 * act01 + B_2 * (act01)^2 + u_i \tag{13}$$

where *totpup02* represents total expenditures per pupil, *act01* represents scores on the ACT Assessment, $(act01)^2$ represents the square of scores on the ACT Assessment, and u_i represents measurement error.[2]

In this instance, the superintendent is the central administrative figure—the chooser or the maximizer—and is assumed to (Niskanen, 1971):

♦ Face a set of possible actions constrained by the sponsor

♦ Have personal preferences among the outcomes of these actions

♦ Choose the action within the possible set that is preferred

As Niskanen assumes correctly, the larger political and organizational environment also is believed to influence the behavior of the bureaucrat by constraining—or enhancing—sets of possible actions; changing relationships between actions and outcomes; and by influencing preferences. The analysis of educational productivity presented below will compare OLS and SFA methodologies to measure levels of technical efficiency present for Tennessee public school districts within the budget-maximizing context.

Measuring Efficiency Using Ordinary Least Squares

An examination of the data indicates the mean OLS-generated CIR for Tennessee public school districts is -0.5% (see Figures 9.1a and 9.1b). In other words, school districts are observed to spend slightly less than the OLS predicted average expenditure given scores on the ACT. These values range from a high of 69.8% to a low of -31.9%. That is, the most inefficient of Tennessee school districts spends approximately 70% above the state average whereas the most efficient spends about 30% less.[3]

---

2 Given that this example is illustrative, other outputs and controls could be incorporated into more complex budget-maximizing statistical models.

3 For all statistical categories, a school district that has the maximum ACT score, for example, does not necessarily correspond to the school district with the highest efficiency ratio. Complete data tables are available from the author on request.

Figure 9.1a. Univariate Statistics
for Tennessee Public School Districts

Academic Year 2001–2002				
Statistics	*ACT Scores*	*Actual total expenditure per pupil*	*Estimated total expenditure per pupil*	*OLS Inefficiency Ratio*
Maximum	23.6	$11,156.34	$9185.09	69.8%
Mean	19.7	$5959.67	$5995.85	–0.5%
Median	19.7	$5736.92	$5797.30	–2.6%
Std. Deviation	1.07	$923.92	$537.86	13.28%
Minimum	16.1	$4900.81	$5710.76	–31.9%
CoV	0.054	0.155	0.090	0.135

Figure 9.1b. OLS Regression Statistics
for Tennessee Public School Districts

Academic Year 2001–2002					
				N = 120	
Source	SS	Df	MS	F $(2,117)$ = 15.64	
Model	21426705	2	10713352.29	**Prob** > F = 0.0000	
Residual	80154934	117	685084.91	R^2 = 0.211	
Total	1.02e+08	119	853627.16	**Adj** R^2 = 0.197	
Dependent Variable: Total Expenditures per Pupil					
Variables	Coeficient	Std. Error	Beta	t	P>|t|
act02	–5863.53	1359.63	–6.813	–4.313	0.000
act02sq	153.91	34.27	7.097	4.492	0.000
constant	61556.32	13484.28		4.565	0.000

At face value, these ranges of inefficiency seem fairly reasonable given varying school characteristics such as teacher quality and student effort. But it is important to note that the CIR evaluated using OLS fails to measure levels of technical inefficiency independent of measurement error. So, in evaluations of educational productivity, using OLS measures will tend to provide inconclusive results with regard to technical efficiency. Also of note is that OLS measures compare varying levels of educational productivity to the best *average* performers in a sample—not to the best performers in a sample. If the veracity of educational productivity research is to be maintained, and excellence in education to be pursued, school districts need to be compared to the best performers in the group to generate authentic measures of efficiency.

Measuring Efficiency Using Stochastic Frontier Analysis

An examination of the same data using MLE techniques indicates the SFA-generated CIR—assuming a half-normal distribution for the composite error term—for Tennessee public school districts is 19.1% (see Figures 9.2a and 9.2b). In other words, school districts spend approximately 20% more than the SFA-predicted average expenditure given scores on the ACT. These values range from a high of 140.0% to a low of 0.1% for school districts closest to the cost frontier. The most technically inefficient of school districts in Tennessee spends more than twice as much as the most efficient.

Figure 9.2a. Univariate Statistics for Tennessee Public School Districts

		Academic Year 2001–2002				
Statistics	*ACT Scores*	*Observed natural log total expenditure per pupil*	*Estimated natural log total expenditure per pupil*	*Observed to estimated expenditure ratio*	*Error due to inefficiency*	*Technical Inefficiency Ratio*
Maximum	23.6	9.3193	8.5956	1.087	0.800	140.0%
Mean	19.7	8.6828	8.5204	1.019	0.165	19.1%
Median	19.7	8.6547	8.5202	1.015	0.139	14.9%
Std. Dev.	1.07	0.1364	0.0228	0.016	0.132	17.8%
Minimum	16.1	8.4972	8.4360	0.997	0.064	0.0%
CoV	0.054	0.0157	0.0027	0.016	0.800	0.149

Figure 9.2b. Maximum Likelihood Estimated Stochastic Frontier Regression Statistics

Tennessee Public School Districts—Academic Year 2001–2002						
Log Likelihood = 94.7814					Wald χ^2 Prob $> \chi^2$	N=120 5.37 0.0683
Variables	*Coefficient*	*Std. Error*	z	*P>|z|*	*95% confidence Interval*	
Lact02	−29.1363	14.7050	−1.98	0.048	−57.9577	−0.3150
Lact02sq	14.7769	7.4123	1.99	0.046	0.2490	29.3048
Constant	7.2758	0.5753		0.000	6.1482	8.4034
Lnsig2v	−9.0236	1.3894	−6.49	0.000	−11.7468	−6.3003
Lnsig2u	−3.1062	0.1439	−21.59	0.000	−3.3882	−2.8242
Sigma-v	0.0110	0.0076			0.0028	0.0428
Sigma-u	0.2116	0.0152			0.1838	0.2436
Sigma2	0.0449	0.0064			0.0323	0.0574
Lambda	19.2727	0.0192			19.2350	19.3103
Likelihood-ratio test of sigma-u=0:			χ^2 bar = 44.06		Prob $\geq \chi^2$ bar = 0.000	

It is important to remember here that the CIR evaluated here separates measurement error from error because of technical inefficiency. And initially, these ranges of inefficiency may seem unreasonable; but a reasonable amount of deference needs to be given to the results because of varying school characteristics such as teacher quality and student effort. Also of note is that SFA measures compare varying levels of educational productivity relative to the best performers in a sample—not to the best average performers in a sample. So, in evaluations of educational productivity, using SFA measures will tend to provide more accurate policy conclusions than OLS when comparing levels of efficiency between similar organizations.

Given the level of efficient producers of educational outcomes in public school districts, the logical next step is to examine the curricular and policy practices of the school districts categorized as relatively efficient and compare them to the curricular and policy practices of the relatively inefficient school districts. At the same time that these educational policies and practices are being examined, state-level policies and policy goals need to be reviewed to determine if the mandated educational goals are being obtained by the high-performing districts. If the current state goals are being obtained by these districts, then a secondary analysis—a determination of the characteristics of the school district that can be altered to improve educational attainment versus those that cannot—needs to be completed to determine a series of best practices that would lead to the improvement of educational services offered by Tennessee public schools. If the stated educational goals are not being obtained by high-performing districts, the state standards need to be reevaluated before embarking on such analyses.

Implications for Education Finance

Traditional cost and production function studies assume that schools act similarly to private businesses and, therefore, act as cost-minimizing agencies. Yet research regarding school administrator behavior and economic theories of bureaucratic organizations indicate that it is highly implausible that public schools act in a similar manner to cost-minimizing agencies. Niskanen's theory of budget-maximizing bureaus offers an alternative framework to traditional economic analyses. As such, Niskanen asserts that in place of salary bonuses and profit sharing that occurs in the private sector, managers of public education agencies seek to maximize such things as the size of their budgets, the scopes of their activities, the ease of their work, and their political prestige. As a result of these activities, the existence of budget maximization will be exhibited by increases in educational expenditures and constancy—or decreases—in organizational outcomes.

Based on the research literature presented here, developers and investigators of education finance policy need to begin examining issues of educational productivity within more politically attuned budget-maximizing frameworks rather than the cost-minimizing frameworks of traditional economic analyses. Furthermore, given the budget-maximizing public policy context within which public schools operate, it seems more appropriate to apply relative measures of economic efficiency—not the absolute measures of typical productivity analyses. As such, when analyzing educational bureaus, using stochastic frontier regression techniques within a budget-maximizing economic framework provides a different, but important, perspective when examining:

- The concept of efficiency as it applies to educational bureaus
- The nature of the input-output relationship assumed to apply to educational bureaus
- The pervasive use of simple linear production functions to predict educational outcomes

With this increased understanding of educational efficiency within a budget-maximizing framework, legislators, education personnel, parents, and the public can address the complex issue of improving the use of public resources to produce higher levels of educational outcomes with greater awareness of the political framework within which education finance policy is developed and administered.

Despite these and other critiques presented in this research, the bases for the theory of budget maximizing bureaus still are strong—the rationality and survival arguments are particularly poignant. Further, given the incentive structures inherent in the legislative process, public sector managers—acting as self-interested individuals seeking to maximize their own welfare—probably do maximize their nonpecuniary benefits (e.g., prestige, scope of activities, or perquisites) through the pursuit of larger agency budgets. In light of these issues, when considering the level of educational efficiency within public school districts, determining how to remove conflicting education legislation, policies, and oversight mechanisms seems to be an appropriate starting point. Increasing the participation of front-line education professionals, practitioners, and researchers in the development of policies and legislation seems to be an appropriate second step. This type of increase in participation and autonomy could be exchanged for increased levels of innovation, parental involvement, and accountability.

As such, spending increases for educational services or programs are designed to achieve both the educational goals desired by the education community as well as political goals desired by legislators, bureaucrats, and influential constituent groups. This duality in desired types of efficiency within public education also generates another question: If all of these constituent groups influence the amounts and types budget increases for education, who—or what group(s)—really is the maximizer? And under what conditions?

If this tension between the desires for technical and allocative efficiency can be corroborated in future research, at least a five-criteria examination needs to be implemented before discussing levels of educational efficiency in public education:

1. What goals are defined specifically for existing—and proposed—state educational programs?
2. Are the program goals deemed valuable for educational purposes (e.g., do the programs increase the learning skills or knowledge base of students)?
3. Can the educational objectives of particular programs be measured with specificity?

4. If an educational program's goals are not designed strictly to achieve measurable educational outcomes, what community, state, or societal goals are being met?

5. Should these noneducational societal goals be financed—and therefore evaluated—as part of the public education system or by some other state sponsored program?

Without such a reassessment of the purpose of educational programs, the true relationship between education budgets and student outcomes—as well as the level of technical efficiency present in the public school system—will remain coupled loosely at best.

References

Aigner, D. J., Lovell, C. A. K., & Schmidt, P. J. (1977). Formulation and estimation of stochastic frontier production function models. *Journal of Econometrics.* 6, 21–37.

Aucoin, P. (1991). The politics and management of restraint budgeting. In A. Blais, & S. Dion (Eds.), *Budget-maximizing bureaucrat: Appraisals and evidence.* Pittsburgh, PA: University of Pittsburgh Press: 119–42.

Barnett, W. S. (1994). Obstacles and opportunities: Some simple economics of school finance reform. *Educational Policy,* 8(4), 436–452.

Barrow, M. M. (1991). Measuring local education authority performance: A frontier approach. *Economics of Education Review,* 10(1), 19–27.

Blais, A., & Dion, S. (1991b). Conclusions: Are bureaucrats budget maximizers? In A. Blais, & S. Dion (Eds.), *Budget-maximizing bureaucrat: Appraisals and evidence* (pp. 355–361). Pittsburgh, PA: University of Pittsburgh Press.

Boyd, W. L., & Hartman, W. T. (1988). Politics of educational productivity In D. H. Monk, & J. Underwood (Eds.), *Micro-level school finance: Issues and implications for policy* (pp. 271–310). Cambridge, MA: Ballinger Publishing Company.

Buchanon, J. M., & Tollison, R. D. (1984). Theory of public choice II. Ann Arbor, MI: University of Michigan Press.

Coelli, T. J., Rao, D. S., & Battese, G. E. (1998). Introduction to Efficiency and Productivity Analysis. Boston, MA: Kluwer Academic Publishers.

Cooper, S. T., & E. Cohn. (1997). "Estimation of a frontier production function for the South Carolina educational process," *Economics of Education Review.* 16(3), 313–327.

Cubberley, E. P. (1906). School funds and their apportionment. New York, NY: Teachers College–Columbia University.

Cubbin, J., & H. Zamani. (1996). Comparison of performance indicators for training and enterprise councils in the UK *Annals of Comparative Economics,* 67(4), 603–632.

Debreu, G. (1951). Coefficient of resource allocation. *Econometrica,* 19(3), 273–292.

Deller, S. C., & Rudnicki, E. (1993). Production efficiency in elementary education: The case of Maine public schools. *Economics of Education Review,* 12(1), 45–57.

Downs, A. (1967). Inside bureaucracy. Boston, MA: Little, Brown, and Company.

Downs, A. (1998). Political theory and public choice. North Hampton, MA: Edward Elgar Publishing Company.

Duncombe, W., Miner, J., & Ruggiero, J. (1997). Empirical evaluation of bureaucratic models of inefficiency. *Public Choice,* 93, 1–18.

Fare, R., Grosskopf, S., & Lovell, C. A. K. (1994). Production frontiers. New York, NY: Cambridge University Press.

Farrell, M. J. (1957). Measurement of production efficiency. *Journal of the Royal Statistical Society.* Series A, 120(3).

Fiorina, M. P., & Noll, R. (1978). Voters, bureaucrats, and legislators: A rational choice perspective on the growth of bureaucracy. *Journal of Public Economics,* 9, 239–254.

Grosskopf, S., & K. Hayes. (1993). Local public sector bureaucrats and their input choices. *Journal of Urban Economics.* 33, 151–166.

Hayes, K. J., Razzolini, L., & Ross, L. B. (1998). Bureaucratic choice and nonoptimal provision of public goods: Theory and evidence. *Public Choice.* 94, 1–20.

Hentschke, G. C. (1988). Budgetary theory and reality: A micro view. In D. H. Monk, & J. Underwood (Eds.), *Micro-level school finance: Issues and implications for policy* (pp. 311–336). Cambridge, MA: Ballinger Publishing Company.

Hoenack, S. A. (1994). Economics, organizations, and learning: Research directions for the economics of education. *Economics of Education Review,* 13(2), 147–162.

Jondrow, J., Materov, I., Lovell, K., & Schmidt, P. (1982). On the estimation of technical inefficiency in the stochastic frontier production function model. *Journal of Econometrics,* 19, 233–238.

Kiewiet, D. R. (1991). Bureaucrats and budgetary outcomes: Quantitative analyses. In A. Blais, & S. Dion (Eds.), *Budget-maximizing bureaucrat: Appraisals and evidence* (pp. 143–174). Pittsburgh, PA: University of Pittsburgh Press.

King, R. A., & MacPhail-Wilcox, B. (1994). Unraveling the production equation. *Journal of Education Finance,* 20(1), 47–65.

Kumbhakar, S. C., & Lovell, C. A. K. (2000). Stochastic frontier analysis. New York, NY: Cambridge University Press.

Levin, H. M. (1974). Measuring efficiency in educational production. *Public Finance Quarterly,* 2(1), 3–24.

Levin, H. M. (1976). Concepts of economic efficiency and educational production. In Froomkin, J.T., Jamison, D.T., & Radner, R. (Eds.), *Education as an Industry* (pp. 149–196). Cambridge, MA: National Bureau of Economic Research and Ballinger Publishing.

Levin, H. M. (1997). Raising School Productivity. *Economics of Education Review,* 16(3), 303–311.

Lynn, L. E. (1991). The budget-maximizing bureaucrat: Is there a case? In A. Blais and S. Dion (Eds.), *The budget-maximizing bureaucrat: Appraisals and evidence.* (pp. 59–84) Pittsburgh, PA: University of Pittsburgh Press.

Mayston, D.J. (1996). "Educational attainment and resource use: Mystery or econometric misspecification?" *Education Economics* 4(2).

Migue, J.L. & Belanger, G. (1974). "Towards a general theory of managerial discretion," *Public Choice.* 17, 1: 24–43.

Mises, L. (1944). *Bureaucracy.* New Haven, CT: Yale University Press.

Monk, D. (1990). Chapter 1—Efficiency and the Use of Private Markets to Produce and Distribute Educational Services. In *Education Finance: An Economic Approach* (pp. 3–11). New York, NY: McGraw-Hill Publishing Company.

Monk, D. H. (1992). Education productivity research: An update and assessment of its role in education finance reform. *Educational Evaluation and Policy Analysis.* 4: 307–32.

Mort, P. R. (1924). *The measurement of educational need.* New York, NY: Columbia University.

Murillia-Zamarano, L. R. (2004). Economic efficiency and frontier techniques. *Journal of Economic Surveys,* 18(1), 33–76.

Niskanen, W. A. (1968). Peculiar economics of bureaucracy. *American Economic Review,* 58(2), 293–305.

Niskanen, W. A. (1971). *Bureaucracy and representative government.* Chicago, IL: Aldine-Atherton Incorporated.

Niskanen, W. A. (1973). *Bureaucracy: Servant or master?* London, England: Institute of Economic Affairs.

Niskanen, W. A. (1975). Bureaucrats and politicians. *Journal of Law and Economics,* 81(3), 617–644.

Niskanen, W. A. (1991). A reflection on "Bureaucracy and representative government." In A. Blais, & S. Dion (Eds.), *Budget-maximizing bureaucrat: Appraisals and evidence.* Pittsburgh: University of Pittsburgh Press, 13–32.

Niskanen, W. A. (1994). *Bureaucracy and public economics.* Vermont: Edward Elgar Publishing.

Peacock, A. T. (1992). *Public choice analysis in historical perspective.* Cambridge, England: Press Syndicate of the University of Cambridge, 1–83.

Pritchett and Filmer (1999). What education production function really show: A positive theory of expenditures. *Economics of Education Review,* 18: 223–239.

Rice, J. K. (2001). Illuminating the black box: The evolving role of education productivity research. In S. Chaikind, & W. J. Fowler, Jr. (Eds.), *Education finance in the new millennium: 2001 yearbook of the American education finance association.* Larchmont, NY: Eye On Education, Inc., 121–139.

Rolle, R. A. (2003). Getting the biggest bang for the educational buck: An empirical analysis of public school corporations as budget-maximizing bureaus. In W. J. Fowler, Jr. (Ed.), *Developments in school finance: 2001–02* (pp. 25–52). Washington, D.C.: National Center for Education Statistics.

Rolle, R. A. (2004a). Out with the old and in with the new: Thoughts on the future of educational productivity and efficiency. *Peabody Journal of Education*, 79(3), 31–56.

Rolle, R. A. (2004b). Empirical discussion of public school districts as budget-maximizing agencies. *Journal of Education Finance*, 29(4), 277–298.

Romer, T., & Rosenthal, H. (1984). Voting models and empirical evidence. *American Scientist*, 72 (September-October): 465–473.

Schwartz, A. E. & Stiefel, L. (2001). Measuring school efficiency: Lessons from economics, implications for practice. In D. H. Monk, H. J. Walberg, & M.C. Wang (Eds.), *Improving educational productivity* (pp. 115–138). Greenwich, CT: Information Age Publishing.

Sowell, T. (1993). Inside American education: The decline, the deception, and the dogmas. New York, NY: The Free Press, 1–18, 285–303.

Stevens, J. B. (1993). Economics of collective choice. Boulder, CO: Westview Press Incorporated, 263–297.

Strayer, G. D., & Haig, R. M. (1923). *Financing of education in the state of New York.* New York, NY: Macmillan Publishing Company.

Tullock, G. (1965). *Politics of bureaucracy.* Washington D.C.: Public Affairs Press.

Verstegen, D. A., & King, R. A. (1998). Relationship between school spending and student achievement: A review and analysis of 35 years of production function research. *Journal of Education Finance,* 24(4), 243–262.

Walberg, H. J., & Fowler, W. J. (1987). Expenditure and size efficiencies of public school districts. *Educational Researcher,* 16(7), 5–13.

Walberg, H. J., & Walberg, H. (1994). Losing local control. *Educational Researcher,* 23(5), 19–26.

Wildavsky, A. (1964). *Politics of the budgetary process.* Boston, MA: Little, Brown, and Company.

Worthington, A. C. (2001). Empirical survey of frontier efficient measurement techniques in education. *Education Economics,* 9(3), 245–268.

Young, R. A. (1991). Budget size and bureaucratic careers. In A. Blais, & S. Dion (Eds.), Budget-maximizing bureaucrat: Appraisals and Evidence. Pittsburgh, PA: University of Pittsburgh Press, 33–58.

Index

Accountability Systems 1–4, 9, 14–15, 120, 126, 132–133, 140, 154

Adequacy vi, 9, 70, 90–91, 123, 133, 134, 163–164, 173–175, 177, 181–183

Adjusted Performance Measures 4, 5, 13, 17–35, 65, 76
    generic 5, 19, 20, 29–32
    tailored 5, 28, 18
    theory 5, 17–19, 65, 76

Aggregation viii, 2–3, 9, 40, 66, 71, 108, 120–124

Aigner, D.J. 194

Alabama 138

Alignment 123–124, 137–139, 152–153, 157

Allocative Efficiency 4, 185 (def.), 192–193, 200

Andrews, M. 68

Annunziata, J. 139, 156

Asian students 20, 22–23, 25, 27–28, 30, 32, 46, 48, 53, 63, 77, 80, 84, 87, 99, 104–106

Attendance Zone 11, 163, 166–168, 173–176, 181

Aucoin, P. 192

Babu, S. 138, 156–157

Baker, B.D. 163

Barbanel, J. 17

Barnett, W.S. 187

Barrow, M.M. 194

Bartelsman, E.J. 40, 66

Bartik, T.J. 165

Battese, G.E. 193–194

Bayer, P. 173

Bel Hadj Amor, H. 5, 7, 19, 76, 185

Belanger, G. 191

Berne, R. 36, 97, 118

Bessent, W. 97, 117

Bias x, 6, 11, 38, 41–43, 54, 56, 64, 75, 80, 82, 97, 133, 155, 167

Bid-Rent function 164–165

Bifulco, R. 98, 117

Black students 63, 77–78, 80–81, 84–85, 87–88, 95, 99, 104–106, 121, 165–166, 170–171, 173, 175–176, 178, 182, 203

Black, S.E. 11, 166, 173

Blais, A. 192

Blinder, A.S. 26

Bogart, W.T. 167, 174

Bommer, W.H. 153, 156

Booker, K. 163

Borman, G.D. 147, 156–157

Boyd, W.L. 187

Bradbury, K. 70

Brasington, D.M. 166–167, 174

Bretschneider, S. 98, 117

Brunner, E.J. 166–167

Buchanon, J.M. 187

Budget-Maximization Theory 12, 14, 185, 188–192, 196, 199

Budget-Output Function 188–191

Bush, J. 121, 128

Capitalization 11, 166–177, 181–182

Carnoy, M. 119, 133

Census 166–167, 172–173

Charnes, A. 96–97, 117

Charter Schools 143–144

Cincinnati 140–141, 146–151

Clauretie, T.M. 70

Coelli, T.J. 193–194

Cohn, E. 195

Cohort (s) 98, 110, 120–121, 123, 127, 168

Coker, H. 138, 157

Constant returns 107–109, 112, 114–116

Conventry 140–143, 150

Cooper, S.T. 195

Cooper, W. W. 96, 117

Correnti, R. 146, 158

Cost Functions 4, 7, 13, 76, 188, 191,199
  adjusted cost measures 76, 80
  cost indices 68, 69, 134
  translog cost function 71, 74

Cromwell, B.J. 166–168, 174

Cubberley, E.P. 195

Cubbin, J. 193

Cullen, J. 128, 132–134

Daneshvary, N. 70

Danielson, C. 138, 139, 141–144, 156

Data Envelopment Analysis (DEA) viii,
  8–9, 12–14, 69, 72–73, 75, 77, 79, 81,
  83–101, 93–94 (def.), 103, 105–117

Debreu, G. 193

Decision-making unit (s) DMU 93,
  95–97, 100

Deere, D. 119, 134

Deller, S.C. 187

Desvousges, W.H. 18–19

Dion, S. 192

Disabilities 128, 132

Discrete Choice Model 164, 171

Doms, M. 41, 66

Downes, T.A. 69–70, 90, 133–134,
  165–168, 182, 187, 202

Downs, A. 187

Duncombe, W. 68–70, 90, 123, 129, 134,
  163, 182, 188, 202

Economic Efficiency 7, 12, 185, 192, 199

Economies of Scale 68–73, 175–177

Elementary schools 6

Ellett, C.D. 139, 156

Empirical Bayes (EB) 145, 149

Endogeneity/endogenous 56, 70, 75,
  166

Enrollment 20, 21, 24, 27, 39, 44, 47, 56,
  61, 64, 68, 70- 71, 73, 78–79, 81–82,
  84, 88, 99, 141, 147, 163, 175–176

Environmental Protection Agency 18

Equalization 130

Equity v, vi, vii, 9, 47, 66, 90, 118, 123,
  126, 131, 133, 134

Evans, W.N. 21

Exogeneity/exogenous 56, 75

Factor Prices 74, 75

Fare, R. 194

Farrell, M.J. 193

Ferriera, F.V. 173

Figlio, D.N. 9, 119–120, 122, 124–126,
  128, 130, 132–133, 165–168, 182

Fiorina, M.P. 192

Fixed Effects 6–8, 11, 13, 14, 19, 38–43,
  52, 54, 56, 65, 68–69, 71–73, 80–82,
  89, 165–170, 173–176, 180
  boundary fixed effects 11, 166, 167,
  173, 174
  house-specific fixed effects 165–167
  neighborhood fixed effects 11, 175
  school-level fixed effects 11, 39–43,
  68, 72, 81, 85, 166, 168–169, 171,
  175, 180, 183

Florida v, 1, 121, 122, 128, 133–135, 168
  A+ Plan 121, 128
  Florida Comprehensive Assessment
  Test (FCAT) 121

Fowler, W.J. 21, 188

Fox, W. 68

Free-lunch 28, 30, 32, 82, 99, 121

Fritsche, L. 138, 156

Index

Frontier 8, 12, 95, 98, 109, 185, 192–194, 198

Fuhrman, S.H. 137, 139, 156

Gains viii, 5, 9–10, 40–42, 49, 52, 59, 61, 71, 73, 103, 105, 113, 117, 126–127, 132–133, 138

Gallagher, H.A. 147, 151, 156–157

Gaming 124–125, 131, 143

Getzler, L. 126, 128, 132, 134

Gordon, N. 130, 134

Grade Span 7, 20–22, 24, 27, 39, 47, 63, 73

Gramlich, E.M. 19- 21

Greenwald, R. 10, 21

Gronberg, T.J. 163

Grosskopf, S. 169, 187, 194

Haddock, C.K. 15, 35, 134, 183

Haig, R.M. 195

Hanushek, E. vii, 10, 15, 21, 35, 119, 124, 134, 175, 183

Hartman, W.T. 187

Haurin, D.R. 166

Hayes, K.J. 168–169, 187, 192

Hedges, L.V. 10, 21

Hedonic Model 11, 164–177, 181, 183

Heneman, H.G. III 156–158

Heneman, R.L. 157

Hentschke, G.C. 187

Hierarchial Linear Model 145

High schools 35, 68

High stakes testing v, 9, 119, 124, 126, 129, 135, 154

Hispanic students 105

Hoenack, S.A. 186

Hogan, A. J. 118

Housing Prices 11, 163–164, 170, 173, 176

Hsiao, C. 43, 66

Iatarola, P. 36, 44, 66

Imazeki, J. 68–69

Incentives 1, 3, 9, 12 34, 116, 129, 131–132, 192, 200

Individual Public Use Microdata Series (IPUMS) 172–173

Jacob, B 119, 124, 126, 128, 132, 135

Jansen, D.W. 163

Jimenez, E. 71

Jondrow, J. 194

Kane, T. 60, 66, 120, 122, 125–126, 135, 166–169, 171, 173, 183

Kane, T.J. 120, 122–123, 125–126, 166–169, 171, 173

Kealy, J.K. 18

Kelley, C. 138, 151, 157, 158

Kellor, E.M. 151, 157

Kennington, J. 117

Kiewiet, D.R. 192

Kimball, S.M. 156, 157

King, R.A. 186

Knapp, C.G. 135

Koretz, D.M. 137, 157

Kumbhakar, S.C. 194

Ladd, H.F. 10, 19, 76

Laine, R.D. 10, 21

Lancaster, K.J. 73

Levels 11, 73, 126, 192, 195, 199–200

Levin, H.M. 185–187

Lewin, A.Y. 117

Limited English Proficiency (LEP) 11, 38, 44, 56, 69, 70, 104, 106

Loeb, S. 119, 133

Loubert, L. 169

Lovell, C.A.K. 96, 194

Lucas, A. 165–168

Lukemeyer, A. 163

Lynn, L.E. 192

Macphail-Wilcox, B. 186
Materov, I. 194
Math Scores 5, 44, 54, 60, 94, 99, 114
Mayston, D.J. 185
McFadden, D. 171
McGreal, T. 139, 156
McMillan, R. 173
Measurement error 43, 120
Middle schools 142
Migue, J.L. 191
Milanowski, A.T. 156–158
Miller, R.J. 1, 15, 146, 158
Miner, J. 70, 186, 188
Minimization 74, 95, 99–100, 103–104,
    106–107, 109–110, 113–116, 170
Mises, L. 187
Monk, D.H. 186
Mort, P.R. 195
Mukherjee, K. 70
Murdoch, J. 166–167
Murillia-Zamarano, L.R. 193
Murray, S. 21

National Assessment of Educational
    Progress (NAEP) 35
Nevada 70, 138, 140, 144, 157
New York City v, vii, ix, xi, 4–6, 8, 17–29,
    33, 35–36, 38, 44, 47–48, 66, 94, 98,
    100, 110–111
    Annual School Reports (ASR) 22, 44
    New York Department of Education
        (DOE) 22, 44, 47
    School Based Expenditure Reports
        (SBER) 26, 44
Niskanen, W.A. 12, 187–192, 195–196,
    199
No Child Left Behind Act of 2001 (NCLB)
    3, 9, 17, 119–124, 127, 130, 132, 134,
    156, 163, 168, 195
Noll, R. 192

Nondiscretionary Inputs 96
North Carolina 19, 122, 168

Oaxaca, R. 26
Odden, A.R. vi, xi, 10, 66, 137–138, 151,
    157–158
Ohio v, ix, xi, 4–8, 17–29, 34, 68, 76–78,
    82, 94, 98, 110–117, 140
    Ohio Department of Education
        (ODE) 21–22, 76, 82
    Ohio Education Association
        (OHEA) 76, 80
Ordinary Least Squares Regression xii,
    7, 42–43, 149, 193, 195–197, 199
Outcome (s) 156, 186, 199–200
Output (s) 57, 68, 74, 89, 96, 112–113,
    188, 194

Page, M. 134
Parsons, G.R. 18
Peacock, A.T. 187
Peer Effects viii, 11, 21, 168–175
Peer group or peers viii, 38–39, 154, 174
Penault, M. 70
Pennsylvania 156
Performance 3–5, 7–9, 14, 26, 83, 110,
    117, 119–120, 126–127, 153–154
Peterson, K.D. 138, 158
Podsakoff, P.M. 156
Pogue, T.F. 69
Porter, A. 138, 158
Principals 14, 189
Production Functions 4, 6, 12, 14, 37–65,
    74–75, 187, 193, 199
    Cobb-Douglas 72–74
    Education Production Functions
        (EPF) 12, 39, 40, 42, 47–49, 52,
        54–56, 64–65
Proficiency 64, 121, 128
Property Values vii, 4, 14, 165, 168, 171,
    183

Index

Public Use Microdata Area (PUMA) 172, 173

Race 10, 20, 44, 82, 141
Random Utility Model 36, 171–172
Rankings 58, 82, 115, 125
Rao, D.S. 193–194
Ratcliffe, K. 69
Ray, S.C. 70
Raymond, M. 119, 124, 134
Razzolini, L. 192
Reagan, B. 117
Reback, R. 126, 128, 132, 134
Regent's Examinations 29
Reiggs, S.K. 166–169, 171, 173
Reliability 8, 93
Reno, NV 140, 144
Reschovsky, A. 68–69, 163
Residual Costs 69, 72
Resources vii, viii, 1–8, 10, 13, 18, 20, 21, 24–25, 27–28, 30, 33, 35–37, 42–45, 47, 56, 62–63, 66–68, 71, 73, 75, 96–97, 117, 126, 133, 152, 157, 177, 183, 185–186, 188, 191–193, 195, 200
Revealed-preference 11, 12, 163–164, 173–177, 181, 189
Rhode Island 140, 142
Rhodes, E. 116–117
Rich, G.A. 156
Riddre, B. 69
Rivkin, S.G. 175
Robustness 34, 84, 110, 167, 176
Rolle, R.A. 12, 186, 188, 191
Romer, T. 188
Rosen, S. 164
Rosenthal, H. 188
Ross, L.B. 192
Rouse, C. 119, 124, 134
Rowan, B. 158

Rubenstein, R. vi, ix, x, 1, 5, 8–9, 15, 19, 34, 36, 66, 72, 91, 93, 97, 101, 110, 118
Rubrics 10, 139, 143–144, 151
Rudnicki, E. 187
Rueben, K. 133–134, 173, 182
Ruggiero, J. 69–70, 188

Samms, G. 166–169, 171, 173
Sanctions 121–122
Schiavone, S. 139, 156
Schmidt, P.J. 194
School size 5, 12, 21, 61, 137
Schwab, R.M. 21
Schwartz, A.E. vii, ix, x, 1, 5–7, 15, 17, 19–20, 34, 37–40, 42, 65–66, 72–73, 76, 91, 110, 118, 185–186
Seiford, L.M. 117
Sensitivity 55
Sexton, T.R. 98, 118
Shadish, W.R. 146, 158
Silkman, R.H. 118
Slack 95–97
Small class 137, 187
Small school 26, 27, 123, 177, 195
Smith, V.K. 165
Snijders, T. 145, 158
Sowell, T. 188
Sparks 144, 157
Special education 9, 11, 44, 48, 56, 63, 70, 127–130, 132–133, 143
Specification 6, 33, 98, 100, 203
Staiger, D.O. 60, 66, 120–123, 125–126, 135, 166–169, 171, 173, 183
Standards-based 138–139, 145, 153
Stevens, J.B. 188
Stiefel et al. 5, 21, 76, 185–186
Stiefel, L. vii, ix, x, 1, 5, 7, 15, 17, 19, 21, 34, 36, 38, 40, 65–67, 72, 76, 91, 97, 110, 118, 185–186, 204

Stochastic Frontier Analysis (SFA) 12, 192–199
Strayer, G.D. 192
Strayer, W. 119, 134, 195, 204
Stronge, J. 138, 156, 158
Sub-groups 123–124
Superintendents 64, 189, 191–192, 196

Taylor, L.L. 11–12, 163, 169, 175
Teacher-pupil ratio 45–47, 53–55, 63–63, 65, 177, 180
Technical Efficiency 2, 12, 70, 93–94, 96, 185 (def.), 188, 193–201
Tennessee 12, 195–199
   Education Improvement Act 195
   Tennessee Small School Systems v. McWherter 195–196
TerraNova 146, 159, 161
Test pool xi, 9, 120, 126, 128, 129
Test scores vii, x, xi, 2, 3, 5–14, 17–18, 20, 26–27, 32, 34–35, 37–62, 64, 69, 71, 73, 75–76, 78, 82, 89, 93–101, 103, 105–107, 109–117, 119–123, 125–127, 133, 137–138, 140, 142, 144–151, 153, 155–159, 163–169, 171–175, 177, 180
Texas vi, vii, viii, 11, 75, 122, 14, 138, 169, 175, 181
Thayer, M. 166–167
Tiebout, C.M. 164, 167, 171, 173–174, 181
Title I 130, 131, 134
Todd, P. 39, 66
Tollison, R.D.   187
Tone, K. 117
Tullock, G. 187

Value-added 8, 10–11, 18, 20, 34, 36–38, 41, 65, 73, 98–117, 120, 125–132, 146, 168–169, 179–181
Varian, H.R. 74
Vaugh 140, 141, 143, 149–150
Vedlitz, A. 163
Verstegen, D.A. 186

Walberg, H.J. 21, 186
Walsh, R.P. 19
Washoe County xi, 140–141, 144, 150–153, 157
Weerasinghe, D. 138, 156
Weights 29, 40, 69, 75, 94, 96–97, 145–146, 175–176
Weimer, D.L. 166
White students 11, 22, 48, 78, 85, 99, 104–106, 126, 141–142, 172, 178
White, B. 147, 157, 158
Wildavsky, A. 192
Winicki, J. 126, 134
Wolkoff, M. 166
Wolpin, K. 39, 66
Worthington, A.C. 193

Yinger, J. 68–69, 90–91, 123, 129, 134, 163, 182
Yingu, J. 70
Young, R.A. 192
Youngs, P. 138, 158

Zabel, J.E. 6, 19–20, 37, 39–40, 42, 66, 165–168, 182–183
Zamani, H. 193

9781596670068